AF444224

Slow Learner

Essays

Jan Shoemaker

trail to table press
eastsound, washington

First Edition. Published by Trail to Table Press,
an imprint of Wandering Aengus Press

Nonfiction: Essays
ISBN: 979-8-218-24150-6
Author Photo: Julie Seraphinoff
Book Design: Jill McCabe Johnson

Trail to Table Press
PO Box 334 Eastsound, WA 98245
trailtotable.net
wanderingaenguspress.com

TABLE OF CONTENTS

For Larry, who made life beautiful.

Slow Learner

VISIBLE

During the week that Notre Dame burned and the Mueller report was released, in a less remarked upon but still, I think, remarkable incident, I was called, "Mrs. Larry Shoemaker." Warming myself by the fire in a cafe, innocently scrolling through emails, I was unprepared for the slight. I'd say it was a slap, but the hand passed right through me, for I had been erased.

The note addressing Larry Shoemaker and some nameless accessory came from the lawyer who was preparing our trust. Staring at my phone, I wondered when western civilization had started disappearing women again. Did it recommence with the advent of that neo-girdle called *Spanx*—an appalling product name, now that I thought about it, that didn't need much unpacking. Vaguely, I wondered if I still had property rights.

At the tables in my vicinity, familiar people were carrying on with their old and new enthusiasms. The half-dozen stiffening septuagenarians who meet weekly to keep their French supple were pouring over a common script, letter pressing Rs, tongue to palate, and rolling out soft vowels like pastry dough. To my left, a middle-aged couple, touching shoulders, bent over *The New York Times* while their third party, belly-heavy and losing his hair, kept up a refrain about redactions and full-disclosure. I nodded my assent to him, then wondered if I'd really caught his eye, having just been deleted myself.

It was true that recently I'd been making breezy, upbeat remarks about erasure—I called it "invisibility"—most publicly at a book launch for my new poetry collection. "Remember when, as a child, you used to deliberate between the advantages of two great superpowers, being able to fly or becoming invisible? Both so enthralling and full of possibilities?" I'd asked my small audience—loyal friends and students who turn out for these things. "Well, I may never fly of my own volition but, as is reliably the case with women over sixty, I *have* become invisible." Then I told a short, true story, outfitted to entertain, about the advantages of moving through life unnoticed, ending with, "and I carried my big red Solo cup of Chardonnay right past the 'No Alcohol on the Beach!' sign and soaked my feet in the lake." The crowd tittered, as I'd hoped they would. There *are* practical advantages to ducking below the world's radar, but then I recalled that my husband had carried his wine to the lake too, and he was still *Larry* Shoemaker. Social convention had not redacted his name as it had mine—in the 21st century, for fuck's sake.

Pouring the last of the tea from the press pot into my cup, I thumbed a reply into my phone. "Dear T________, 'Mrs. Larry Shoemaker'? Really? What a quaint and dismissive anachronism; I thought it had been euthanized decades ago. I'm honestly shocked." Then I hit *send* and made my way to the barista, managing at least enough visibility to come away with a refill of hot water and a blueberry scone.

I sometimes have the sense to be interested in what I'm overlooking, what I don't see. A couple of Christmases ago, thoughtful, name-retaining Larry gave me a digital microscope and I couldn't stop pushing things into its saucer of light and ogling their images which were magnified on a screen. I slid stones and seed pods and thistles and nests under that small, bright eye at the end of a swan's neck which bent over a plastic plate with a clip for holding the item of interest in place. Worlds opened before my astonished eyes. Mosses turned to forests, fungi to canyons of spires, the scales of pinecones to battered canoes. I eased back the covers of old leather books, slid them beneath the small, bright lens and what once had been smooth and uniform planes were sliced with rivers and plateaus; the threads of their bindings scattered to the prisms of peacocks' tails. I'd been fumbling blindly through a landscape of textures and hues to which I'd been oblivious.

Morocco recently taught me a few things about invisibility when my daughter Maddie and I spent a few days in Fez. We never did learn to negotiate the shadowy passages of that crowded, ancient medina with the vaguest idea of where we'd spill out into a square. Some of its stone lanes were so narrow we had to walk single-file and you never knew when a turn would lead you to an abrupt face-to-face with a goat's head stuck on a pike announcing another butcher's stall in the souk. We were grateful for our good day-guide, Muhammad, who kept track of us for a few hours each afternoon and steered us to a handful of sites on our itinerary, among them the tannery dye vats featured in every guidebook about the old, walled city.

Leather is everywhere in Moroccan souks: in bags and belts and ottoman pouffes and most noticeably in babouches—brightly-colored, pointy-toed slippers that line the walls of countless small shops. And the animal hides that make up these goods pass through the fabled Fez tanneries. The dye vats and the hidden men who work in them to produce the bright wares strung up in markets can be seen from wooden balconies that overlook them.

Through a door in a dim lane of the medina, beneath an overhead lattice that scattered the light, Muhammad led Maddie and me into a leather-goods shop festooned with the ubiquitous slippers and bags, where we followed him through a series of rooms, climbing half a dozen steps here and half a dozen steps there. Finally, he led us outside, onto a few planks of a third-story porch that overlooked the tannery and pressed a mint leaf into each of our hands. "To hold like this," he said, delicately lifting a leaf to his nose to filter the assault of air that reeked suddenly of a thousand outhouses.

Below us a honeycomb of stone vessels, each deep enough to hold a man to the hips and twice as wide, were filled to the brim—some with dyes and others with a sharp stew of animal urine and feces that softened the tough sheets of cow and camel and goat hides. Balancing on the rims, men moved, as they had moved for centuries, among the vats or stood thigh-deep in their putrid soup, kneading the hides with their feet and hands. Voyeurs, we gaped from the lip of some ring of an *inferno* into which humans are tossed to toil in shit. We lifted our mint leaves like porcelain cups.

After a few minutes, Maddie and I retreated into the shop and retraced our route through the jungle of handbags, deflecting sales pitches with apologetic "*la shukran*"s (no thanks) and "*vegetarians*"—as if that were a regrettable condition we were forced to endure—refrains that could only have sounded senseless and effete.

Though they're not all quite so literal, the world is full of shit jobs performed by invisible people that those of us living scaffolded lives seldom glimpse. Coal mining comes to mind. Because I teach high school English, which involves mountains of papers that you literally grade everywhere—on vacation, during concert intermissions, in surgical waiting rooms and sports arenas—I keep a couple of pictures torn from *National Geographic* magazine taped inside a closet door in my classroom. They are for the bad days, the buried-and-I-can't-get-out days. One photograph shows a thin man inching toward an enormous beehive on a tree limb that sprawls several stories above ground. "Honey-gatherer," the caption reads. In the other picture a woman in a lab coat presses her nose into the armpit of a shirtless, middle-aged man: "Deodorant tester." On days when the academic earth's plates collide and thrust up new alpine peaks on my desk, I open that cabinet door and gaze at those pictures, then—with a fresh dose of perspective—go back to my desk and pick up a pen.

I know as little about the invisible person who tested my deodorant as I do about the men in the tannery vats; presumably, in a narrow field of choices, some choice was made; none of them, to my knowledge, were actually enslaved, as the truly invisible are. Visibility, it turns out, varies by degree. And it's not, of course, determined by your corporeality but by how much interest the world takes in you and by how comfortable or uneasy you make people feel.

It was a few days after leaving Fez, when Maddie and I were spectacle-browsing in the big, dusty square called Jemaa el-Fna in Marrakech, that I first noticed the advantage of *female geriatric invisibility*. It's a dynamic that relies on a lack of interest so profound in the predatory male for a post-menopausal female who is not his mama or auntie, that he is unable to register her presence. Doubtless a chemical as well as a social phenomenon, like dirty dancing in high school gyms, it hails from the pole opposite arousal and adds a great deal of agreeability to the daily life of aging women. But not to their daughters.

Strolling through the square, Maddie moved without being accosted as long as the light lasted. In the warm but not hot April sun, we loitered among the notoriously surly snake-charmers—bored as assembly-line workers by the repetitions of serpent-handling—and water-sellers draped in brass cups, and lantern-venders overseeing their glass-and-tin wares spread out on the ground. As the sun set, the scene began changing. The snake-men packed up their asps; the lantern-men lit up their wicks. Tent canopies were unfurled, grills fired up, and picnic tables conjured out of the dry air were laid out in lines in a flash-restauranteuring routine that predated the stampede of American food trucks by centuries. Storytellers and magicians materialized and bejeweled men dancing in satin pantaloons and gauzy veils, as every street that met the square discharged its throng. Women in western sundresses and women in head-to-toe hijab, men in tight American jeans and men in *djellabas*—traditional, Berber robes with pointed hoods—crowded the square. We had stepped into a tale from the *Arabian Nights*—tweaked by the times— and I gave myself up to its enchantments. Until Maddie leaned in and asked, "Can we go back to our room? I can't take anymore groping."

The groping—right. From the free pass of invisibility, I'd nearly forgotten the intrusions young women encounter in the world. As the crowd pressed us toward a small band of Berber drummers, the grabbing hands on subways came back to me, the calls from construction sites, the whole, male world that once wanted to know, it seemed, if I didn't *want some of this?*

"Of course," I said, recalled to the realm of fertile women—a place improved, I'd thought, over several decades, but suddenly so very still the same. Withdrawing with Maddie to the courtyard of the *riad* where we were staying, I felt a spasm of gratitude for the years between us that set me outside the world's glance—which I recognized immediately as an absurd and demeaning gratitude and an inadequate response to the paradoxical problem of invisibility and visibility for women. Because visibility alone has never guaranteed value.

My friend Beckie likes to tell a story about visibility and value from her years as a biology student at Cornell in the 1950s. Sitting near the front of the lecture hall, the only other woman enrolled in the class was knitting as she listened to the professor hold forth. Noticing her—a woman whose very presence violated the sciences—the estimable Doctor of Philosophy addressed her directly. "Knitting," he paused in his remarks to observe, "is just another form of masturbation." Looking up, she replied without losing a stitch, "Professor, when I knit, I knit and when I masturbate, I masturbate." I love this woman for her refusal to be devalued and excommunicated, for maintaining her composure, for defending her visible right to be.

Women *and* men with an eye out for justice keep fighting and, as my own years of witness and work accumulate, I see how very much those of us doing so will have to, as Martin Luther King Jr. instructed, as every folk singer and tee shirt printer in the upstart sixties repeated, *keep on keeping on*. Not enough has been gained and nothing is gained that can't be lost.

"Fifty-three percent," I intoned—again—to my friend Janet who was sitting with me in a small pub. We were waiting for drinks at a *Planned Parenthood* fundraiser, stacking little foil squares of condoms that had been dropped on our table like salt and pepper packets. "Fifty-three percent of American white women voted for a man who bragged he could 'grab them by the pussy.'"

"How do women let that go?"

"*I* will never let that go." Now the Republican Party was gunning for women's reproductive healthcare, which was why we'd accepted the invitation to sip wine and write checks that night.

There is a postcard I keep propped on a bookshelf in my study showing a woman—easily in her seventies—holding a sign that reads: "I Can't Believe I Still Have to Protest This Fucking Shit!" But the truth is, we do. This week, in 2019, Alabama arrested a woman because her fetus died of a gunshot wound she sustained in a fight. She wasn't invisible. Alabama saw her and Alabama *sent her to jail*. She was lucky; outraged people around the country saw her too and got her out. But, I wondered, in the emboldened conservatism of these times, how many flesh and blood women would not be seen?

Because I am invisible now, I keep props at the ready; they're like the bandages H.G. Wells' Invisible Man used to wrap himself in when he needed to be seen. Gathering lint and dog hair in the back of my car, homemade signs duct-taped to dowels and dented by bags of groceries read "FACTS Absolutely Matter!" and "Women's Rights are Human Rights!" Somewhere there's a pussy-hat back there too. You never know when you might need to jump out in a median or swing by a university or detour by a capitol lawn to join a protest in progress.

The fire at Notre Dame and the Mueller Report both left the world in the dark. The cathedral's spire illuminated against the night sky was, for many people, both a monument to truth and the visible face of France. From the American Midwest, I wept as it burned; people wept all over the world. Robert Mueller's report—as censored with inky black bars as any World War II letter sent home from the front—seemed to promise but failed to illuminate the shadowy machinations of the Trump cartel. Like lots of disappointed people, I've hitched my wagon to the glimmer of ongoing investigations in the hope they'll turn up actionable evidence of what is obvious and noisome malfeasance. In the meantime—visibly, doggedly, hopefully—I keep on. I keep on keeping on.

CURIOSITIES

My friend Stephanie was lecturing her son Tom about white male privilege again. He was five and blond and had refused to pick up his toys. "*No one* in this world is cleaning up after you," she warned him. "If I get to them first, they're mine." Her storage room was now packed like a theme park shed.

I felt a little sympathy for Tom-the-Defiler-of-Public-Space. As a person who is always dragging home more detritus than can be stowed away, I have long left small cairns of the world's best stuff around the house: fossils, seeds, abandoned hives. For quite a few years, whenever my patient husband sank onto the couch to watch basketball on TV, he was in danger of setting his beer down in a bird's nest.

Then I read Oliver Sacks' description of Philadelphia's old Natural History Museum—*like a Victorian cabinet of curiosities,* he said—a term I promptly googled. And what an infinite world of shelves and drawers and pigeonholes opened up.

I knew the Victorians were hoarders like me. I'd read heavily from their canon. But for their corsets and consumption, I could happily have lived among them in smoggy London. I will take one Dorothea Brooke to your dozen Bridget Joneses any day. I knew the sorts of things Darwin, seasick and swinging in his hammock below deck, had dragged home from all over the world. I pine for the British Museum. But I had never laid eyes on a cabinet of curiosities, though I could see at once in its degraded form it had become the American "curio" cabinet into which mid-century ladies with strikingly little curiosity had stashed their Hummels.

I was immediately mad for one. And who more than I and my wary family and friends, their elbows tucked cautiously to their sides as they angled from room to room in our house, could claim such need? We were all thinking the same thing: finally, a dedicated shelf for that saucer of coyote toe bones that kept turning up.

Inspired by photographs of skulls and shells and fungi and vials of small, pickled amphibians, I grabbed my daughter Anna and we headed to a sprawling antiques mall outside of town. There we spent an afternoon happily rummaging through old incubators, great scrolls of concrete molding pried from who knows what now-naked or collapsed edifices, and rusty electric fans repurposed as edgy, industrial chandeliers. At one point I shuddered at a cobwebby, wooden wheelchair. "I used to think those were the most jarring discards you come across in places like this," I told Anna. "Then, when we were talking about gruesome finds in junk shops, a woman in one of my writing classes shut that down with, 'Depression-era prosthetics.' Did she have *that* right. Nothing like one of those old, hinged, wood and leather monstrosities moldering in a corner to put the fear of a vengeful God in you."

Anna and I did not come home with a peeling, green, pigeon coop that my husband, who makes no fine distinction between rubbish and eclectic plunder, would have hated, though I thought it would make an excellent wine rack. We did, however, buy a cabinet—a very large and heavy cabinet—which he helped haul into our living room before heading off to play tennis. There Anna and I eyeballed it and strolled its perimeter, frowning because something was wrong. "It's upside down," she finally sighed. So we made ourselves a pot of tea and sank into a couple of old rockers and kept it company until my son-in-law Jon arrived and carefully flipped it over. Then we shoved it against a wall and decided what it really wanted was the contents of another cupboard occupying the opposite flank of the room. There followed a great migration of big art books and atlases and family photos, and our original, now empty cabinet was ready to receive its curiosities. I made a great sweep of the house, harvesting its shelves and end tables and baskets and bureaus and deposited all those bits of nature's poetry—all that dried, mineral, sometimes rickety good loot—on a big farm table adjacent to the cabinet. Anna, who is an artist, took it from there.

Poking around online while she worked, I learned that a few years ago, one of Darwin's own cabinets was discovered in a dark corner of the British Geological Survey. Unopened and forgotten since 1851, it had been abandoned by one of his friends, a botanist in charge of cataloguing its contents but who ran off to the Himalayas to look at plants instead. What the young paleontologist who fumbled upon it discovered inside were shelves of fossil slices placed between glass slides for viewing under a microscope. Among other specimens, the cabinet contained a 40-million-year-old piece of wood that Darwin brought back from Chile on the *HMS Beagle*.

What piqued my interest in this story was not just the looseness of the British repository machine, or the dating of Darwin's wood to the Paleogene Period; fossils are utterly democratizing, and any child can mine a beach and come away with equal treasures. My Petoskey stones, plucked out of Lake Michigan, are older than Darwin's bit of lumber. It's the idea of finding something "new" brought back on the mythic *Beagle* that set me to marveling. Most of my finds come home in a Kia.

It took Anna a couple of hours to assemble our cabinet of curiosities. Stacking, draping, tilting, layering, she filled five shelves and, defying gravity, the airy spaces between them, with wonders. When she was done, a horsehair bird's nest dangled from a twig, an emu eggshell rested against a Moroccan ammonite, a paper-wasp hive floated like a pinata, and a canoe of eucalyptus bark teetered on the steeple of a wedge of jasper shaped like a New England church. Every inch of space was filled with rocks and minerals, pinecones and pods, columns of selenite, spiraling shells, bones and seeds and lichens and leaves. Our cabinet was a temple of curiosities.

In the next room, backed up against the same place on their common wall, a bookshelf almost exactly the size of the cabinet holds the world's religious texts in a juxtaposition I can observe by standing beneath the lintel bridging the two rooms, as if demonstrating that, however combative their history and claims, in their quest for truth, science and religion are two sides of the same coin. Leaning there when Anna finally closed the glass doors on our curiosities, I recalled that, before the South American fossil record put Darwin squarely in the scientific camp, he'd been preparing to enter a seminary.

There was no order to our cabinet beyond a simple code of aesthetics: how pretty the patina of copper rupees dropped on a canvas of sand-dollars. Standing before the cabinet a couple of times a week—or month, life being busy—I read its natural artifacts like a collection of poems, like the *Book of Psalms*. The imbricate leaves of its pinecones, its nautilus spirals, the etched fronds of its fossilized ferns suggested some hidden hand or hinge in a complex apparatus too great to wholly know.

Like Tom, who was scheduled to get his toys back in a few days if he followed a more socially responsible clean-up protocol, I was making progress in curtailing my profligate household littering—though I dropped an entire sycamore branch on the front porch bench the other day. Knocked down by the wind, its stanzas of molting bark had sung to me in the woods. But most of the treasures that came home these days made their way straight to the tabernacle.

A Better View

Mallory Cho ambushed me again the other day when I got to school. It's become more the rule than the exception this year. My classroom is only a dozen linear feet and a sharp turn to the left inside the front door and that right angle works to her advantage. Three out of five mornings she lays in wait and pounces when I round the bend fumbling with my keys, her mind percolating with catastrophes *du jour*. Mallory Cho has autism and, along with Belarus and Turkish prisons, I am one of her grand enthusiasms.

Although she wasn't in any of my classes, I invited Mallory's attentions when I paused in the hall one day to compliment her on her voice. She has a sweet, high chirrup and often sings softly to herself as she picks through the contents of her locker, which is twenty discrete gallops down the hall from my door. More wren than filly to look at—she is eighty pounds at best—Mallory Cho is a terrific galloper and every day is Derby day as she races between bells. She only pauses at the corner of the track where I stand between classes to alert me to the latest outrage that has turned up on the rolodex of crises that plays incessantly in her head, fanned by the cyclones of her indignation.

"The Indonesian government *persecutes its own people—its own people, Mrs. Shoemaker!* Mrs. Shoemaker, Mrs. Shoemaker, that's like a mother *hurting her own child!*" she once cried, mentoring me in her native tongue, which is *ITALICS*.

"That *is* terrible, Mallory—aren't you *late for class?*" I've learned to reply in my new second language. And off she gallops for another hour. One day after school early in the year Mallory Cho, spitting fire about Istanbul's penal system, followed me out to the parking lot where I stood stupidly beside my car with a bag full of essays on *The Crucible,* waiting for her to wind down. I had not yet learned to redirect her thoughts or successfully navigate her effluence of denunciations which were rising around our ankles. Mallory Cho has huge reservoirs of empathy and a highly developed sense of social justice which, I would learn, the world often rubs raw.

She is also keen on my agnosticism, which she somehow got wind of. That and my unsurpassable niceness. "Mrs. Shoemaker is *so nice!*" she testifies up and down the halls when she can't find me in my classroom because, having rerouted myself to avoid running into her, I selfishly reconnoiter down a back hall with an ear out for her light cantor. Sometimes, before or after school, she flickers in my peripheral vision, hovering in the window outside my locked door and, coming up empty of all that niceness she sings about, I glance over, wave at her, and resume entering grades into my computer. End of encounter, I think. But Mallory Cho is an accomplished waiter and often when I step through my door ten minutes after I last glimpsed her, there she'll be, idling in place, ready to spring into action. "Mrs. Shoemaker!" she once cried, pulling up alongside as I high-tailed it for the teacher workroom. "Mrs. Shoemaker! You're an *agnostic* but I *respect* that even though I'm a *Christian!*"

"*Thank you*, Mallory. I *appreciate* that!" And then I veered off, dodged through a door, and left her to pursue her emphatic trajectory down the hall.

Amy and Cindy, the smart, saintly women who run our school's busy front office on irony and coffee and some thermal spring of good will, are Mallory's regular sounding-boards too and they both threw me dark looks when I left her at their door the other day before first period and headed for the copy machines. "What that girl needs," I called, "is her own radio show. *It's Mallory in the Morning!*"

As a person with autism, Mallory Cho brims with quirks of cognition and personality that make her seem *other*. My sense that she belongs to a small fringe tribe while I belong to the dominant one, however unarticulated, is at the forefront of my mind in all our encounters. I see where our tribes overlap, in our common humanity and nationality and sex, like the crescent moon in a Venn diagram. But in our daily intercourse, which draws on my skimpy patience, I am more inclined to see a big gibbous moon where they do not— which is a lazy default habit that people with better lights keep trying to help me change. It is easy to fall into drawing lines; most of us fashion identity in large part by carving out our differences, and I love the crisp cuff of a clean boundary. It is an addiction probably exacerbated by all my working-class, Anglo blood: God grant me the serenity of a straight hedgerow and a good English garden.

Years ago, I heard a man talking on the radio who had learned to distinguish between flotsam and jetsam, and for that I would nearly have had his child. Flotsam, it turns out, is the floating refuse of a shipwreck; jetsam is jettisoned cargo that is deliberately thrown from a foundering ship. For years, I hammered away at my American Literature students about the difference between metaphor and symbol and even more arcanely about the difference between symbol and synecdoche—fussy English-teachery stuff as useful to the world at large as the philatelic distinctions of gum skips and creases on the back of a stamp. Enthralled with these nice minutiae as any day trader with his blue chips and bids and dividends, I watched a handful of students, boundary-aficionados like me, quicken in their seats, their raised hands quivering like antennae, while the rest started to congeal and sneak out their phones.

Mallory is a mixed bag when it comes to drawing lines and making distinctions. On the one hand, she is magnanimous, solidly on board with Second Isaiah's vision of turning weapons into tools for the community garden, and a terrific dismisser of wrongs she's been done. "I FORGIVE her!" she trumpeted up and down the halls when a student with myriad, tough disabilities slapped her. On the other hand, she likes a good rule, one that if broken comes with clear consequences—even when she was on the receiving end. Someone must have observed the drawn, hunted look I sometimes let myself wear when, in a rush to make copies between classes, I try to outpace her in the hall, and reported it to our autism director because Mallory turned up at my door one morning with a typed contract in her hand, erupting with approval over its black and white lines of demarcation.

"I'm to have *boundaries*, Mrs. Shoemaker, *boundaries!*" she cried and proceeded to read emphatically from a numbered list of rules. "I will *NOT* talk to Mrs. Shoemaker when she is *working!* I will *NOT* talk to Mrs. Shoemaker when she is *with a colleague!* I will *NOT* follow Mrs. Shoemaker when she is *walking down the hall!*" Then she pushed the contract and a pen at me, indicating I was to sign it at the bottom next to where she had already signed it herself. "If I do these things there will be *consequences!*" she sang, adding—which nudged the little bud of shame I was feeling into the full brief bloom of regret—"If I do these things *I won't get to go to Cedar Point!*" Wordlessly I signed and returned the contract to her and she galloped off down the hall.

Researchers have long reported that people with autism perceive the world differently than most of us do. Their central vision may blur while their peripheral vision sharpens—or vice-versa. Images may fragment or it may be easier for them to focus on a single detail instead of an entire object. I don't know if any of these anomalies applies to Mallory's visual field, but my own reliable—as in steady if not always accurate—perception altered suddenly last summer when I stood up quickly after squinting into a computer monitor at the library. Ironically, I'd been scouring the nearby university's catalogue for books on perception, and especially on the perception of boundaries—a concept about which I'd been growing increasingly suspicious. Over the blank white wall before me a dozen slim brown tadpoles dove and rose like synchronized swimmers. I studied their antics for a minute, then called my ophthalmologist who told me to come in immediately.

"It's called posterior vitreous detachment," I explained to my friend, Dave, as we stood with our feet in Lake Michigan a few weeks later. Only a couple of tadpoles remained but were putting on quite a show, leaping out of the blue lake into the blue sky, like flying-fish, oblivious to the seam of horizon that separated worlds. "Bits of blood from the retinal wall can tear off as our eyes age," I recited from the brochure I'd filed away back home. "They float around in the vitreous fluid until they're absorbed."

"Age," Dave sighed. A year back from a stroke he'd suffered the previous summer, he had returned to his former regimen of tennis and running, but the trauma still dogged him. "Are they always absorbed?"

"I don't know, but the two out there"—I pointed to where the tadpoles were summersaulting in the lake—"haven't been yet. I don't see them when we're hiking in the woods so much—they get lost in the trees. But they're distracting when I read." And when Dave walked down the beach to talk with my husband Larry, who was throwing a stick for our dog, I stepped out of the lake and sat down in the sand to brood about strokes and retinal tears and the vexingness of infirmity—which is generally, maybe always, traceable to our old, established boundaries giving way like the tumbled rocks in the wall Robert Frost met his neighbor at once a year to mend. *Something there is that doesn't love a wall.*

The undoing of borders, or possibly their fiction, preoccupied my thoughts increasingly as even the dependable, identifying lines of my own body—the clean jaw, taut arm, edge of lip—give way and blurred with the background. Another survivor of stroke, neuroanatomist Jill Bolte Taylor describes the way she lost all track of herself as separate from her surroundings when a bleed shut down the left hemisphere of her brain. Confronting "a fluid world where everything exists in motion," unable to distinguish her own body or anyone else's among the "trillions and trillions of particles in soft vibration," she concludes that our perception of ourselves as discrete entities is nothing but a product of our "neurological circuitry" and joyfully celebrates the moment she realized "I had really been a figment of my own imagination!" Joyful, rather than dismayed or alarmed because, with no sense of herself as solid or separate, it was impossible for her to experience the threat or fact of loss. In the thrall of a crisis that threatened the very fact of her*self,* of existence as we all know it, she understood she was sublimely safe.

Frowning at the lake, which was glinting like sapphires as far as I could see, I considered its celebrated blueness—a condition more equivocal than I'd ever imagined, I'd recently learned, when I returned to the library to pick up the book about perception I'd abandoned the day the tadpoles invaded the aquarium of my left eye. In *Through the Language Glass*, Guy Deutscher, a British linguist, points out that exactly where borders fall in the light spectrum can migrate (like my lips) by language and culture. A number of languages make no distinction between green and blue at all, he claims, and treat these shades as one color. And it's not only the color wheel distinctions that can melt and disappear. Physical anthropologists now dismiss biological divisions of race. And where exactly is that crack in the perceptual sidewalk a person steps over to land on the autism spectrum? Digging my heels into the cooler sand below the surface as I tracked my tadpoles leaping through clouds and waves alike, as nimble in the sky full of water as they were in the lake full of sun, I wondered idly about the lines those of us who are not M.C. Escher draw between the fishes and birds— those edible off-landers of the disputable blue. And I made an effort to steer my thoughts clear of the time zones, which seemed especially vulnerable to boundary-bashing, because brooding on time only leads, I have learned, to brooding on eternity which leads straight to the vertigo I find at the top of a stepladder.

As a teacher, I used to think it was my job to know many things and answer many questions, and while there is still a bit of that tiresomeness where those tidy, linguistic categories I love to defend are concerned, I've come to see that, if the questions are any good, the answers won't be easily or maybe ever known. At least where ultimate things are concerned, which is the stock and trade of poetry. God only knows what goes on, as the British say, in the maths.

The best of our three-pound brains—poor equipment and not much of it—squinting away at the universe, are unable as ever to answer the big questions, I like to point out as we suit up to meet the interrogatory poetry of that fierce inquisitor, Emily Dickinson. We can calculate the age of our universe but have no idea what is beyond its edges or if there are edges at all. Our better brains can explain how our universe rose out of a few chemicals but they can't explain where those proto-chemicals came from or answer that perennial question—Why does anything exist instead of nothing at all?— which still hangs over our heads, as luminous and terrifying as the northern lights. I like to lead my students through Plato's "Allegory of the Cave," then give them a little Pascal to chew on, which we tackle together.

"Emma," I'll say (or Katie or Jake), "Please read this passage out loud."

And Emma will begin, "I am in a terrible ignorance about everything." I wait for yawns or snickers, but they almost never come. "I do not know what my body is, or my senses, or my soul or even that part of me which thinks what I am saying, which reflects on itself…I see only infinity on every side, enclosing me like an atom, or a shadow that vanishes in an instant." There is usually a bit of silence that follows and then the conjectures begin to roll—about truth and consciousness, the curved spine of space, the likelihood of God. Lots of my students enjoy poking at these big, troubling questions; they seem genuinely drawn to the examined life, and I am always surprised at how few easy platitudes they trot out. Come to think of it, I suppose it is just this kind of exercise that put Mallory Cho onto my agnosticism.

"Try to love the questions themselves," Rilke says, which sounds like the kind of mantra a tortured existentialist might pick up in a cognitive therapy session. I picture the poet repeating it earnestly to himself as he combed his beard in the mirror, as he pulled on his boots and buttoned his coat to the Paris rain. But why not love the questions, if you can manage it, when human answers are so various and contradictory? The transcendentalists, with whom Jill Bolte Taylor would agree, tell my sophomores that we are nothing more than temporary lenses through which, for a few seconds, a spoonful of undifferentiated spirit peers before it returns to the soupy Oversoul, which provides a little contrast to the narrative some of these sixteen-year-olds get from their youth pastors. *"Oversoul,"* they repeat, writing it down—some of them genuinely turning it over in their heads, others simply warehousing it—fodder for future flash cards.

"It's hard to be in love and wise," the poet Keith Flynn says, reminding me of the error I suspect I kept making. Enamored with the view of my own lens, which scores in bars like lead in glass, I keep seeing borders, margins, lines—illusory as tadpoles, it may turn out. When I am thoughtful instead of harried and irritable, I see in the overlapping areas of that Venn diagram where Mallory Cho and I find congruence, the sliding lenses an optometrist uses to correct our vision. "A or B?"…the lenses shift, the images blur…"A or B?" Eventually the circles synch and a clearer field unfolds.

Each September I introduce myself to 150 new students and explain how exacting my courses will be—trying to get the numbers down. Over the next few months a few of them drop, undone by four tribes of irony and the clamor of too many allusions. Lately September has also become my taking-stock month as I note how the larger mechanism of the universe, operating with its own agenda, or none, keeps chipping away at my tidy, faux-separate self. There was the September of The New Reading Glasses, the September of The Upstart Varicose Vein, the September of The Lost Passwords—which maybe flew off like diving birds or flying fish and are living below the sea or above the clouds. Any way you look at it, I am coming apart. *Something there is that doesn't love a wall.* All this dissolution puts me to wondering about what it is that lasts—and so is worth including in a literary canon. Ecclesiastes warns us "All is vanity," but, as I told my students as soon as I discovered it myself, "that's a mistranslation of the Hebrew *hevel:* All is mist, vapor, breath." Nebulous, this world, with no boundaries at all.

So, *what can last?*—at least for the short span of a culture, the shorter span of a human life—I hear myself wondering in Mallory's native tongue. Habits of mind, perhaps, if they are passed on. Not a single view, but the will to find a better view that goes with a healthy suspicion about what we think we see. And kindness, of course. Mallory Cho, who was elected to the homecoming court this year in a popular, student-driven movement to erase boundaries, reminds me in her total blindness to figures of speech but unmitigated outrage at every case of cruelty her global radar picks up, that in our spotty understanding, we are all autistic before the God she knows, the God in which I try and sometimes do believe.

Not long ago my friend Mark had dinner at his friend Judy Pluto's house to help celebrate her husband's birthday. Mark had never met Judy's husband, which was why he was invited. "Judy Pluto always brings a stranger home for dinner on her husband's birthday, he explained, which is a quirky tradition that never stops delighting me. I do not plan to take it up myself, of course. Mallory Cho, I am certain, would thoroughly approve.

In considering Mallory's post-secondary options, I see that a morning show is selling her way too short and that her native tongue is not italics at all. Truth is her first—and only—language. Career-wise, what she'd make is a top-notch president. "Mrs. Shoemaker, Mrs. Shoemaker!" she blurted, storming my room the other day and stepping right between me and a student I was helping with an essay. "The Chinese are *killing their baby girls— their baby girls,* Mrs. Shoemaker!" We could do worse than put Mallory Cho in charge of running the world. *NO* one would *EVER* get hurt on her watch.

THROUGH THE DARK

Nothing cries, "You're a crone!" like losing a tooth. The first time it happens, you can put a brave face on it and make edgy quips about womynhood (with a y) and systerhood (with a y) and wysdom (with a y), and you can laugh along with anyone brave enough to challenge that shit. The second time it happens—the second time a tooth *falls out of your head*—when you've used up all the jokes and squandered all your insouciance, you hold a finger to the wind and tense at the direction things are taking. Perhaps you recall your toothless Uncle Chet gumming saltines in his undershirt. And that is when you high tail it to the oral surgeon's office.

Down a couple of burly, proletariat molars, whose work I only really admired when they were gone, I was installed in a chair in my oral surgeon's examining room, waiting for the anesthesia-fairy to arrive. It cost three-hundred bucks out of pocket to get the stuff that actually knocks you out, which I was more than willing to pay. Although the dental assistant had assured me that a hefty dose of Novocain would be sufficient for bolting down the implant I'd agreed to have installed, I had no desire to be awake for any of it. I closed my eyes and waited.

"Hellooo." I started at the deep voice and opened my eyes as something—*someone*—lanky and uncommonly tall, whose dimensions recalled Dr. Will's, swept into the room. Dr. Will, who would be performing the procedure, was a well-established surgeon with degrees from solid colleges (I'd checked) and two busy offices to boot. This person, tossing back the hair of a wild black wig, had a face covered with white greasepaint and a black star stenciled around one eye. I nodded at him, accepting my crone's role as the adult in the room.

"*Kiss*," I said, "you're from *Kiss*."

He bowed, breaking character, then intoned, in Dr. Will's voice, "And you're here for the cadaver bone." I laughed, going along: it was October 31st, which explained the costume: we were doing Halloween. "No, *really*," he said, "we're going to pack cadaver bone in your jaw to give the implant something to sink into. We'll add the new tooth later." And then someone dressed as a nurse anesthetist materialized and placed a plastic cup on my face and the hard world softened and gravity gave up its pull and I levitated, out of ordinary time.

That was a couple of Halloweens ago. I went to sleep, woke up with part of a dead person's freeze-dried femur or maybe sternum packed into my mandible, wrote a check for a chunk of money, and headed home. I felt a little ghoulish leaving the surgeon's office—having just transitioned to the walking dead, after all—and on Halloween day, and a little titillated by it. No one knew exactly what lurked among them as I browsed in a bookstore later that afternoon; no one knew exactly who handed candy to their children on our porch that night. "She's a teacher," I heard one father tell his little boy, a dragon with a runny nose, as they walked down our driveway. I smiled my new B-movie smile. *That's not all she is*, I thought.

Until I became, practically speaking, a zombie, I have never been what anyone would call frightening. I've been selfish and dishonest and vain, but never unnerving. People don't cross themselves or lock their car doors when I walk down a sidewalk. But my own initiation into the tribe of the reanimated dead, creatures we've dubbed evil rather than spectacularly unlucky, proves that we never know who's in the checkout line behind us.

Some time ago, I learned that every Roman Catholic diocese has an exorcist—an actual *exorcist*. As there are, give or take, 3000 dioceses in the world, that means the Catholic Church— the church of Chief Justice John Roberts and Joe Biden and, for the love of God, Stephen Colbert—has deployed an army of demon-fighters that are, as we sip out lattes and microbrews, swarming the globe, crucifixes holstered and at the ready. I couldn't stop thinking about it. Does genial Father Joe, who was handing around the Host at a wedding I recently attended, do a little demon-chasing on the side? And this collared fellow in front of me ordering soup at Panera's—did he spend the odd Saturday night driving devils from the deranged faithful with a raised cross and some Latin version of "Scram!"? And as for demonic possession itself, was it a chronic and democratic phenomenon, spread equally around the world like color-blindness, or did it flare up disproportionately in places like Mara Lago and Saudi embassies? And how does a person end up an exorcist? Did he choose it, like a minor, in seminary—a few credits of demon-shaming to balance out that major in liberation theology? Or was there some short stick involved?

My sister Sue, recently retired, worked for twenty-five years in the ICU of a Midwestern hospital. She occasionally talks about the lives saved by the high-tech interventions of cutting-edge intensive care, but she also tells the story of a failing, elderly patient in her unit who had locked eyes firmly with death. Not all the chemicals or cords or valves in the modern medical arsenal were helping her turn back toward the living world. "One night her family brought in a priest—who cleared us all out of the room," Sue said. "They claimed he was an exorcist." My immediate response to that story was not a scoff, but a question: "Did it work?" I caught myself before I asked this out loud and am therefore still considered to be a mostly sane person by my family. "It probably didn't work," I thought. *Probably* not.

I was, at the time I heard this story, worshipping at the shrine of the periodic table, studying it, actually—adding and subtracting electrons, sketching out orbitals in a little notebook—mining it for poetry. (You can do a lot, I'd discovered, with hydrogen and some of the heavy metals.) My heroes were all rational feminists and Enlightenment men; I owned property at science camp. My roots led right to the Age of Reason. "Exorcism *probably* didn't work?"

The truth is, I do and do not know what is happening around here, in this place I believe we occupy, without knowing who we are, in this time I suspect we invented or, at best, misunderstand. I do and do not know evil. Like goodness, it sometimes feels greater than the sum of its parts, beyond anything explained by the social and neurosciences. A mystery: shapeless and terrifying. Pooling here and there, with no atomic weight at all.

We gave evil shapes, of course, and names to contain it. It was Mara hurling fiery rocks at the Buddha. It was a Gorgon turning flesh to stone, Leviathan rising from boiling seas, Lucifer falling from Heaven. As Incubus and Succubus, it came in dreams. It was Moloch, Shayton, Satan, Baal. It often shape-shifted, assuming familiars as it did in Salem where two dogs were executed with 19 "witches"—which makes that national madness so much worse.

As a child, I had an extravagant fear of evil, for reasons I don't fully understand. There was no Devil in the little matchbox church I was raised in—just a children's choir and Easter hats and an affable Jesus who looked like a homebrewer in Birkenstocks, like everyone's cousin Benny who dropped out of college.

Nevertheless, familiars filled my daily world which tripped my panic switches. Feathers strewn on the lawn or loosened from my own pillow were weighted with a malice that set me screaming. Dock weed and Queen Anne's Lace reached toward me like cursed and bony fingers from alongside the dirt roads that scored our fresh little neighborhood carved out of an orchard. The orange life-saving vest that hung in our garage crept down from its hook after dark and waited in a corner to snap at my feet as I climbed from the car. And once I was tucked into my own bed, there was the waiting thing in the sinister dark.

People grow out of their irrational fears. Or they don't. When my husband was away or when I was alone in a hotel room, I left a low light on when I slept and not just because crones have to shuffle to the bathroom several times a night. I simply hadn't figured out how to sift the noisome possibility of evil from out of the dark. And where would you put that stuff anyway? Even the best exorcists are in the removal, not the exterminating business. Even Jesus, who set the industry standard for exorcism, had to settle for driving demons from a man into a herd of swine, which seems an unfair, if suitably kosher move. Every movie about the mob, every Irish love story or Italian food story, had a crucifix hanging over somebody's bed, running defense during the night. *I pray the Lord my soul to keep.* If Larry died before I did, as every actuarial report insisted he would, I'd probably hang a cross on a nail over my bed too.

After the 2016 presidential election, when the most basic respect for reason began to erode, I felt my private nemesis, the Irrational, rise from the dead and take on new flesh. Climate change deniers, immigrant demonizers, white supremacists, EPA dismantlers, seemed to appear out of nowhere to walk the world with the rest of us. I remember making some crack to friends about how we were heading down the road to Salem again, how—a little uneasily—we laughed. We're not laughing anymore and I dread what's ahead if we don't get a national grip. Deflecting our personal hobgoblins with the Hand of Fatima or a smudging of sage or a bowl of medallions emblazoned with saints is entirely our own half-baked business—protected by a rationally conceived constitution—but letting the crazy in us drive policy or collective action leads to places that only sound pretty: *Inquisitio, Guyana, Kristelnacht.* I could hang a cross over my bed, but the end is near when the mob gets a green light to paint one on a mosque or burn one on a lawn. Flipping through the *New York Times* these days seemed increasingly like reading something from Stephen King or Poe—or Arthur Miller—and I wondered just how much of our ransacked republic we were willing to burn at the stake of our fears.

Facing his philosophical options, the writer Poe Ballantine states, "Whatever I believe in must have depth and power to repel evil, insanity, loneliness, and despair. It must be built on the observation of what is good and true." It was a tall order, but not unfillable. For a couple of hundred years, after all, our good American democracy had continuously rebuilt itself on reason and on the "observation of what is good and true," and though it hadn't filled the whole prescription yet, its rising vials gave us hope. Gradually, our reason eliminated the number of things we had to be afraid of—dentistry among them. It was not our country's father's wooden teeth anymore

On Halloween, we tried to tame what scares us by mocking it, getting inside it, throwing it off when we're done. Those *Glo-Brite* bones on a spandex bodysuit may get a gasp in the dark, but nothing exorcises their terror to exhaustion like shucking them off on the laundry room floor.

I downloaded the dead into my own body one Halloween day, in the most literal way. I still carried someone's old rib cage around. And I never did get those molar implants. I learned to chew on the other side.

It was October again, a month that inspires speculation—so full, as it is, of the end of things: the leaves, the light, the year. A couple of weeks ago, as if on cue, I had a sugar addict's hankering for candy corn, that quintessentially American confection in which corn syrup finally knows itself and ascends to its perfect form—terrible for the crone-teeth that remain and may be fixing to jump ship. But just days before Halloween, there was an inexplicable dearth of it in my suburban neck of the woods, absolutely no one was selling it: not Target, not Kroger, not the rickety old 7-11 near our house. Curious, I went looking online, googling, "Where is the candy corn?" To which the rational, irrational cyber-world replied, in all its fearsome passing strange, "Why does candy corn exist?"

The question *why* abounds. Why must we suffer? Why must we die? Why was everything changing so fast? The most commonly googled *why* is, "Why is there a leap year?" And then the cat people get hold of the world's keyboards ("Why does my cat lick my eyelashes, roll olives, wedge his face between my toes?") and it was all over for the curious rest of us. But this wasn't really a why moment anymore. It was time for more practical questions. Like how. How do we hold onto what's left of our teeth? How do we find our discarded humanity, our better vision, our democratic resolve? How do we find our way through the dark to that half-remembered, old high road?

Kryptonite

"Come on in!" I heard Larry call from the front door one Friday evening in January. "You must be freezing!" There followed the thud of boots being pulled off and dropped on the foyer floor. Hunkered down with a heating pad on the couch, I was riding the bucks of a bad cold. Suddenly, we had company. I groped for the remote and snapped off Netflix.

"Honey," Larry announced, leading two very young women, teenagers it looked like from what you could see of them, into the family room and depositing them on the opposite couch, "these girls need to warm up." I didn't doubt him; it was ten degrees outside and, at six o'clock, had been dark for an hour. I heaved myself into what I hoped was an upright position, though it was hard to be sure with the room spinning like it was. Still wrapped up in down coats, the girls pulled their scarves below their chins and steamed their gratitude.

Larry disappeared into the kitchen as I blinked at our company, then was back a minute later, pressing them with a plate of the generic cardboard cookies he keeps stacked in the pantry like poker chips. The girls, who he'd found on our front porch and who each politely took a cookie were, of course, Latter Day Saints. The fact that they were proselytizing door to door put them roughly at nineteen. And the additional fact that they were doing it in the middle of winter in Michigan, rather than in Hawaii or Kuala Lampur, meant that in the match-game of Mormon missionary assignments, they had drawn the short stick.

"So, are you both in college?" I—or someone—asked in a fuzzy voice that might have been coming from beneath the floorboards. They were. "And are you from…"

"Utah," they answered, more or less in sync, shouldering their share of the small talk, when Larry suddenly interrupted, "Well, I'm off to tennis." Then he picked up his gym bag and walked out the door.

Now, I have no problem with scooping young women from the winter wind so they can thaw out by the fire and return to the work that drives them, but it seemed to me that if you brought Mormon missionaries into the house, they were wholly and unequivocally *your Mormons*, for as long as they stayed. Ditto missionaries from the Jehovah's Witnesses and Clean Water Action and the disciples of whoever is running for county clerk. Was this not obvious? Did everyone not know this? Was it not abundantly clear to all that you do not hand them cheap cookies, then walk away, leaving them to your stupefied spouse?

"Um," I gurgled after a longish pause, "would you like—um—tea?" Fever had driven out a lot of my facts, like the one about caffeine being anathema to observant members of the LDS Church. They declined politely. One of them (Kaylee, I think) did so with a raspy whisper, hoarse from her own whopping head cold. And then I asked about their families, milking the subject for as long as I could ("And what is it again that your fifth brother does?") as I groped my way toward their college majors. I thought I saw Elizabeth watching for the natural segue to the Lord while debating if she should take it at all, given the rescue-nature of their invitation inside. I figured she would find it when she explained, "I've been working in Michigan for the past year but Kaylee just got here two days ago." This, then, was not only about my salvation or swelling the ranks of the faithful; it was a mentoring session. And after I explained, when she inquired about my work, that I teach a comparative religion class, she found her ramp.

"So, what do you think about Jesus?" she asked gently and I began making a list in my head of ways that Larry would pay for this.

"Would you like some tea?" I asked again, thinking I'd just heard that somewhere, and rising unsteadily to tilt across the room to put another log on the fire. "How late are you, um, working?" They were knocking on doors, they said, until nine.

"Jesus," I repeated, sitting back down in my nest of blankets and trying to think thoughts that would breed words. "A good man." I coughed into my sleeve. "Wise. Probably gay. Excuse me." I got up and shuffled to the bathroom and returned with a box of Kleenex. "What did you say your fourth brother does?"

"He's a biology teacher in middle school."

"I heard that male Latter Day Saints get their own planets when they die," I said. "That will be an upgrade for him." There were a few seconds of empty air.

"So why do you think Jesus was *gay*?" Kaylee or Elizabeth—they sort of shimmered in and out of each other, with the way the mucus in my eyes was bending light—asked. I thought they'd come back to that. Turns out, I had set them up; turns out, I'm pretty canny with a cold. I could have left their heretofore heterosexual Lord alone, but I do think there is a more than good chance that Jesus, who chose the company of men almost exclusively and died unmarried in his thirties, was gay and if we're going to extoll and celebrate his life, shouldn't we all acknowledge and celebrate that too? They came to my door; I didn't go to theirs.

So I said things about that, which maybe helped warm them up because they left pretty quickly, gushing thanks. Of all the people who turned up on our porch, Joseph Smith's tidy, disciplined Saints were the most unfalteringly polite. And because I was feeling pretty pleased with myself, I let Larry live when he finally came home. He has not always gotten off so lightly.

He had not, for instance, walked away with a spring in his step when I'd overheard him refer to me as "old" a few years earlier. "It was a joke!" he'd pled to no, and I mean zero, avail. Here, for the conjugal record, is how that went down:

It was a dark and wintry night—a portentous beginning to any tale—and I was grading papers by the fire in a *rocking* chair, a situation loaded with incoming irony that was nowhere on my radar. Larry's side of a conversation on the phone in the kitchen drifted in as an ambient hum, nothing more, until one phrase tore away from the rest and distinguished itself. "I had to drive Jan to the eye doctor today; that's how it is with an old wife." He chortled—funny guy.

The floater in my left eye drifted up toward the mantle. I put down my pen. Old?

The speed at which my vanity drew itself up for retaliation must have been something to behold; working from the inside, I couldn't really see it myself. "O-o-old?" I asked, when he clicked out of his call and wandered into the room, milking the long, ominous o. "O-o-old?" He started, surprised. "You have eight and a half years on me, *friend,* which we will now and forever be rounding up to nine."

"I was kidding!"

"I'm *not* kidding. Can *old* people teach high school? No"—I cut him off and tossed down my pile of essays on *Huck Finn*—"they can't. Here's what else they can't do: they can't walk a fourteen-minute mile, they can't climb to the top bunk in a second-class compartment on an Indian train, they can't hoist themselves into that beech tree I scale every June when we hike to the dunes." I fired off a few more salvos—about his retirement and my toil, if memory serves, about his empty days and my brilliant, purposeful, full ones. It went on. Somewhere in there the dogs slid off the couch and withdrew from the front.

"It was a joke!"

But I was already through the Maginot Line and well into France. Because at some point in this diatribe, I realized he was right. Like it or not,

I *was* pretty old, and if there were things I wanted to do, I saw I'd better get to them. "I'm going to Paris," I told him. "I'm going to study French."

Stunned, he stammered, "Well, you had that locked and loaded." He was right. Ever since I'd begun tinkering with the French language a year earlier before traveling to Morocco, I'd been thirsty for more of those lovely liquid syllables.

"Yes," I said, "I think I did."

And because he is a loving man who hates to leave home, but worries when I am away, he asked, mildly, for just one thing. "Will you take someone with you?"

"I can do that," I said. Which is how our daughter Anna and I came to spend that year's spring break in Paris, a trip for which I started planning a few days later by taking an online test in order to attend, for a week, a class at the *Alliance française*. That I found the test itself nearly incomprehensible should have been an indicator there would be rocky *rues* ahead.

"How'd it go?" Larry called from the kitchen after I finished the test and closed my laptop.

"Let's go get your wife drunk," I answered.

A couple of months later, after maneuvering through the Charles de Gaulle Airport, after clapping madly at our first glimpse of Paris's signature chimneys when we taxied into the city, after settling into our small, functional hotel room on the Left Bank, I lasted for exactly two days in a class that was skylines over my head at the *Alliance*. To be fair to the school, which had presumably used the results of my test to register me in what it considered to be a suitable course, my placement *may* not have been entirely uncalibrated. To be fair to myself, to the test's essay question that inquired about what I thought would be an effective outcome for a collaborative team project, I wrote, "*Mon ami a Paris est un grand chien noir*": "My friend in Paris is a big black dog." So when it came down to spending the few days we had among les boulangeries et les patisseries et les musees, or in befuddlement at the back of a class, I cut and ran. On the week's Tuesday, as the other highly discursive students streamed out for a break, I took a breath and addressed our teacher, a trim, brisk woman of my own age, at the front of the room. She had labored visibly over the problem of what to do with me. "Madame," I said evenly, "*Vous etudiez la trigonometrie, mais j'etudie l'addition*." I waved a hand sweepingly to indicate the plural "you," while inviting her into my metaphor: *You study trigonometry while I study addition.*

"Oui," she finally agreed, not unkindly, but in what even I could translate as unmistakable resignation.

"Merci, Madame," I said, meaning it. Then I walked out the door and headed for the Seine where I ran right into Anna browsing the book stalls. We had a lovely day at the Picasso Museum, a lovely rest of the week—all the result of Larry's little *faux pas*. Talk about your lemons and lemonade.

What I appreciate about the French is how they roll right over the low bar for amiability you set for them--how they are so much friendlier than you expect them to be. What I appreciate about the LDS Church is the dogged and loving way its adherents will baptize your outlier self right into their salvation even after you die. I have known people who bristle at this, which makes no sense to me, no matter how you run at it. I am nothing but grateful for such astonishing generosity. What I appreciate about Larry is, well—that list is endless. But on it, certainly, is the fact that, however entitled he is to it, he has never activated the lever I added to our marriage that late-winter night—let's call it the Reparations Clause. Infinitely generous, he is a super-man whose defining power is magnanimity—though I do wonder if he recognizes that winter nights are his kryptonite, that before the solstice he ought to step softly and watch where he puts his feet.

DOE

Full disclaimer: the deer dies, so you might want to bail on this story here and find something less painful to do than read on, like weed the poison ivy out of your myrtle or get a full-torso tattoo or thread a catheter through your urethra. The doe at the side of the road was broken and will absolutely die by the end of this, maybe sooner, so let's be clear about that. Me, I'd cut and run.

But I didn't cut and run on that cold night in December when my headlights caught the doe, folded swanlike, with her legs tucked beneath her, on the shoulder of Park Lake Road. She held her graceful neck erect as a treble clef; her face—perfect as only a doe's can be, so made in God's image, presumably—was composed, her thoughts inscrutable. I veered onto the nearest side street and pulled up behind the SUV that had struck her.

Next to the wrinkled car, a young woman holding a baby was speaking into her phone, which she put away when I approached. I could see her breath. She was almost out of gas, I learned, and her husband was working, but her mother was on the way from just across town; she'd be there soon. And, almost before I could ask after her and her baby—were they okay?—her mom pulled up and popped the car seat and infant into her own warm station wagon then joined the two of us by the vehicle's ruined hood. "Have you called the police?" I asked. Yes, she had, about twenty minutes earlier. I took out my phone and headed for the deer.

It's not an un-busy road, Park Lake, slicing north to south through three major arteries that take people in and out of Lansing. Politicians line its two lanes with signs during election years. And it was very dark that night. The doe never shied when I drew near her and I kept a few feet between us as I stepped into the street and flipped on my phone light. The power of its beam—like everything else about these phones—astonished me. Who knew I'd been packing a lightsaber? I pointed it toward an approaching car, which slowed down. Then, making a big, dramatic half-circle, I directed the driver into the other lane, as far from the deer, who had sunk to the asphalt right on the shoulder's white line—in sorely re-strikable distance of whoever drove by—as the road permitted. As other cars appeared—six, maybe, or eight—I waved them clear of the deer.

Then I called the police. "Hello, "I began, streamlining the facts for the sake of clarity. "My name is Jan Shoemaker. I am standing in the middle of Park Lake Road directing traffic away from a wounded deer. There is also a lady with a baby here. Please send an officer."

"We have that call already," a voice replied. "We're sending someone. Get out of the road."

"It's been twenty minutes," I cut in. "I'm as old as the hills and I'll snap like a twig and I'm not getting out of the road until an officer arrives."

"You need to get out of the road."

"You need to send someone *now*." Then another pair of headlights appeared and I hung up, clicked on my beam and waved the driver away from the doe. Several minutes later, I called the police again.

"Hi, I called recently about the lady and the baby and the deer, but no one has come. I'm still in the middle of this very dark road."

"You *need* to get out of the road."

"I *won't* get out of the road." It had occurred to me when I pulled over that I'd stumbled into one of those moments when the universe allows you to be a little bit useful, out of your ordinary way. I kept thinking my defiance, not to mention concern for the little PR scandal that might ignite if I were run down and the local news picked it up: "Mentally Ill Woman Struck On Road; Police Refuse Aid," would set a fire under someone sworn to protect and serve—but half an hour rolled by, punctuated by my calls to the same dispatcher at five minute intervals.

"We need an officer! What's taking so long?" Someone, I was assured every time, would be there soon. But, in the developing plot, shifts were changing, which added to the delay. I wondered how valuable a shift-changing timetable might be to aspiring housebreakers. *Window* of opportunity suddenly acquired an extra dimension. Every few minutes, the younger woman's mother climbed out of her car to stand with her daughter in the wind, then retreated to the warmth of her front seat. The doe never stirred.

"Hi, it's me—lady with the deer."

"You need to get *out* of the road!" And so it went for nearly an hour—the doe stoic and austere, the young woman sighing by her car, me dancing in the street. To be clear, I was there for the deer. The driver with the baby, fully rigged with thoughts and thumbs and therefore access to the human engines of benevolence, wherever the hell they were just then, was fine; plus she had a mom on hand with a spare car. "I'm always afraid I'll hit a deer," I had commiserated with her (maybe not that helpfully), which is true, and my specific fear is of wounding rather than killing one because what would I do? My brave friend Terry stopped and dismounted his bicycle one day to dispatch a ruined kitten with a rock, but my little well of moral courage has nothing like that kind of depth. Because the terrible frailty of animals homesteads my head *a lot,* I slow down when driving through corridors of trees and at dusk and dawn, tapping my car's horn in a staccato of warning: five-thousand pounds of steel coming through! The possibility of striking any creature is a reasonable argument for carrying a handgun in my car, but I don't.

Eventually, a police car pulled up and an officer and the baby and the driver-mom and *her* mom and I—also a mom and butting into these strangers' crisis whenever traffic cleared—gathered by the damaged car. There was a lot of matriarchy going on in our huddle. There was also, I thought, way too much interest in the mangled but insensate front of the car. The officer opened its hood and introduced the relevant, if not critical, topic of insurance. Everyone who wasn't me peered inside and made small sounds of concern.

"I'm sorry," I finally blurted at the officer, "but that deer (I pointed my beam at the doe) is suffering. "Will you *please* put her out of her misery?" I glanced at the gun on his belt.

Standing in the road during the previous almost-an-hour, I'd thought, of course, what might, what should, what likely would become of the deer. I knew of no local wildlife rescue organizations with the equipment to convey a damaged deer to an ICU; my own veterinarian's office had been closed for hours, and I believed, at that time, that the slender, broken legs of a deer would never heal to hold the animal. To be struck by a car, I thought, was *it.* All I really had was, "Traveling Through the Dark," that William Stafford poem about his finding a deer along the side of a road, in my head. The scene he confronted was made more morally ambiguous by the fact that his doe, while dead, was carrying her living, unborn fawn. If you're looking for a poem to tear out your heart, this one will do it.

It was euthanasia I had on my mind—a merciful shot, quick and clean—to release this doe from her agony. But the officer had produced a document and was taking the other two women through its intricacies while I agitated at the edge of the group and sprinted back to the deer, who continued in the guise of a bodhisattva, erect and serene, even as each new set of headlights bore down on her. Waving my fellow humans around the doe, I marveled at her equanimity and wondered if shock had subdued her, or if she simply accepted this moment as another among the uncounted moments of her life before an SUV had intersected it, because acceptance was all there was. I had no idea what sort of narrative enlivened the mind of a deer, if discrete windfalls and catastrophes were connected at all in some intimate story of self. When it seemed like another quarter hour had gone by, I jogged over to check on the driver-mom's mom, who'd rejoined her grandson in her own car. I was bending to their window when I heard the pistol fire.

A doe's legs can mend, it turns out, and deer have survived in the wild on three. But even if I'd known this, I'm not sure any of us on the side of that road could have managed a better outcome for the doe. Though he hesitated in the listening wilderness and half-light of his own vehicle, Stafford famously pushed his deer "over the edge into the river."

Crossing a dark patch of lawn to where the doe lay emptied of her old desires and drives and fears, a gentle heap making its way, not across human roads anymore, but into the waiting all-of-it, I thanked the officer who'd finally shown up to open her way. Then I got in my car and drove home.

GRACE

I am not *usually* profane, by which I mean I am not *always* profane, which is to say *sometimes I don't mean to be* profane—a little profanity *just slips out*, but that was not the case last week when I carried the broken mouse, curled like a comma on a paper towel padding a shoebox, into the wildlife rescue center at a nearby university. This was performance. I wanted the receptionist absorbed in her computer at the intake desk to notice my mouse, who had last stirred when I placed him beside me on the front seat of the car.

Let me preface this by pointing out that I'd just finished reading Ron Chernow's big *Hamilton* biography and had been listening to the *Hamilton* soundtrack every time I drove anywhere in the car for the previous six months. I knew Aaron Burr's grandfather, the "fire and brimstone preacher (preacher preacher preacher)" had been the formidable Jonathan Edwards. I had seen repeatedly and firsthand that immigrants "get the job done." I knew, should I ever be inclined to duel, to "pick a place to die where it's high and dry." So when I scooped up the little mouse—just an adolescent mouse at the very most, and so delicate—from a skittish friend's living room floor, I thought naming him after a hero might help his chances.

"HELLO," I said firmly to the distracted receptionist. "This is Hercules Mulligan. Can you help him get the fuck back up again?"

She never flinched—neither in recognition (wasn't *everyone* listening to that soundtrack?) or offense—the effect of living in a college town, I suppose. But when we peered together into the box, it was evident to us both that little Hercules had passed on to the next adventure, whatever that might be. She kept his ounce of body to add to what I supposed was a discreetly placed bag of small corpses headed for an incinerator, also judiciously hidden, which saved me the trouble of stopping by a field on the way home.

Not long after Hercules Mulligan was folded back into the all-of-it, a desperate, injured dove hopped a curb and hightailed it across my path as I was out admiring the big, mottled sycamores in my neighborhood. Clearly in a panic to be somewhere else, she was working to get there cross-country, as fast as her toothpick legs could propel her. My left eye caught a peripheral movement—a cat slinking down a driveway across the street. I sighed, remembering the old *Wild Kingdom* television show my dad had watched every Sunday afternoon of the 1960s, where no one on camera or crew ever intervened to save the terrified prey from teeth at the bloody end of the hunt, the food chain being some unwinding of holy purpose too sacred to defile.

Possibly that's where the delicate concept of *bullshit* first took root in my mind. I stamped my foot at the cat, who merely rerouted his advance by a few sly inches, and glanced around for a neighbor likely to have a box.

Two houses away, a balding man I'd never met was propping up the limbs of his pear tree, which were drooping with a bumper-crop of cannonball pears, on step ladders he must have scavenged up and down the street. Seven ladders circled the trunk in his jury-rigged war against gravity, and he was busy tucking in an eighth. With a whole tree in traction on his hands, I gave him a pass, made another run at the cat, and checked the whereabouts of the dove, which was headed longitudinally down the sidewalk in a doomed, direct path to the cat, who seemed to be protracting angles. As the dove approached a mailbox set on a post rising from a bucket full of rocks, I noted that, at the very least, we were scrambling in the applied problem-solving corner of the neighborhood. And just then a door opened, a young woman with an empty box appeared—she was helping friends move in, she explained—and we bore down on the bird. Twenty minutes later, she was scrabbling in her box next to me in the car as I drove to a new wildlife-rescue operation I'd heard about, which turned out to be a kind lady named Cheryl who lived in a farmhouse filled with cages of recuperating animals.

"This dove is probably just bruised," she assured me, calmly cupping her hands around it and lifting it from the box. "She'll be flying again in a couple of days." Then she placed the dove gently in a cage in a room that looked like the step-down unit of an ICU and I wrote a small check—a tiny donation to her cost of saving the world.

The world. I'd been feeling pretty roughed up by it myself—and I hadn't personally been laid out on a rug or knocked to the earth. My town wasn't flooded or flattened or burned, but lately the news had been full of people who'd lost everything to hurricanes and earthquakes and fires. Added to that, militant evangelical Christians, to whom the Republican party had sold itself piece by piece at some decades-long, Faustian swap meet, held the reins of government and, among other things, were attacking my gay friends, hacking away at my daughters' birth control, and scheming to put guns in my school. So when NPR topped it all off by telling me one morning, as I drove to the high school where I teach, that 45 billion bacteria were homesteading my kitchen sponge, pushing my teetering list of fears past the tipping point by one, it was too much; I burst into tears and bore down on the messenger. "Damn you NPR!" I wept. "Damn you and your filthy, fucking sponge!" It was a while before I could compose myself enough to walk into school.

A year after the 2016 election, everyone I knew was bruised and teetering—it was like we were walking the pickets of a fence that ran all the way to the horizon.

In the first months following the election—once I reoriented myself in space and time—I boiled over in outrage and purpose. I joined the ACLU. I called senators every day, signed petitions, hauled big, homemade signs to the state capitol and stood holding them in the wind.

Early that spring, incensed by threats to women's healthcare, my husband Larry and I threw a fundraiser for Planned Parenthood in our home—a soup supper. Peeling carrots and potatoes at the kitchen sink, I blasted that *Hamilton* CD. "Gotta rise up when you're down on your knees!" I sang, raising my fist and flinging peelings over the counters and floor. I bought a uterus cookie cutter, rolled out dozens of doughy uteruses on the kitchen island, frosted them pink and piped in fallopian tubes with red icing. On the day of the event, my daughter Maddie and I crawled over our driveway and the sidewalk running in front of our house with a bucket of chalk. "I get a little itchy when I don't have some control—Amy Poehler," we scrawled, and "Knowing what must be done does away with fear—Rosa Parks," and "Every woman should have a blowtorch—Julia Child." As friends poured in the door to sip soup and stuff money in a shoebox wrapped in pink tissue paper, from the living room window I watched passersby pause outside to absorb the vitriol of our inscriptions. Counting contributions at the end of the day, the victory we felt was heady and the success of our little skirmish made us feel like we were winning the war against civilization as we'd known it.

Half a year later, as the war waged on and casualties littered the battleground—climate protections, national monuments, children's healthcare among them—I felt sad and as ragged as that broken dove and wondered, "Is this how political prisoners feel when they are thrown in a cell, pulled out for regular drubbings, and thrown back in? Do intervals of despondency follow periods of hope in some rhythm you can get used to? Because all I wanted to do was pull inward and take cover—in poetry—on my rare strong days, in *Netflix* on the rest.

From their bookcase in the living room, the poets rose up and made what scruffy, small noises they could. "When despair for the world grows in me," Wendell Berry advised, "I go and lie down where the wood drake rests in his beauty on the water, and the great heron feeds." And, he concluded, "For a time I rest in the grace of the world and am free."

The grace of the world.

Taking Berry's cue, I'd been seeking shelter most afternoons in a small woods a few blocks from our home. Skulking under giant beeches and craggy oaks, and trespassing on quite a few properties, determined as Thoreau to reach the edge of a pond, I foraged for leaves and reeds and seed pods—which tell me with their symmetry, that there is an order and in that way maybe a grace to things. From their pulpits in the creaking tree canopy, crows bellowed their wild heresies with the bombast of Baptist ministers and, riding half-submerged logs, frogs elvised their velvety *love me tenders*. It was a better noise than I got from the news.

As fall stripped the shorelines and woods of their frills, the good bones of the world, which day after day threw down its treasures, emerged. Formerly hidden limbs scored the sky. Wildflower discs, barnacled with tiny florets usually screened by petals, rose like upholstered knobs among grasses fringing a marsh. Milkweed carapaces hung like little canoes on their stalks, their floss teased away by the wind. A plastic, gallon-size Ziploc in hand, which Larry drolly advised me to stop calling my "specimen bag," I bent to retrieve what loot the landlord threw down, hauled it back to the house, and spread it out on the kitchen island. Then piece by piece, I carried it into the living room, which is where I kept the digital microscope Larry brought home to aid my investigations, and ogled each artifact, projected in detailed relief on a screen.

"Larry!" I cried when a bit of beehive opened into a priory of monk's cells, and "Larry!" when a dime-sized lichen grew tentacled as a squid. The rachis of a wren's feather was straight as a stalactite, its barbs as regular as a Rockettes kick line. Mathematics was everywhere. Knit from an algorithm eons older than the pattern for a fisherman's sweater, the imbricate scales of an acorn cap fanned out in Fibonacci spirals and the pinnate veins of a beech leaf ran in perfect parallels from blade base to tip.

Is pattern *grace*? Is it this regular unfolding of things, so precise and dependable you could hang a hammock on it, that Berry rests in? If so, grace would have to include the cat stalking the dove, its instincts in perfect sync with millennia of cats that came before it. Plenty of people do make their peace with the natural world's innocent teeth and are no doubt the wiser for it.

Of course, human behavior—from a woman nursing injured animals to a president waging a war on truth—brings the real rub. Even before we constructed our informing modern *ologies*—psycho and neuro—about the things our frontal lobes got up to, whose functions appeared to muck up the natural world's narrative, our ancient mythmakers took up tweezers and extracted us from the pattern-minding matrix of determinism. They gave us forbidden fruit. They dispatched us from Eden. They explained how one day a president might come by the dishonorable ambitions that threaten democracy and how people with better lights would choose to stand against him. Decanting seeds from my pockets and folding leaves into books, I saw that the path to the woods, and the refuge those woods provided for reflection to open and bloom, led back to the world, *must* lead back to the world—and maybe therein lies grace.

I did not call kindly Cheryl to check on the progress of the rehabbing dove. I pictured her moving from cage to cage in her living room and kitchen and big, enclosed breezeway—filling water saucers, replacing bedding, speaking softly to the animals and I wondered where such powerful, shaping empathy comes from in a ravening world. High principles may be part of nature's complicated grammar, or they may be non-sequiturs, but her unequivocal call to kindness sure seemed to be coming from inside the house.

I don't know what thoughts entertained or bewildered Hercules Mulligan during his handful of minutes being a mouse. Like me, he probably thought a lot about food and predators. Nor do I know what quarter note in the world's sheet music flung him to the floor, not having been "in the room where it happened."

One of my students told me the other day that his grandmother prays the Rosary for every squirrel that runs by her window. And I found there was not one thing I had to overthink about that. For a time—but only, I told myself, for a time—I rested in the grace of the world and was free.

Through the Trees

"You can't take things from a *grave*, Mom." My teenage daughters were bringing down the gavel as I plucked a sheet of paper from Thoreau's grave where it had been pinned under a pebble amid the offerings of pilgrims. Placed on top of the small, upright stone in the Thoreau family plot that read only "Henry," rather than among the coins and pens and flowers scattered more broadly, it had caught my eye.

"Watch me," I said, backing under a big pine where, unrepentantly, I opened the creased page to a poem and slowly read the half-dozen stanzas scrawled in longhand.

"Did you hear the planes fly over?" it began. This was July of 2002—the first summer following 9/11, and it quickly became clear that Corinne Smith, whose name was signed at the bottom of the page, had brought her bewilderment and sorrow to Concord's sages who are buried near one another in Sleepy Hollow Cemetery. "Did Concord's best decipher all the meanings of that act?" she asked. "Did Waldo make pronouncements?...Did Bronson take the other side?...And what about the voices of the women on the hill?" Nearby, the graves of Louisa May Alcott, Elizabeth Peabody, and Thoreau's passionately abolitionist mother, Cynthia Dunbar Thoreau, bore their own bounty in offerings. "Did you honor their opinions? Does the air carry them still?" Reasoning that one good rain would be the end of it, I refolded the poem and put it in my pocket.

Back home in Michigan the following week, I slipped the poem inside a frame and hung it on a wall in my high school classroom. Its handful of stanzas—so earnest and bemused, in the way of that disoriented summer—would usher my students into our study of transcendentalism in the following years as, for its part, the world steadily became more complicated. And as complication goes with being sixteen like breathing goes with air, it was a natural fit.

Sixteen, I noticed more than ever, was seriously young—younger than most of my clothes, half the age—give or take—of my own daughters these days. All of my students were post-9/11 babies. I felt the distance between us as I never did before. Last fall one of the Zoes in my 2nd hour showed me an app that matched selfies to classic works of art. "See," she said, offering me her phone. "I'm the Lady of Shalott." I downloaded the app and submitted my own picture. "Old Woman Cooking an Egg," it said.

On the last day of summer this past year, I sat on a broad, flat rock in my garden among the hosta blossoms that overlook the lawn like consumptives, all lavender-gray and fading fast. Teaching, itself, was beginning to feel like a young person's game, most pointedly in its emphasis on the shiny stream of technologies that seemed to hatch daily from the genius of small gods working off stage. It was hard to keep up. It was hard to *almost* keep up.

A few days earlier, during my school's open house a parent in the back row, sitting below a string of Tibetan prayer flags, called up, "And what technology do you use in class?" I had to admit that I didn't use much. I certainly don't arrange a platform for my students to chat up Hester Prynne online from their bedrooms. "Technology is great where it's needed," I answered, "like for distance learning, when students don't have the benefit of discussing ideas with people in the same room." I heard the pedantic tin in my tone, felt the rush of wind as I launched into a screed. "But we are living, beating hearts and minds who do convene in a room together—and what a rich and lively experience that is!" Those were all the cards I laid on the table—for the most part, they were the only cards I ever had. Like the words stamped onto the prayer flags that rustled near the air-conditioner, I hoped my students' thoughts, generated by our reading and refined by our spirited give-and-take analysis, would lift and take flight.

Draped in a sheet on an examining table a few weeks earlier, I listened as my good doctor—a woman my own age—said, "There are three doors a woman walks through in life." We were talking about aging and the changing workplace. "The first leads to preparation—you're a student. The second door leads to a career and, for most of us, motherhood, and that long period where you give yourself to your job and family. The third door is menopause. After menopause, a woman's *only* job is to speak the truth."

Alone again in the examining room, I thought about truth-speaking as I put my clothes back on, about how aging can make us doubt our own conclusions—am I correct or merely a curmudgeon in a world that has rightly, naturally moved on?—and the extent to which our views will be valued. And I considered (again) the "professional" lines I sometimes crossed in class when the President put out some barbarous new lie or blast of hate. Politically, teachers are supposed to remain neutral in class, which was to say, opaque as those eyeless old statues overlooking the atrocities of the Colosseum. But lately I'd been too outraged for silence, which felt like complicity, and I'd found myself making pointed remarks in our class discussions—most recently regarding "men who boast about building walls while having so few boundaries they brag about grabbing women's genitals." Gamely, I scrawled *HYPOCRISY* on the board, then asked, "What does *this* mean?" Almost daily, my mind drifted to the authoritarian rise of the Third Reich and I wondered how teachers in Germany had felt during the thirties. Did horrified Weimar democrats censor themselves among the ranks of true believers when their country made that murderous right turn that led straight to dictatorship and genocide? And weren't terms like "professionalism" and "neutrality" just uniforms we donned to take the heat off our squeamish moral responsibilities? And, day after day, I wondered if I might be getting too angry to teach.

Schlepping on my jacket, I exited the examining room, turned the wrong way, as I always do, and let someone direct me to the parking lot. The next day I flew to New Hampshire, rented a car, and drove south to Concord, Massachusetts. Sixteen years after swiping a poem from Thoreau's grave, I was returning to the scene of the crime.

The Walden Woods Project, in its own words, "preserves the land, literature, and legacy of Henry David Thoreau to foster an ethic of environmental stewardship and social responsibility." As a part of this mission, twenty or so teachers from around the U.S. are invited to convene for a week each summer at the headquarters of the Thoreau Institute on a wooded slope overlooking Walden Pond.

On the morning of our first day, I drove into busy, bucolic Concord and met the five other teachers with whom I'd be sharing digs, all of us introducing ourselves as we hauled bags up the old, steep steps of a cottage in town. Then we squeezed into my car and wove the winding few miles to Walden Woods to meet our larger group and push chairs into a circle in the manor house that serves as headquarters for the Institute. Paneled wood walls rose up around us and shelves at both ends of the room were thick with books.

We were young and old, from both coasts and the middle of the country. One of us had ridden horses in rodeos. Two had driven from Texas, camping in the rain with their indispensable third, a stolid bottle of Jim Beam. One of us was a novelist. One of us was pregnant with a child that we would all insist, as the week wore on and we got comfortable together, she name *Henry*. There was lots of time to talk as we hiked.

"This was Thoreau's bean field, "our trail guide Brian, an environmentalist from Brandeis, announced as our single-file group accordioned in around him where the path in the woods broadened. A few days into our week, we were just uphill from Thoreau's pond, the deepest freshwater lake in Massachusetts. Every summer morning, quite a few swimmers bisect it, most of them with flotation "bubbles" bobbing over their backs.

"All trees now," someone murmured. In Thoreau's day, much of the forest had been cleared to feed Boston's stoves and he'd planted and tended, not very successfully, a small crop of beans.

"None of these trees are more than eighty years old." Brian told us, "It's mostly pitch pine and oak." As we jotted field notes, he added, "Animals ate a tenth of his crop; Thoreau said it was a kind of tithe." I pulled a cluster or "fascicle" of pine needles from a sapling; its three needles told me it was pitch pine; red pines have only two needles per bundle, white pines five, we were learning.

We moved on through the woods, over a landscape that rose and dipped among geological kettles—basins left behind by stranded icebergs that had slowly melted away. "Henry used to drink here," Matt, our resident naturalist, remarked, pointing to a spring fringed by ferns and mossy boulders. I was noticing how often the staff referred to Thoreau as *Henry*— a friend. More noticeable was the way they pronounced his name: *thorough*, as in, *a thorough explanation,* which was what, secretly, we were all waiting for regarding that jarring inflection.

"Yes," we were told when one of us finally asked. "Thoreau is rightly pronounced *thorough;* that's how Henry said it." I imagined taking that insider's scoop back to the Midwest—back to anywhere, really—and saw at once how *thoroughly* it couldn't be exported. You can't return from a week in London and start taking the *lift* or grow up sticking a fistful of dandelions in a *vace* and show up at a family dinner twenty years later with lilacs in a *vahz*. I stashed *thorough* away among the other private mementos I'd haul home, most of them rocks dug out of the pond.

Sitting in loose rings around a big conference table in the library at the Thoreau Institute, we began our days with Jeff, who curates the manuscript collections at Walden, and Whitney, whose vision and grit organized our days and corralled us through them. We'd read all of the same materials sent to us with a syllabus the previous spring but I, at least, had never dug into Thoreau's journals, never read the entry where he describes encountering God in his own root cellar. "How many communications may we not lose through inattention?" he asks.

When Jeff brought out some of the Institute's actual manuscripts for us to hold, we lined up like novitiates and received the pages—Thoreau's slanted goose quill scrawl running over them—with awe. "One hundred and sixty-four Bibles:" Jeff said, "that's the length of Thoreau's journals."

Our afternoons were spent hiking and swimming and gliding in canoes along the serene Concord River where lawns roll down to the water from enormous, gabled homes. There was a lot of money in Concord these days. "Fooh-kin' gaw-geous is what we call this in Massachusetts!" Patty, who'd grown up nearby, called from her seat in the middle of a canoe Cindy-from-Missouri and I were paddling.

But lovely as our Walden days were, we carried the desperation of the times with us and everyone seemed to have descended on Walden Woods with the same visceral fear of the demolition machine that had been threatening to clear-cut the institutions of our democracy for the past couple of years. Would razed institutions simply grow back like trees? And what was our classroom role? No one was sure. By the time he wrote *Civil Disobedience*, Thoreau's own school had long been closed. But the transcendentalists' days had been fraught too, the future of *their* democracy threatened by the question of abolition: the *question*. There was nothing new about rampant American wrong-headedness.

Back in my classroom in Michigan, I thumb-tacked a map of the United States, the words: "America is Sacred: No Lies!" running across it at a diagonal, and thought about Thoreau's habitual, impolitic truth-talking. Then, on the first morning of class, when we all rose to recite *The Pledge of Allegiance*, I concluded my own pledge with a resounding, "with liberty and justice for *all races, all religions, all genders*!" and—big finish: "because this is America!" My students, startled at first, moved on to smiling and rolling their eyes, then to just eye-rolling, and finally to ignoring me altogether while they scrolled on their phones as I laid it out there day after day.

During the third week of school, I asked them, "Will Americans support national leaders who are bullies? Egomaniacs who rant and lie? Shameless power-grabbers who exploit people's fears while pretending to be patriots?" Eyes blinked in the little gulf of uneasy silence that followed. Then I threw a picture of Joe McCarthy on the *Smartboard* screen in preparation for reading *The Crucible* and we examined the way McCarthy lost the support of the American people once his character and abuses were fully known. "What *are* the obligations as citizenship?" I asked. "When do we say *enough?* We'll think about that for the rest of the year." Oblique or transparent, it's a question that has to be asked. And after a week at Walden Pond, I had good reason to believe that teachers across the country were feeling their way forward, no two in the same way, asking, asking, asking.

Concord was busy the day I drove in from New Hampshire and parked in the driveway of a white, columned church shouldering an enormous steeple, in the way of old Puritan meeting houses. As the door was open, I wandered into the vestibule and was greeted by a couple of friendly twenty-somethings sitting at a card table. "What's happening inside?" I asked.

"The Thoreau Society is having its annual meeting," the young woman replied as a question formed in my mind.

"You don't—by any chance—know a Thoreau-loving poet named Corinne Smith, do you?" It was a ridiculous longshot.

"I do," she answered and joined me at the small window where we squinted into the sanctuary at the backs of a hundred or so people spread throughout the pews. From the high pulpit in front, a genial-looking man with a stand of silver hair was speaking. "She's there, in the middle, in the white shirt." My eyes settled on the back of a gray-haired woman sitting next to the center board that bisected the pews into equal segments. I eased open the door and slipped inside.

Halfway up the left aisle, I lit on the end of the plank I was suddenly sharing with the woman whose purloined poem hung on my classroom wall. As the Chair of *The Committee on Selections of Officers* replaced the society's president at the lectern, I began my slow slide along the empty-on-my-side pew. On each side of the pulpit, black-eyed Susans and Queen Anne's lace in old jugs stirred in the small wind of oscillating fans. "One hundred and eight people voted in our election," the Chair reported, pausing: "with no evidence of Russian involvement." A light laughter rippled through the pews as, inch by inch, I bore down on Corinne. When I reached the bisecting plank that separated us like an old Yankee bundling board, a man to our left rose to address the troubling acrimony between members of the Thoreau Society and members of the Emerson Society. Polarization was *everywhere*.

Snaking my arm up the side of the partition in our pew, I slipped Corinne a note on a page torn from my journal and watched her give it a quick scan. "I am Jan Shoemaker," it said. "I took your poem from Thoreau's grave 16 years ago." When she turned to look at me, I like to think a bit of transcendentalist awe opened in us both.

Later that week, Corinne showed me around town, pointing out the stone marker where Thoreau's infamous jail cell once squatted, the saltbox house he died in (up for sale for a couple of million bucks), the busts of Concord's luminaries in the Free Public Library. Among them, Bronson Alcott's famous daughter Louisa looked down from its pedestal. Despite reprisals threatened by the Fugitive Slave Law, that murderous legislation enacted by the governing scoundrels of their day, the Alcotts had made their home a stop along the Underground Railroad.

In the transcendentalists' divided nation, it took a war to dismantle the scabrous institution of slavery which, as newly free African Americans made economic and political strides, was replaced by Jim Crow. Even my current students, with their handful of years, can recall the times before gay men and women could marry, and I remind them that at least one local chain store in our town *legally* denies birth control coverage to its employees. "What is once well done is done forever," Thoreau maintained, mistakenly. Even in its errors, Concord seemed to emphasize the way we inch forward and slide back, inch forward and slide back. Apparently, hard-won human rights were never *fait accompli* and vigilance was not something we could afford to let slide. It seemed that only by paying attention, by keeping about us a bit of the root cellar, could we hold a higher ground.

Naturally, during my week in Walden Woods, I revisited Sleepy Hollow—you don't go to Concord without stopping by to see *Henry*. The usual trinkets littered his grave—but no poems. At the cairn of boulders that marked the site of his cabin, however, I found another sheet of notebook paper with a message scrawled sloppily by someone bent over a knee.

"I know of no method or discipline that can supersede the necessity of being ever on the alert," it read. "HDT"—then, "Thank you Henry."

"Thank you, Henry," I echoed. And, in keeping with that old wisdom about paper covering rock, I replaced the note where I'd found it and walked down to the pond.

WHAT THE WHELK SHELLS TELL

Skirting the tables at *Les Deux Magots*, the little tabloid vender issued a salacious trill and patted his stack of papers. He seemed to have the goods on *"un triste scandaleuse!"* but he might have been calling, "Caps for Sale!" by the looks of him. Slim and mustachioed, in a small green blazer and flat cap, its tongue-tip of brim shading his brow, he was flirting with café-sitters in Saint-Germaine-des-Pres, urging them to swap a euro or two for a morsel of gossip, its probability as weightless and delicious as meringue.

When no one on our corner nipped at the bait, he scampered across the street to have another go at it and Anna and I finished our tea and headed out to find *un tire-bouchon,* a corkscrew.

In Paris for the chilly first week of April, we'd brought along short shopping lists; Anna wanted vintage fashion prints from a flea market and I wanted olive-wood salad-servers and the aforementioned corkscrew. I'd recently begun quite a radical purging campaign at home, dropping big bags off at the Goodwill on my way to school each morning, and I was too old to be much interested in acquiring new things. But if there was anything I'd learned in my almost sixty years on the planet, a sound corkscrew is indispensable to good living and when I ran my current acquisitions and divestitures program through the Jesus sieve—the particular wisdom tradition I grew up in—it came out: "Take everything you have and give it to the poor, but keep your corkscrew."

We also had wedding gifts to buy, which took us down a few rabbit holes in search of boutiques described in detail online but nonexistent in the narrow *rues* of real life and finally led us to the famous department store, *Galeries Lafayette. Galeries Lafayette* is *un grand magasin* as tufted and gilded as an opera house, an only slightly smaller version (it seemed) of *Versailles.* Entering one of a thousand doors, Anna and I made our way through sundry, glinting, smart salons that angled into one another like a couture house of mirrors. Eventually, we escalated to a higher tier from which we gazed down at the ground-floor—the interior of the building is circular as a hive and all floors or *galeries* open to a vast atrium in the middle—and up at the magnificent, stained-glass dome, which filtered light like a blessing on all that well-heeled wanting and scheming and getting and spending, blurring the old boundaries between the sacred and profane. Up to another floor, and up again, then down we went until, completely overwhelmed by the pulsing pageantry of it all, we accosted what seemed to be a customer au pair (God bless him), an impeccably dressed idler in the land of *parfumeries* keeping an eye out for the lost likes of us. And there between the opulent fiefdoms of Givenchy and Chanel, I broke out my hunchbacked French.

"S'il vous plait, Monsieur, ou est…les choses…pour la maison?" ("Where is…the things…for the house?") And he directed us across a broad street to another colony in the *Galeries* empire, where we orienteered through villages of chocolates and cheese, veered around mountains of sea salts and hillocks of herbs, navigated nations of olives and pastries and oils before making our way upstairs to linens and glass, the sorts of things that would box up nicely, we thought, and make suitable gifts. Which they did. And a few months later, the weddings we attended were *tres beaux.*

Who knew why people wanted what they did? Sometimes it was simple, of course. I wanted to go to Paris to play with language. I loved looping words together and stringing them all over the patient people I knew, the way I festooned our living room with paper chains when I was the single mom of two small girls and we had too little money, really, even to leave the house.

But it wasn't always clear, I thought, watching the stepmother-of-the-bride cross the banquet hall at the second wedding I went to after returning from Paris. Mothers-of-the-bride were in a terrible pickle, it must be allowed. They wanted to look nice on their daughter's big day. But confronting what should be the simple task of dressing themselves for the occasion, no one in the wedding industrial complex had their backs, and inevitably they are pointed by prim sadists to racks of satin hanging at the back of every bridal store. I knew this from experience and I think my own reaction to it was telling. When I found a dead bat interred behind a row of books in our family room shortly after my daughter Maddie announced her engagement, my response leapt on light feet from horror to glee. "If I have rabies," I beamed at my husband, as he carried the little mummy out of the house, "I won't have to shop for a mother-of-the-bride dress!" In the quest for suitable apparel, too many of us end up looking like Queen Elizabeth—all jowls in some ghastly pastel at the opening of Parliament.

But this stepmother I'd never met of a bride I barely knew had headed off down the road less traveled by turning up in her own wedding dress: a white, abundantly beaded gown with a train. Mesmerized, I watched as she advanced down the aisle at the start of the ceremony, veering just short of the altar to her seat in the front row, and later I couldn't pry my eyes off her as, bent slightly forward, all cheekbones and chin, she darted busily among the tables and dancers, her train brushing over people's shoes and wrapping itself around the legs of chairs. What she wanted—besides the obvious limelight—and what she was able to take from the evening is anyone's guess.

We all knew that, according to wry Jane Austen, what men wanted, at least what single men "in possession of a good fortune" wanted, was a wife. Women, by contrast, wanted power—at least over their husbands, according to centuries of instruction from Chaucer's randy Wife of Bath, or over their own bodies and lives according to more reliable narrators. But as we are a baffling and often perverse species, mucking things up is this: what we should want and what we do want, so often didn't align. There was a reason we never see an "All You Should Eat!" buffet.

The question of what I wanted would certainly have baffled my socially conscious friends had any of them spied me slinking into a Walmart shortly after I returned from Paris. I finally caved is all—finally decided to stop raging against the machine—against Asian sweatshops, anti-Labor, cheap crap. Against the obliteration of the little guys with their quaint mom and pop shops, most of them long gone, having limped off with Opie and Aunt Bee. Just one person, what could I do? And what had I accomplished during all those years of my Great Big Boycott? Way past time to let it go.

On W-Day, I parked in the middle of the vast, paved acreage flanking the giant Walmart box, which felt, I imagined, like docking on the Death Star, but I shrugged it off and head slightly down, resolutely ducked inside. "Grim," I muttered out loud, glancing around what looked like an enormous, crowded bunker, but what was I expecting—*Galeries Lafayette?*— which had been a lark anyway, a glitzy little trespass out of my working class world. This was more like a warehouse grafted to one of those cheerless flea markets hawking batteries and beer coolers in dead strip malls. I turned into a maze of alleys, high-rise shelves on each side, the depressing modern medina of the global economy.

Soon, however, things started looking up. My shoulder caught the edge of a quilt, which was what I'd come for. Our bedspread had literally gone to the dogs and company was coming, so we needed a replacement and they were far too expensive everywhere else, at every *possible other store* I'd shook down first. I unfolded the quilt, dismissed it as pretty ugly—no, just ugly—but the same color as our dogs—a boon. I peeked at the label, hoping for "Labrador Yellow," but adjectives cost extra so "Yellow" it read. Then: $19.97—less than twenty bucks—for an ugly, (king-size!) quilt at Walmart! Hugging it to my chest, I cautiously moved on and spied what I thought was a hot tub, but which turned out better—a volcano, a crater, a vast plastic sinkhole chockfull of candy. Plucking out a box of Junior Mints, I felt a flutter of excitement. This was okay—no—better than that; this was getting a little bit *fun*. Gripping my quilt and clutching my chocolate, I paused to take stock, feeling the squeeze of the "close place," all at once channeling Huck Finn who, risking hell to free the slave Jim, recklessly cried, "If I could think up anything worse, I would do that too!" I took a big lungful of air and headed back for a cart.

It was easy after that. As I rolled along aisle after aisle, my uppity principles broke free of their tethers to conscience—that pedant, that bore—and I felt almost buoyant. This, I thought, must be how Rush Limbaugh felt every day of his life—and laughed at the thought, laughed out loud at Rush and Walmart and me. Rolling into cosmetics, I pulled up alongside a monolith of mailbox-sized bottles of aloe lotion and hoisted one into my cart. Ditto a colander on short legs to replace my suddenly untenable old one which wallowed on its belly at the bottom of the sink. Meeting needs I never knew I had, those wizards at Walmart! Then I turned a corner—into a line of artillery.

A gun department. No segue—no shelves of fatigues or magazines—no *Soldier of Fortune* stacked on a rack. Just suddenly there—assault rifles, lined up like smokestacks, like pikes on a bridge awaiting the next unlucky head, not twenty feet from hand towels, not fifty feet from pinwheels and bubbles with wands.

I did not storm out in a righteous huff. Instead, I scanned for witnesses, found no one nearby, and reconnoitered to the counter, revulsed and enthralled—like the first time I'd sidled coffin-side to gape at an uncle when I was a kid. The remains of an uncle, no longer a man—a slab of something strangely boxed, something ruined, something wrong. I'd fled that room.

No one was supervising the Walmart arsenal as I bent over the handguns in the display case. Short-handled, long snouted, they looked hard to balance, like they'd want to tip forward, blast off a foot. Later, researching gun lexicon online—feeling every inch the voyeur and ghoul—it occurred to me that the *stock* or *grip* must be weighted, the *barrel* light steel—the better to keep it aimed at whomever you mean to put a hole in, a neat little puncture for life to leak out.

Not often, but too often, I dreamt I was being tugged toward the nucleus of some force or entity I sensed as evil. Sometimes aroused and surrendered, sometimes futilely resisting, I was drawn into a darkness I knew would be the end of me. It was primal and mythic and, frankly, terrifying and no doubt would drive a lively dinner party discussion among Freudians and Jungians and my own people, the feminists, but the point being, it was a bit the way I felt about those guns. Attracted to annihilation, back-pedaling for my life. This was just where chumming with Rush would get you in broad daylight.

In a handful of minutes, that good angel, Reason, swept in to remind me that guns kill kids. I left my cart in the store.

Huston Smith makes the at once sweeping and incisive claim that "People can never get enough of what they do not really want." I made a big deal of this paradox with my students early in the semester. "If that dozen pair of boots in my closet didn't satisfy me, if I'm still rooting around at the mall, what did that suggest?

"Maybe it's not boots you actually want?" Alex or Emma or Rachel would risk—which launched our investigation of the nature of self and desire.

"Then what do you think *I really* want?"

My tabletops at home whispered hints. Gradually dispatched lamps and picture frames and baskets and bowls were supplanted by wonders I couldn't keep my greedy fingers from hauling home. Petoskey stones. Horn and honeycomb and chain corrals. Pinecones and acorns. An ammonite the size of a softball lugged back from Morocco, a robin's nest lowered from the steel pulleys and tracks that open our garage door—its blue egg, abandoned, still tucked inside. Whelk shells from Normandy, pin curls of birch, a wren's nest from the rafters of a friend's dairy barn. When I carried in an enormous hive dangling from a branch like a Japanese lantern last fall, Larry gave me a startled look so we let it winter on the porch where the brutal north took it down to twenty below, then, satisfied there were no intransigent wasps hunkered down inside, I placed it on the library table. Its poetry startled me every time I walked into the room.

I'd been slipping these artifacts into our house for years, but had picked up the pace, intrigued by the mechanism that shaped every scale and leaf and spiral to its niche. The ferns outside the window by my desk unfurled like sonnets in the spring; their blades, regular as iambs, soothed me with their meter, their promise that this buckling world was an orderly place, that if I could only enter its rhythm and find my step, its beautiful, brutal choreography would carry and not crush me.

This summer I shared separate lunches with two former students, Meghan and Matt, who'd both recently finished college, returned from traveling abroad, and had stories to tell I was happy to hear. Meghan, who'd been homeschooled until ninth grade, had grown up in a conservative, evangelical family and gone off to a small, parochial college. Though she was bright and animated and reflective, I stupidly wrote the end of her story and never expected to read it. Matt, who was raised by British expats in Africa, had turned up in my classroom when his father took a job with the university down the road. Jocular and cosmopolitan, he tracked political machinations in Africa like the BBC, held his breath during the elections of its war-torn nations, grieved the grinding of nascent leaders into despots. His mind was always in Africa.

Just back from a year in Mali, where his humanitarian ambitions were thwarted by bureaucrats, Matt had joined the Jesuits, he explained, picking up his sandwich and putting it down again, not getting many bites in as he enthused about his next adventure. He was affable and burly and in his plaid shirt he looked like his Calvinist father's son, but he'd thrown in his hat with the serving Catholics and was heading off to work with refugees.

Slight and blond, Meghan met me a couple of weeks later, lit up by lupines in Iceland and peaks in the Alps, but solemn and composed when I pressed her for the other stories, the ones about hauling laundry up flights of stairs at the Mother Teresa House in Kolkata, of sitting bedside among people dying in another language. "You just hold their hands," she said, putting down her fork, her falling voice telling me a little of what she'd learned about limitations and perseverance and the simple gift of presence. She had just accepted a teaching job abroad. Matt and Meghan's futures both loomed exotic and a little frightening, I thought, though Meghan was only going to Uganda while Matt was headed for Texas.

The great thing about teaching is, of course, what you learn. Only in their twenties, Matt and Meghan heard a rhythm running through the world's discord, felt the pulse below its thin skin of squabbling doctrines, dueling politics, insistent sirens. Fueled by hope and driven by Faith in the Small Difference theology—that belief in the bit of good we can do if we put our shoulder to it—they were singing "the tune without the words" or swapping words as required, for all they were worth. They reminded me that the tune was the thing. I wasn't getting on a plane, as they would be soon, but I went home and wrote a little midsummer "thinking of you" note to a student who struggled with a learning disability and put it in the mailbox.

Nestled in a wooden bowl with a honeycomb hive the size of a child's fist, a finch's nest woven of twigs and down, a bit of rusty sumac, and a couple of small, basalt boulders that fit in the socket of my palm, were a few pinecones. I used to make a little joke that, after poetry had spent itself tracking it, Truth would be revealed in an equation, the maths would take all, and mathematicians everywhere would celebrate by waving their graphic calculators and sinking drunkenly into their lumbar cushions.

The scales on pinecones are imbricate, meaning they overlapped like shingles. It was a soothing design, which is why I liked to keep a couple of artichokes, which do the same thing, in a bowl on our kitchen counter. But the big punchbowl of nature, of course, was spiked with mathematics and, like the leaves of a fiddlehead fern and the spiral of a nautilus, pinecone scales were also arranged according to the Fibonacci ratio, the famous ordering sequence that came out like a flash of light from what we like to call the late Dark Ages, wherein each number in a list is the sum of the previous two. The Fibonacci choreography goes like this: 1, 1, 2, 3, 5, 8 and so on, infinitely. Peering into my pinecone I searched for but couldn't find the numbers, which is how it goes with math and me. Still, I had faith in the unseen—like any true believer.

"People can never get enough of what they do not really want." Smith makes his observation from the Hindu point of view, which sees each of our true selves as a droplet of God, bottled up in our bodies and pining for the ocean of God surrounding us. Sufism agrees. "I have a thirsty fish in me that can never find enough of what it's thirsty for! Show me the way to the ocean!" Rumi cries. We crave reunion with our Source, whether it's Deity or the universe itself; new boots will simply never do.

Cascading from a single point in spirals and fronds, what the ferns and cones and whelk shells I've gathered up tell is this: I wanted my life to ripple right. Not in perfect Fibonacci emanations like the chambers of an ammonite, which I would never pull off—it was the rare day I didn't curse at someone in traffic or toss out another appeal for money that came in the mail. Nothing mucked up the math like free will.

It wasn't likely I'd ever discover if the universe was home-made with love like apple pie, the sweet and sour worked thoughtfully into the recipe, or if it was the intention-less rippling of some mysterious proto particle accelerator the good physicists at nearby Michigan State University were trying to reproduce. Being made of the same stuff about which we endlessly inquire, I suppose, was limiting—that old forest for the trees business, but scientists and shamans kept showing up at work, pressing for a glimpse. What we did know was this: about fourteen billion years ago an explosion occurred, and as a result of that audacious Bang, out of nowhere and nothing at all, our universe was born, voila!—not a thing most of us could wrap our poor minds around. And way down the line, Bill Bryson explained to non-scientists like me, on a newly formed planet, "some tiny bag of chemicals twitched and became animate." The *how* it managed to twitch was where we still hit a wall, which was what kept quite a few of even my scientist friends—biologists, chemists, physicists—going to church.

I believed in form and pattern. In sequence and rhythm. And I believed in ripples. It mattered today that four thousand years ago a shepherd in Sicily or Peru offered a crust to an orphaned child.

My own life was a small disturbance—a pebble tossed into the sea—but I wanted this life to ripple right, at least as right as it could ripple in the days I have left. Which I saw, casting about my little niche in the universe—the high school, Midwest, American, Earth in the 21st century niche—meant remembering to drive my whole humanity to school each day and marching it into class and offering it up to my students—a big, fat, full, human presence—gratuitous, it could seem, in an educational climate that, driven increasingly by machines rather than people, appeared to value humanity less every year. A climate that trumpeted a test score but ignored the poetry of a young life and wanted us to believe Emma's Data > Emma Herself. It meant, even as they went out of style, steadfastly donning half a dozen human hats at once—teacher, mentor, parent, confidante, counselor, coach: *Caps for Sale*!

Like poor old Prufrock, "I grow old," my back reminded me every time I hacked away at our marauding ferns, which rose in midsummer and threatened to take our neighbor's front porch. And as my days dwindled, this concern for their rippling was more on my mind, in a stark equation aging threw up. "Maybe you could join Special Forces," Larry remarked drily at breakfast the other day as I mused out loud about volunteering to help in the next African Ebola outbreak where my sister, an actual nurse, assured me I'd only be in the way. So instead, as it closed in on August, I went to the mall to pick up a few back-to-school basics, mindful not to get much since my teaching years ahead were down to single digits, and in doing so, ran into a clearance sale where I bought a bathing suit—with an old-lady skirt. "Ask not," I told the cashier darkly, "for whom the bell tolls."

"Thanks!" she smiled brightly and handed me my bag.

Slow Learner

Summer interrupts a teaching life like a refrain following a series of erratic free verses. Last year's final verse, launched by an upturned mop (six scrawny feet and tousled hair) that clattered into my room with a gym bag and lacrosse gear just after I'd turned in final grades and was locking my file cabinets, went like this:

"Dude! I gotta have a B!"

"Dude, you gotta *earn* a B! And did you call me *Dude?* I'm your uppity English teacher—that's '*Ms.* Dude' to you!"

"Duuude!"

"*I know you!*" I thought, stepping lightly through the high school door into the sunny second week of June and picking the tune right up. "Na na na na"—a glance at the school parking lot in my rearview mirror—"hey hey hey: goodbye!" I drove with the windows down, belting the old lyrics through the whipping strands of my hair, singing to my fellow humans buttoned up in lawyer and accountant and optometrist-suits as we paused together at traffic lights, wailing to the car-wash guys in their rubber boots and the cashiers tethered to display counters in the low-sprawling mall. "Hey hey hey: goodbye!"

But when I pulled into the driveway at home all that breezy *vive la liberation!* sputtered and died. Having driven to the lip of summer, which loomed vast and deep as the Grand Canyon, I teetered there, disoriented and overwhelmed. Dropping my bag inside the front door, I worked the short line of our ecstatic dogs—Lab Gracie and Lab-ish Scout—reminded them they are "*Good* girls! *Good* girls!" and fed them each a gruesome little gummy-steak from the treat-bag in the cupboard. Then I made a tentative tour of the house, unsure where to turn—*knowing how way leads on to way* and all that.

Blinking at the stacks of books foresting our end tables, which would only be hewn with reading, I turned to the paper shards torn from notebooks and menus and magazines—frowzy split-ends sticking out of folders piled on my desk and heaped on the laptop. They were scrawled with anecdotes, sudden insights, turns of phrase—little skid-marks of my fickle, dine-and-dash muse. I peeled back a folder and read: "Things I was promised in the 1970s: my own jetpack and a four-day work week," "Aphrodite transformed into Virgin Mary," "the peppery scent of my mother." In the "Elephant Room," a bay of windows named for a former student's painting that hangs there, I scanned bowls and bowls of rocks: knobby fossils from Lake Huron, creamy disks from Lake Michigan as thin as guitar picks, black lozenges from the coast of Maine, pearly buttons from Hampstead Heath, and more—all clamoring to be labeled by site.

Withdrawing back outside, I veered around the house and tried not to trample the small ferns that have shot on a syndicate of underground runners into my garden path—impudent street-kids maybe still young enough to find good homes for. Which led me to the garage to assess the state of the spades and shovels and trowels stuffed into pots among wadded-up gloves stiff with dried soil—lazy, late-fall shelving. Returning to the house, I made a cup of tea and resumed my standoff with the books.

After a couple of flummoxed days in the Land-of-Where-to-Begin? my shoulders relaxed and the undifferentiated hours of summer started sorting themselves into their own verses, almost always about the home projects I saved up for the non-teaching months: the hideous wallpaper that will have to come off in slivers with a spackling knife, the window blinds to remove and scrub on the patio table, the grisly de-webbing of the basement windows—their packed little mausoleums sucked into the long snout of the wet-vac. Sorry spiders.

In the last couple of years, without even registering for classes, I had become something of a student again myself, was busy learning myriad new things about what happens to a human body in its sixth decade. And by way of gearing up philosophically for the seventh, which I could practically reach out and touch from here, I'd added a new refrain to fold a little poetry into my days and maybe shore up small terraces in the landslide toward…well, oblivion. "So we're doing *this* now," I thought shortly after the first time I rocketed out of bed with foot cramps in the middle of the night and, "So we're doing *this* now," when little geysers of stomach acid began erupting into my throat and, "So we're doing *this* now when floaters invaded my left eye. It was also a distancing device, I saw (onto my own wiles), one that, in dividing body from consciousness—object from observer, story from narrator—gave me a neat shield of protection: an illusion, of course. Self-as-scientist and science-project: collecting data, falling apart.

This summer the Detroit Institute of Arts, which had lately groaned through its own struggle to keep body and soul together as the city's creditors threatened to ransack its few treasures, featured a Frida Kahlo / Diego Rivera exhibit. Detroit itself had shrunken in recent decades to small archipelagos of cultural and sporting venues in a sea of hapless city blocks, thousands of its abandoned homes razed, long grasses between the occupied dwellings that remain blowing in the wind. As the city tried to shore up its meager resources over the past few years, light and water became unreliable in whole neighborhoods—it might have been Baghdad; besieged Detroit was doing *this* now. When I googled "Detroit neighborhoods" for information on the city's stretched police and fire services, "Detroit neighborhoods to avoid" came up—anger and despair in volatile doses apparently being inseparable from abandonment.

My friends and I took the luck-of-birth luxury of avoiding those desperate enclaves by zipping over them on I-96 when we drove down to see the exhibition—by a second stroke of luck, as there was cake—on Frida Kahlo's birthday. The DIA was best known for the Rivera murals covering the four walls of its interior courtyard, a monolithic tribute (and a somewhat romantic one, in which black and white men are depicted working side by side in Ford factories which were, at the time, segregated) to the automobile industry and its workers. Rivera's additional paintings, acquired for the exhibition, were impressive, but it was one of Kahlo's pictures that I found most arresting and I settled down in front of it holding the audio-speaker to my ear like a shoe-phone, very Maxwell Smart.

Kahlo's *The Suicide of Dorothy Hale* depicts the sensational and tragic fall of a beautiful, penniless socialite who leapt to her death from a New York apartment building in the 1930s. It's a painting rife with curiosities. Commissioned by the victim's friend as a gift for Hale's mother, Kahlo knew she was expected to produce a memorial portrait suitable for hanging in a grief-stricken house. Why then did Kahlo paint the suicide itself—in stages, no less: the leap, the fall, the body sprawled on the ground? Why does Hale's foot slip out of the painting and into the inscription at the bottom, blurring the boundary between art and life? And why did Kahlo paint it as an *Ex-Voto*—a type of Mexican folk art that depicts both a tragedy and the saint who intervened to help the victim, when clearly no hand pulled Hale back inside her little rented room? These were compelling questions about compassion and faith and estrangement and artistic intent and maybe responsibility. But the thought that nagged me as I leaned in and squinted at the falling figure was, why *head-first?* A question for physics, or at the very least, meteorology.

Poets and pastors and, of course, psychologists, out of their deep humanness, have colonized suicide, explored its jungles, written it epitaphs. Many have thrown up nets—just there, near the cliff—catching, catching, catching in the deep and rippling rye. God bless them, every one. The public discussion about people who leap to their deaths—the jumpers as well as the divers—rightly concerned itself with depression, its warning signs, and the pretty good drugs that existed now for treating it. There was little if any hard data about what happened to a body as it fell.

As one who had long evaded the sciences to truck with the arts and letters, this peering under the world's hood and squinting at its nuts and bolts came late to me. Unable to ignore my own dismantling ("You lost half an inch in height," a nurse reported at my last yearly exam as I stretched below the damning little lever resting on my head. "Hmmm," I thought, "We're doing *this* now."), I was dogged by the idea that time was running out, which turned my thoughts increasingly to this windy, watery world I'd have to "leave" when death, indifferently razing this old house, closed me down and sentience slipped away like a wisp of smoke. *What's going on around here anyway?*

"Why *head-first?*" was not a question that came up in poetry or philosophy or theology—those disciplines whose structures and musings informed my own, and for an hour a day, at least, my students' world. There was a collective, audible gasp the first time I read that famous, last line of "Richard Cory" to my high school sophomores. *Why* he committed suicide, (when "he was... richer than a king") not *how* (with "a bullet through his head") drove our discussion of estrangement and hopelessness and the terrible dark places to which they could lead. Kahlo, of course, didn't see Hale fall; she simply painted the plunge as she imagined it, but now she had me wondering, why *head-first?* Did Hale jump or dive? Does a body in freefall tip forward, a clumsy kite for gravity and wind? Does a leap inevitably end in a dive?

That was the question that nagged me as I renovated the laundry room after returning from the Kahlo exhibit, lugging old shelves outside, sheering corkboard from drywall with a putty knife, excavating under the ancient utility sink with a flashlight and spray-bottle of Lysol—trigger finger poised; I'd once seen a centipede crawl out from under there which had sent me howling to the curb. This neglected room had hovered near the top of my to-do list ever since the rusting washing machine had begun hobbling across the floor during the spin cycle (it was doing *this* now), pulling the hose out and flooding the place. I'd spent quite a few evenings over the past year sitting on top of it with a book and a glass of wine but finally new appliances were on their way and I wanted fresh, clean everything. Fidgeting with the old light fixture at the top of a stepladder, I wobbled at a little spasm of vertigo and braced myself on a new cabinet. Whatever flavor of despair might await me in the coming years, I would never be a jumper, would never apply the scientific method to the problem of falling.

Each evening during the week or so it took me to muck out the laundry room, I pushed aside the fabric softener and buckets and batteries and dog shampoo cluttering the kitchen table, sat down with a notebook, and worked on a list straightforwardly titled: *Things to Learn Before I Die.* Some of the questions seemed embarrassingly simple. *1.) What is a watershed?* I'd been driving by a sign that read "Mud Creek Watershed" every day on my way to school for fifteen years. "A watershed, Mrs. Shoemaker, is where all the rivers and streams flow from surrounding high places into the same lower place," the barista at my favorite café (and a student at my school) kindly explained as he steamed my milk. Check. *2.)* Borrowed from a friend's three-year-old: *When you pour water from a pail, why doesn't it pile up like sand? 3.) What is fire? 4.) What do I feel when the wind blows? 5.) Why do Ginkgo trees lose their leaves on the same day all over town?* And so on.

Building my list, I began to see how much my questions resembled the mess on my kitchen table—no order to them at all, and realized I'd have to get organized. But how, after ignoring the actual contraption of the universe for the better part of a lifetime, do you begin rummaging around inside it? Do you unscrew it from the top, start with the most nearly perfect specimens evolution has so far produced—a Mother Teresa, say, or Marie Curie, or Michelle Obama?—and work your way down, deconstructing as you go? Or do you begin in the basement, with a single trembling atom, and work your way up? I opted for the cellar and, just after the new washer and dryer were installed, ordered a copy of the Periodic Table, all done up in jellybean colors, which looked non-threatening in an Easter basket way and made the columns easy to see. Then, jumping verses, I flew to France for a week.

Normandy brooded, even in July, and there was an elemental feel to its fieldstone houses, its fierce tides, its slate sky. I had wanted to visit this place for most of my life—especially Utah Beach, where my father had come ashore on D-Day and saved, well—civilization. Although Housman was talking about the massacre of British soldiers in Belgium during the First World War when he wrote, "Their shoulders held the sky suspended; they stood—and Earth's foundations stay," I had always automatically transposed his words, like a banner, over the men who slogged their way out of the sea onto the beaches of northern France.

My husband Larry, an entrenched homebody who usually stayed put when I traveled (which pleased our dogs—one of the several reasons they loved him best), planned our trip, and when they heard us talking about it, my brother-in-law Kim, and his brother Tim decided to come along too. So it was four of us, eyes glazed with jetlag and the hour or two it took us to lay hands on our rental car at Charles de Gaulle Airport, who folded ourselves inside what the droll French call a mid-size vehicle and headed north out of Paris. Though I was the only one in our group whose dad had actually been at the beaches, just a generation removed from the men who arrived in waves on France's *J-Jour*, one way or another, we all walked in our fathers' footsteps.

As a group, we pooled our strengths. I had just enough French to keep myself in *vin rouge* and the guys in *biere*. Larry, with years of teaching history under his belt, brought our battle narratives. Tim and Kim, men undaunted by technology, manned the navigation device which—*Dieu merci!*—spoke English. After nipping along the motorway, then winding through mazes of hedgerows, we finally pushed the doorbell at our inn like good, Skinnerian mice, and following standard travel protocol, made a point to stay awake until after supper, which we pieced together at a little storybook cheese shop. Then we hit the sack and tossed sleeplessly through the night. We'd all traveled west of our fiftieth birthdays years before, a crossing more telling than the ocean and the half dozen time zones to the east we'd ticked off in a night so, despite their desperate need for sleep, our restless bodies were doing insomnia now. Gradually, over the following days, we adjusted to most things Norman, including time, and found a jagged little rhythm, as tourists do, by which to conduct our explorations.

Although along its Swiss border, where it cohosts the world's largest particle collider, France was all science, its northern coast, which had been a busy pilgrimage destination since the Middle Ages, ran to religion with throngs of Christians trooping over its wet sand to *Mont Saint Michel*, the Benedictine Abbey that commanded a small, rocky island jutting into *la Manche*, ("the sleeve"), as the French called the English Channel. We weren't pilgrims—at least I didn't think we were—but when we decided to visit Normandy's beaches I added *le Mont* to our list of destinations. The UNESCO World Heritage guys had put it on *their list,* after all, and after poking around the planet a bit I'd learned how very often they got these things right.

Lashed by a cold rain that slanted sideways off the growling sea, it was certainly the thousand-year-old pilgrim's chill we felt as we trudged through an ocean of parking lots to the tram stop and again as we trooped off the tram itself, which had sped us over a causeway, to the gate of the fortified town, which spiraled upward in cobbled streets and culminated in the Abbey. Inside the walls, shops, and restaurants, which had been serving pilgrims for a millennium, lined the lanes you climb. Because pilgrimage sites were among the few places where tourism was authentic, their established kitsch was not so irritating, and I was grateful for the wool gloves I found (*Thinsulate*, their tag said: Middle Ages, meet the global economy) hanging between cheap Saint Michael medallions and leering gargoyle garden spigots. We were all happy to be wedged into a sea of small tables and fed hot food at one of the crowded hostelries, but when we'd devoured every crumb and our dishes were cleared and the men sat waiting for their profiteroles, I wandered across the cobbles, climbed half a dozen stone steps that seemed to lead to a vault of some kind, and stepped inside a small church.

This was not the Abbey, which topped off the *mont* like a crown on a wedding cake. This was the parish church, *Eglise St-Pierre*, consecrated to St. Peter, patron saint of fishermen, I learned. Crossing the nave where a handful of worshippers prayed in the church's dozen pews, I slipped below a gothic arch into a small chapel where votives flickered under the timeless gaze of Mary, who presided in a statue and in window glass too, which seemed redundant, but I supposed the people who installed her there twice felt this broken world needed all the mother-love it could get, and they wouldn't be wrong about that. I slipped a coin in the cash box.

Despite my doubts about there being an omnipotent Mother or Father looking out for anyone at all, I always lit these little candles in church alcoves. Like the American poet Mary Rose O'Reilly, a former Catholic turned Quaker and skeptic, who answers, "Maybe," when evangelical preachers ask through her car radio if she's been born again, I was covering my bases, I supposed. And I prayed too. "Dear God," my prayers always began, "I know this probably isn't how things work, but please keep my children safe"— though even as my silent words formed, my head was full of toddlers in oncology wards and refugee kids drowning at sea. "NO LIFEGUARD ON DUTY—SWIM AT YOUR OWN RISK!" the world warned millions of times a day, though I kept hoping there was ONE (or a crew), working in ways we simply couldn't see.

What was clear is that we were all riding the tectonic plates like surfers, and I sometimes wondered if it was only the prayers of mothers who floated anyone at all. I was sure my mother prayed for my sister and me, so I took my responsibility seriously and made a point to step up. Choosing a candle in the little, double-Mary chapel, I groped futilely for a fresh match among the discarded ones, then lit my votive from the flame of one already burning, careful not to douse the first with my spilling wax. Next to me a middle-aged woman in a long wool skirt knelt down and, holding her beads aloft, began praying, in some eastern language, a plaintive Rosary. Here was a pilgrim.

By the time our little group made it all the way up to the Abbey itself, the sky had cleared and we could lean onto the ramparts and look out over a sea as gray and flat as a cast iron pan. Along the coast, the tide had gone out and a dozen or so people, some with small children, squatted in the wet sand, digging for clams. To the east, on the far side of the Cotentin Peninsula and farther than we could see, the D-Day beaches sprawled.

Like the beaches of Michigan, a peninsula that stretches into the heart of the Great Lakes basin, which is comprised of several watersheds, the five D-Day beaches differed in character. Turn a corner, round a cove, and the whole terrain changed. Omaha Beach, the scene of so much slaughter, which ran below the American Cemetery overlooking it from a cliff, was an idyll of powdery sand, a magnet for beach towels and lawn chairs—irreconcilable in my head with a massacre, the only association I had for it. I recently read that American geologists studying sand from Omaha Beach under microscopes discovered that four percent of the sand-granules were bits of shrapnel rolled smooth by the sea. Every August when Paris emptied out, Omaha Beach acquired its squadrons of French boys, the same age, more or less, as the Americans who died there, who kicked soccer balls around while clusters of girls in bikinis draped themselves languidly under the feckless Norman sun. Though it was only July, a dozen or so were sprawled on towels. How the planet tills itself, I thought, pushing life up and out, folding each generation back into the earth.

Utah Beach, by contrast, consisted of a sucking sand that tarred your shoes and gummed up your journal if you happened to drop it while making your way around shallow tide pools to the water's edge. Scored by strong tidal currents, it was a raised braille script you felt through your shoes as you picked your way down to its gray blade of sea. The sky scowled and lugworm castings littered the beach at low tide—it was no place to have a picnic or kick a ball, and if you wanted the somber feel of it to hit you full-on when you arrived, you could view it from behind barbed wire, as the beleaguered German army who put it there would have done, which ran the length of a short dune dividing the beach from what was these days, a parking lot. Unlike sunny Omaha, it was exactly what I needed it to be, and when the men headed into the museum, I lagged behind them on the beach.

"Is this Omaha?" a big, ruddy American in a windbreaker stumped onto the sand and asked.

"Utah!" I barked. Then, nicer, "Utah." How could he not *know* where he was? It struck me then, I was, in fact, a pilgrim after all.

My father, a rumbling mystery-behind-the-newspaper, who always-sat-in-the-same- chair, watched-the-Tigers-on-TV, bowled-on-Mondays, and sometimes went-to-the-Red-Horse-bar, rarely spoke of the war. He'd lost friends in France, our mother said. My toe turned up a seashell, which I bent to inspect. How long, I wondered, does it take a human skeleton to decompose in the sea; how long for its calcium to be drawn into a shell? Groping for the dead who'd sanctified this shore, I was beachcombing on holy ground.

Squatting, the hem of my coat splayed like a scallop shell, I unrolled a plastic, zip-lock bag and began palming handfuls of sand inside. Another bag for seashells, which I examined gently for occupants, leaving what offended mollusks I startled—Desole, mes amis!—to the tides, before slipping the small, abandoned properties—ornately domed and whorled and pleated motor-homes with crown molding—inside. Larry was toting a softball-sized rock I'd pried out of the beach to the car when I caught up with him, which he would gamely pack in his suitcase and haul home for me too.

The Periodic Table had arrived by the time we returned from France and, as soon as we shoved our tired travel clothes into the new washing machine and ran the dogs, I slipped it eagerly from its cardboard tube and spread it out on the kitchen island. Mysterious as the Kabbalah, its code winked at me under the pendant lights in clear, incomprehensible columns. But it was a beautiful, and I thought maybe a holy thing, so I installed it in a poster frame and set it on a chair beneath a sketch of India's cave temples which hangs to the left of my writing desk, where it could occupy my periphery in space and thought. Then I ran out to the bookstore and returned with a gorgeous, pictorial book by Theodore Gray called *The Elements*, which, in its introduction of the Periodic Table, begins, "The elements in the first column, not counting hydrogen, are called the alkali metals, and they are all fun to throw into a lake," and concludes, "Almost everything you see in this book is sitting somewhere in my office, except that one thing the FBI confiscated." Encouraged by its friendliness, I set the book on the kitchen table along with *Chemistry for Dummies*, which I also picked up, determined to proceed realistically now that I was a scientist.

When August—which I filled with bone density scans and appointments with the ophthalmologist to adjust my *trifocals* (my summers *were doing this now)*—ran out of weeks, and school rolled around again, I placed my tea-tray by the new books. Each morning at breakfast, as Larry glanced over the newspaper, I tucked into my toast, a couple of pages of increasingly complicated chemistry, and the Periodic Table. It was a modest regimen, by almost anyone's standards: an element-a-day, every morning with a pot of

Earl Grey.

It didn't take me long, however—about the time I hit valence electrons in early October—to become flummoxed. But what is an American high school, after all, if not a vast, rich terrain just begging to be mined? So when my novitiate in the sub-atomic world ground to a halt, I went prospecting and turned up gold: an affable, 12th-grade genius who agreed to tutor me one afternoon a week, a project which paid his hard labor in service hours required by the National Honor Society.

Now every Wednesday at three o'clock, Brad and I sat near a wall of windows in our school's library, amid a sea of bewildered fifteen and sixteen-year-olds struggling to work out ornery equations and scrambled phrases and impossible conjugations with their own tutors. Occasionally I glanced up to see one or two of them staring at me. "Science is haaard!" I called, scrunching my nose.

Patiently drawing covalently bonded atoms in the spiral notebook on which I'd penned "*Chemistry!*" with a proud flourish, Brad tried to lead me to the light. "See," he asked kindly, "how hydrogen and oxygen both *want* an electron?" And I looked over his little Venn diagrams and *tried* to see and sometimes *did* see how the shared custody of electrons made the whole extended family of particles, which comprises the universe, run.

However slow I might be, I am an enthusiastic student. Last week, crying out with the joy of a real break-through when I realized that atomic energy levels are stacked like condos in the Periodic Table, Brad replied, "We go over this every week and you're always so happy when you discover it!"

We'd been studying the same material for a month? "But Mr. Bingley," I protested, "I am all astonishment!" On Tuesday afternoons Brad worked with his other client—a ninth-grade boy with a pretty serious learning disability; we'll see who gives him a better run for no money.

Writing for *The New York Times*, as he was rounding the last ragged corner of cancer, Oliver Sacks, enamored since childhood with the elegant order of the Periodic Table, described how friends had been sending him samples of the elements for his recent birthdays. Thallium (element 81) came "in a charming box" for his eighty-first birthday, and lead (element 82) arrived on his eighty-second. And though he would not live to see his eighty-third birthday, he placed bismuth, (element 83) "a modest, gray metal often…ignored even by metal lovers" on his writing table, explaining, "My feeling for the mistreated or marginalized…extends into the inorganic world." Approaching death, he was surrounding himself "with metals and minerals, little emblems of eternity."

Of course, though their atoms stick around in future liaisons, there is nothing eternal about the particular rocks I dragged home and piled on our shelves. But they were good on daily wear and tear and so gave the impression of lasting forever, which was a pretty fallacy and maybe all I was looking for, despite all my noise about wanting the merciless truth. "Does *nothing* last?" I'd wanted to wail like a child and stamp my foot and throw myself down. A woman held her prayer beads up. Minerals rattled in the tide. The boys who bled on the beach were gone, but the shrapnel winked in the sand.

Recently, I returned to Detroit to look at art, but not at the DIA this time. This time I drove with friends deeper into the excised heart of the city, to one of the ravaged neighborhoods where the few surviving houses, often blackened by arson and boarded up, hunched by the curb wearing the haunted look of casualties. Thirty years ago, in this disintegrating world, Tyree Guyton began cleaning up the sidewalks and yards on his blighted street and decorating abandoned homes he didn't own with the detritus he found. The result of his efforts, *The Heidelberg Project*, fell into the edgy, controversial genre of public art. We parked under a dead, branchless tree which an upturned shopping cart topped like a rusty tiara.

Sculptures of junk rose everywhere—towering, squatting, sprawling in yards, and heaped in the corners of open cellars that pock the city block like the blasted bunkers of Normandy—evidence of a violence that Guyton, like the French, seemed determined to let no one forget. Old shoes upholstered a chain-link fence. Tilting from the second-story window of a house painted in polka-dots the size of satellite dishes, the figure of a superhero was fastened in mid-launch; whether he would someday tumble feet or head-first, like Frieda Kahlo's falling woman, was anyone's guess. Up and down the street, painted wooden clocks perched in the trees—time was on Guyton's mind. "*Souls* too," the woman working the information table inside one of the sagging houses told us; "think of all those *shoes*." Moldering stuffed animals climbed telephone poles, typewriters and gutted televisions and old vacuum cleaners covered lawns—symbols that snaked back, if you cared to trace them, to God only knew how many violations and abandonments. Here and there, plastic dolls were nailed onto boards— Heidelberg Street was rife with crucifixions. Then, carved into the stoop of a house: "Say nice things about Detroit."

Weirdly, in its gritty promotion of shit-to-art, you felt in Guyton's work a will for resurrection which, I'm told, was growing in pockets all around Detroit as young artists and fledgling businesses slipped into the city and bravely set up shop. *Old things are passed away; behold, all things are become new.*

Slow learner that I am, moving among students wedged into desks in my crowded classroom, swept up in the current as rivers of them course through our high school's halls, I don't hear the ruckus of resurrection happening around me, don't see it's here, amid banging lockers and bulging backpacks, that eternity shows its hand, flashing yellow-green in these fresh shoots that jostle my old joints. They are not their great-grandparents and they are.

We want it to be personal—I, forever me—which is not, it seems, in the nature of things, so our only imprint on forever is whatever we pass on— what pebble of sympathy or truth we turn up as we move through.

This morning I took tea with Cu, Element 29. The first pennies, minted in 1792, were made of pure copper, which means each atom comprising each penny was identical to the others. But as the old coins thin with use, their sloughed-off atoms slip back into the air and soil to rebond with other atoms in a refrain the world is constantly singing. Though its verses slipped beneath the radar of our five senses, the elemental music of creation was inscribed right there in the Periodic Table, on the wall of every high school chemistry room. Hail Mary full of grace; resurrection is everywhere we look, just beyond what we can see.

At Sixty

Last fall I took myself to The Plaza in New York City for a celebratory tea. "Happy Birthday!" to the cortical troupe of atoms which have been collaborating these seven decades to produce what I fondly think of as *me,* which in its confusion sometimes segues to *mine,* but that's another story.

The cast that creates the better part of me has changed over the years, as casts do in any long-running show, with skittish skin cells bolting constantly—20,000 or so down the shower drain every day in search of new productions. In fact, nearly the whole body recasts itself every seven years, with only the cells in the cerebral cortex arguably sticking around from opening to closing nights. My own show has surpassed (by a good margin) even *Phantom of the Opera,* the longest running play on Broadway, which has been keening around the stage only since 1988. Thirty-seven trillion cells, give or take a trillion, comprise a human body; that's some stage director keeping them all on cue. Neuroscientists and Buddhists deny that there is any stage director, any discrete you or me taking charge, looking out. "I" am whatever consciousness this chorus of atoms kicks up, an accidental diva, wholly dependent on a changing cast to keep coming to work, finished when the final curtain comes down.

Nevertheless, faithfully practicing the willing suspension of disbelief (good patron of the arts) from the inside out, I allowed it was the same old me I'd always known that sank solidly into a chair in the Palm Court and ordered the *New Yorker Tea,* vegetarian-style—heavy on the egg salad. My friend Jan, who was indulging me in this extravagance, sat down gratefully too; we'd hiked up from our hotel on 26th Street and were ready to be off our feet. Though we are roughly the same age, her current atoms are dancing to different choreographies than mine are, clustering prettily in lipids and collagens. Daintily lifting her china cup, she looked great.

Because, unlike the Syrian refugees who were pouring into Europe the November I turned sixty, or Liberians limping back from the last Ebola outbreak, or Hondurans doggedly slogging north, or so many of the world's people, I have the luxury to imagine such things, sixty felt like a threshold, or a whole new book: *The Silver Years:* Chapter One. And, chastened as I tried to make myself feel by juxtaposing my privileged life with the lives of so many desperate others, I still felt like celebrating, which is nearly always a good thing, I think. I've been told Auden always made his birthday a fête—no shabby endorsement.

I had celebrated my actual birthday, a few days before we flew to New York, by leaping into good-fairy mode—a role I believe all of us who are not actual psychopaths savor playing when we can—sending a little money to the MSU libraries, springing ahead of a single mom checking out her groceries to swipe my credit card with a grand, birthday flourish, running rawhides out to the animal shelter during my planning hour at school. "Sprinkle joy!" a daisy and butterfly-clad poster, taped to the ceiling over my gurney, reminded me during the bone-density scan I'd had the week before I stepped into the next decade. The payoff for my day of peppy, birthday largesse was huge in Happy—a buoyancy which left me thinking I definitely need to take more advice from posters.

All around the Palm Court, the Art-Deco atrium where tea is served at The Plaza, deferential men in suits scrambled to deliver pots of Earl Grey to well-heeled women and the odd table of men. Also, we noticed as there were several of them, two very privileged little girls who were celebrating their eighth or ninth birthdays with an *Eloise Tea* that came with cumulous tufts of cotton candy tethered to their tea caddies. There was more than one tiara. Even so, though I was sure (having waited tables for most of my twenties) the grown men rushing to serve these children had socked away a thousand *princess* complaints, every little girl we saw behaved herself splendidly—a credit to the good mothers of the five boroughs and New Jersey.

Jan and I dug into our scones, fueling up for an afternoon walk through Central Park, and left with a few dainty sandwiches and most of the sweets tucked into a fancy bag, which I toted around with the idea of handing it off to someone homeless, thus prolonging my good-fairy narcissism. But it was too early in the day for men to be burritoed in bedrolls or tucked into church stoops, so I carried the food around until I worried the mayonnaise had gone bad then went back to the hotel and ate the cakes myself.

A week later, back in the Midwest and hunkered down at the high school where I live and move and have my being, I was hauling home a bag of papers to grade when I turned on the car radio to learn that Paris had been torn up by terror again. I was still receiving weekly editions of *Charlie Hebdo,* which I'd subscribed to the previous winter, raising my fist for free speech in my family room as I mainlined CNN, following the slaughter of French satirists who had been warned they'd be killed if they persisted in wanton, western *liberte d'expression.* As my French is more miss than hit, I puzzle over each issue for a few minutes then add it to the pile in the cupboard where I keep my *601 French Verbs* and the flash cards I drag out and study before traveling to France or French-speaking countries. Now this.

My sixteen-year-old students, who have grown up with terror, have plenty of knowledge but no memory of the collapsing Twin Towers. Their September eleventh is my generation's Pearl Harbor—something a person's parents recount. They shared stories about their childhood demons one day when we were discussing the way, without adults even knowing it, kids ingest the poisons of their times like peeling lead paint. "My sister told me if I didn't do what she said, *al Qaeda* would get me!" Anna exclaimed while, suddenly quickening in the back corner, Jake cut in, "I thought *Osama bin Laden* was under my bed!" These stories might have surprised me if I didn't recall so vividly a dream I had, my five-year-old self, of communists invading my elementary school. They'd stormed the place to make us all stop believing in God and it was up to me to get to the principal's office and warn her. No pressure there. Born into time, we all inherit a trunkful of stuff that's been in the making. Life, as Lauren Slater observes, is a "box of snakes and daisies."

Still, if we have the luck not to be born in Spain during the Inquisition, or in Cambodia during the rise of the Khmer Rouge, or in Uganda with Idi Amin, we might note the great fortune of our near miss. But even acknowledging such dumb luck doesn't make us less fearful. "I can't go to Silver Bells this year," Amy, a sweet, sophomore girl told me sadly in the hall outside my classroom one day. She was talking about the festive evening of shopping and caroling that accompanies the annual lighting of the Christmas tree at the capitol in Lansing. Kids around here grow up on it. "I'm afraid of ISIS," she whispered. "My mom is too." Maybe because she caught me by surprise, or maybe because all of the obvious responses—"If you change your life, the terrorists win," and "Anything can happen anywhere," and "We're too small-town for terror,"—seemed hollow and cavalier, I had nothing to offer her but, "Lots of people are afraid"—not very soothing or inspired.

A few times a year, I pull inward and leave the newspaper unread and the radio turned off, in an effort to protect what Thich Nhat Hanh calls "the ecology of the mind." I read poetry at breakfast, listen to Tom Waits or YoYo Ma on the drive to school, make my life very very local. I cook and bake and rearrange our books. Chopping vegetables and stirring them into broth, steam turns the windowpanes to cataracts through which I briefly, happily see no evil. Lots of soup comes out of these retreats—and while it cools I stump along on the treadmill in the basement, watching old DVDs and shoring up my dwindling bone mass. What mail I can afford to ignore piles up: bank statements, public radio appeals, newsletters from *The ASPCA* and *League of Women Voters*. I don't withdraw for long—a couple of weeks at a time is all. As the very *raisin d'etre* of teaching is to prepare young people to take a thoughtful, responsible place in the world, teachers are obliged, I think, to stay alertly in the loop, even when it feels like a noose.

For the past week, however, I've been on hiatus again, having swapped *The New York Times* for *The Jefferson Bible* at breakfast. *The Jefferson Bible* is a literary montage of biography and ethics extracted from the Christian Gospel. An Enlightenment man to the core, Thomas Jefferson literally clipped passages from New Testaments in English, French, Latin, and Greek, and aligned them four columns to a page, retaining Jesus's moral teachings but excising the reason-taxing miracles he believed the evangelists invented for the man, Jesus. He labored privately. Understanding religious faith to be an entirely individual affair, consisting "in the internal persuasion or belief of the mind," Jefferson spoke little about his own religious views, maintaining, like the Buddha, a "noble silence." Publicly, of course, he worked to secure religious freedom for all people, as well as people of no religion at all. My, did he take shit for that. My own copy of *The Jefferson Bible* comes from The Smithsonian Institution with a forward co-written by Harry Rubenstein and Barbara Clark Smith who tell us, "Jefferson increasingly found himself charged with being an infidel, atheist, or worse—not only unchristian but anti-Christian in his aspirations"—and this long before he produced his Bible, a document compiled for his own use and never intended for publication. It was not, in fact, published until 1904.

I have a beaded bracelet that forms the word, *HERETIC*, a gift from my student Johanna, who shares my birthday. Each year, when we are studying Puritanism in my American Lit class, my students toss around the idea of heresy. Puritans, who were about as open-minded as jihadists, had their holy fingers on the trigger of the state—aka the church—when it came to religious dissent of any kind. Anne Hutchinson famously got herself thrown out of Massachusetts for her heterodox views, but in seeking to silence the clergymen with whom she disagreed, she was as intolerant as the rest of them, and as any ayatollah you care to shake a stick at. In following the path of the Reformation that produced those indomitable men and women who commandeered the "new" continent, it doesn't take us long to discover that we are all heretics in someone's estimation—you can't be a Catholic and a Calvinist, if you can manage to be either, at the same time. "It's not a bad pedigree," I reassure my students, pointing to their distinguished family tree: Galileo, Martin Luther, Isaac Newton, Joan of Arc. Sweep Einstein and Edison, Voltaire and Twain, Jesus and Muhammad and their like behind the big escutcheon of those who courageously denounced the orthodoxy to which they were born and we have maybe the greatest tribe, the noblest house in human history: Infidels All.

Buried under essays that grumbled to be graded, I didn't go to Silver Bells this year either, but I did go down to the Capitol for a vigil to protest gun violence a couple of weeks later, after a mass shooting in San Bernardino. The big Christmas tree, whose lighting Amy had mourned missing, dominated the lawn, and in its glow the usual crowd was gathered—a hundred or so shivering liberals, lots of wiry gray tendrils sprouting from beneath wool caps, mine included. We seemed a dispirited lot, confused by the violence of our times and by America's listless, anorexic response to it. A few people gripped little, battery-powered votives in their gloved hands and occasionally held them over their heads in support of a remark one of the speakers made from the Capitol steps. My husband Larry and I listened from the back of the quiet crowd as a rabbi, an imam, and a few ministers took turns at the lectern and spoke mildly about peace, and prayed, and spoke mildly about peace some more, which wore on my patience.

Scrunching up my toes, which were cooling down inside my boots, I pictured the angry heretics of the civil rights movement who defied the orthodoxy of servitude and humiliation. I pictured the loud, in-your-face, fury of AIDS activists who Acted Up and refused to lie down and die. I pictured Jesus spitting fire in the Temple, turning over the money-changers' tables like he'd grown up brawling in bars and I started bristling. When the last minister's prayer ran into the fifth, milquetoast minute, I whispered to Larry, "It's a good thing I don't have a gun. If he doesn't shut up I'd be tempted to shoot him myself." Not very peace-vigil-esque of me. Apparently at sixty I'm a tad pissed off, a little flinty, shooting sparks.

And weighted with my own helplessness: there's the crux of it, which is not an easy thing for a teacher to concede. More than a little hubris leads a lot of us into the profession. "*I can fix this,*" I think every year, handing my syllabus out to the bright and curious sophomores who sit, nearly new-minted, before me with their mountains of intelligence and their chasms of ignorance, empty vaults just waiting to be filled with all that good loot I've loaded into my file cabinets and power points. Years ago, one of them wondered out loud if we might take a vote on a due date for an assignment and I met that question with my own. All incredulity, I hit them with, "Do you think this is a *democracy?* This right here is an absolute dictatorship; this, friends, is my little Cuba!" As a result, there remains to this day quite a good sketch of Castro taped to my lectern—a gift from an artist in that year's third row—with what are clearly my glasses, my hair, my earrings. In other words, you bet your ass I'm in charge. But dammit it if their parents don't still get divorced and if their hearts don't break when their good dogs die. There is almost nothing I can fix.

I try to help them at least suit up for the world's dogmas and banalities—the rightful province of literature—by distributing some of the reliable gifts I've warehoused—one of teaching's perks. Last week in my World Religions class, as I was pulling up a screenful of notes on the *Torah*, Kelsey, a thoughtful senior, asked if I had a favorite poet. "Not really—I can't commit, but there are a few poems that…feed me." And rifling through a drawer in a file cabinet, I pulled out a poem wholly unrelated to our social science curriculum on Judaism and therefore wonderfully impossible to benchmark to the state's Common Core, and put it in her hands. Wendell Berry's Mad Farmer, sowing seeds. "Ask the questions that have no answers," he urges. Kelsey, who could play Varsity for the Mad Farmer's philosophical team, can't help doing this anyway, but there is solace in affirmation, and in company.

Chopping carrots in the kitchen the other night for a kettle of soup, I had a sudden hunger for gifts, myself, which come to most of us, more often than not, in shutter-shots of beauty. Light enters the iris, hits the cornea at the back of the eye, signaling the brain to open the vault and store the image. Now I wanted to get inside that vault and run my hands through its riches. Pouring a glass of wine, I scraped the last of the carrots into the pot and, while the windows steamed up, sat down with a fresh sheet of paper to inventory what winking gems I'd spied in the world's fat jewel chest over the past few months.

When I clicked my pen open, memory spilled them out on the page like they'd been piled against a door—I've either had a good year or I'm getting better at looking. Out tumbled the satin shirt you see inside a milkweed pod when its little jacket opens down the front exposing the neat, tweed vest of its imbricate seeds; the double-spiral staircase in the Gustav Moreau Museum in Paris; rusty fungi sprouting like awnings from the mossy trunks of maples; the cantilevered terraces of the new Whitney Museum in Manhattan; the Fibonacci spirals of a sunflower; light leaking though summer leaves; meanders in the wet sand of the Lake Michigan shore; a poem by Verushka Gray, delivered out of the darkness on social media the day after the Paris massacre:

later that night
I held an atlas in my lap
ran my fingers across the whole
world
and whispered
where does it hurt?
it answered
everywhere
everywhere
everywhere

and finally, a feather installation in the refectory of Mont St Michel, and Mont St Michel, itself—that rocky island culminating in the vaulting, Romanesque arches of an abbey, achieving its aim and finding its song. I put down my pen and sat there breathing.

Where, if anywhere, does nature leave off and the human mind begin? "Ask the questions that have no answer."

Every time I am appalled at the violence of my own species, I remember the food chain and the director in my head, whether she's a hologram of brain, or a holy soul, shudders at the ruthless design woven into the heart of things. Even when we try, through our loftiest aspirations, to extricate ourselves from the fabric of atrocities great and small, we loop back into the all-of-it, part of the world's warp and weft. The mythologies we write—most of them—call us to peace, call us to kill.

I don't know if my student Amy, who forsook the carols and the lights in Lansing, knows it or not, but ISIS, pushing so brutally toward the end prophesied in its own apocalyptic myth, recently rolled out a picture of Times Square on its website. I certainly won't be telling her about it.

At sixty, I am aware of how much more the world belongs to my students than it does to me, and I'm more than a little relieved about that. At sixty, I've lost patience with its dueling orthodoxies and mislaid the ones I grew up with—they're around here somewhere, but not likely to turn up and I can't be bothered to look for them.

Common lore tells us that wisdom comes with age, but if that's true I would certainly know a thing or three more, when a lot of answers have gone the way of bone mass for me. I leave them to the squabbling of True Believers, who hoist them up like idols on jihadist websites and at NRA rallies and carry them around on pedestals and are outfitted for murder by them.

Like Pascal, "I do not know who put me in the world, nor what the world is, nor what I am myself." Perhaps these ongoing, intermittent sequestrations among poets and rationalists in which I indulge is practice for retirement—a startling proposition that's within stick-throwing distance now, or maybe they are manifestations of what Emily Dickinson called "the soul selecting her own society." Reluctantly, I've had to place even the idea of soul, that weightless, wraith—unverifiable in the atomic ruckus of the universe—if not under the cleaver, at least on the chopping block, and I do not know if this is enlightened and brave, or the worst sort of betrayal.

Is it narcissism whispering that maybe wisdom, after all, is just the concession of ignorance—in that way putting me back on top? I like a paradox as well as the next person, and this one has its appeal. For when it comes to what I do know, it's not much more than this: the chilly edge of mystery and a river of tea.

A Crack in Everything

I lost a corkscrew recently on my way to New York, where I'd gone to share digs for a few days with my daughter Maddie, who was attending a conference there. I had set my sights on a Leonard Cohen exhibit at the Jewish Museum called *A Crack in Everything* and Maddie and I booked a night on Broadway too. The corkscrew was confiscated by a TSA screener who disarmed me at DEPARTURES in Detroit. "It's a good corkscrew; you should keep it," I told the large, amiable woman who, with a zip and a pluck, made it property of the state. I have no beef with the TSA keeping our skies blade-free and only think it would be friendly of those vintners, whose bottom-shelf wines I can afford, to go with more screw tops.

I am often pulled out of line in ARRIVALS, as well, to be patted down and have my bags searched. And it's been years since I've opened a checked suitcase without finding the familiar calling card: "Inspected by TSA" on top of my ransacked clothes and unwrapped souvenirs. They actually locked me out of my own luggage recently when, after rifling through my soiled tee shirts and unsexy underwear, they snapped the little TSA-approved padlock, to which I'd lost the key and left dangling on a zipper, shut. My husband had to drag the bag into the garage and break into it with a hacksaw.

I am, I believe, what the TSA uses to prove they are not profiling: a sixty-something white woman in Birkenstocks; I look like I tap my own maple trees. Once, arriving from Budapest at Newark (an especially belligerent airport that requires you to order your drinks through only occasionally working touch screens at bars where human bartenders, in very tempting slapping distance, deflect your pleas by pointing you back to your frozen screen) I was extracted from the line of tousled and bleary-eyed travelers at Customs and channeled alone through an Orwellian series of echoing rooms with wide-belted overseers and special scanners. It was the *deep TSA*. After quite a while and no explanation, I and my ravaged bag were returned to the *regular* airport of melting-down toddlers and heartless bartenders. I was happy to see them.

My encounters with the TSA peaked over a ten-year period as I treated my two, twenty-something daughters to a series of trips abroad. About the time they became thirty-somethings, I realized that if I were ever going to break out of teaching high school to enjoy more languid days of making soup and reading after lunch, I would have to stop flinging money into the void. It had been a fine—and yes, perversely crowded—void, full of ancient ruins and olive groves and spice markets and libraries and cathedrals, but for all its furnishings, my bank account declared it a clear financial vacuum. Its only dividend was high, intangible satisfaction that won't cough up a co-pay for those inevitable hip replacements which are not so far off as they once were. Still, I expect to have as few regrets about all of that delicious travel as the belly-man of the Szechenyi Baths in Budapest appeared to have about his *Speedo*.

As people have been doing for centuries, my daughter Anna and I went to Budapest for the baths. First built by the Romans, who took enthusiastically to the thermal springs they discovered along the Danube, and further developed by the Turks who'd learned to bathe beneath the graceful domes and arches of Ottoman bath houses, the grand old city's spas are its global come hither--and come we did.

I sometimes dream about gardens comprised entirely of pools and fountains, one spilling giddily into the next. Gliding through their spouts and basins, I am an otter, a sprite, a slight and somersaulting child. *Unless you become as a little child you cannot enter the kingdom of heaven*, Jesus says in The Bible, while in The Qur'an God promises, *The righteous will be amid gardens and fountains*. And because I am a person who has earned her regrets and has no clear claim to the future idylls at least two of the world's scriptures dangle before us, Budapest's "Here it is now!" made me an offer I couldn't refuse—or didn't want to.

The Szechenyi Baths are a network of thermal pools—most of them inside a neo-Baroque, yellow wedding cake of a palace. Once you've pulled on your bathing suit and locked your clothes inside a small, rented locker or (for a few extra euros) changing cabin, you are free to wander through a hive of tiled rooms and dip into their various mineral baths which are warm and warmer. Submerged ledges encircle each pool at just the right height to give average Eastern-European adults, who cling to them like barnacles, water to the neck as they chat with friends like they were in a coffee shop. Though there are fountains you can loiter beneath, we sensed that human splashing would be a grave faux pas and were careful to leave no wake as we slipped inside each basin. Then, surrendering to the physics of buoyancy, we soaked quietly, gripping our bit of ledge with our hands as our legs floated like kelp on the water's surface.

You can also soak outside at Szechenyi, in a triptych of splendid, large pools surrounded by a smooth and tiered cement terrace strewn with lounge chairs—which, to secure, you have to arrive earlier than we did.

Planting ourselves on towels that we spread out on the cement, Anna and I set to people-watching which, in my experience, figures largely in what a person leaves America to do.

In the pool nearest us, a group of middle-aged men, submerged to their chests, captured each other's rooks on chessboards laid out along a narrow platform that extended like a diving board a few inches above the water. Slow as manatees, people glided in breast strokes or pushed across the pools on foot while, around us, the hum of Hungarian gossip rose in a lazy froth.

"This is the first time she's worn that bathing suit," Anna remarked, nodding toward a teenage girl shyly approaching the pool in a thong bikini. She was perfect—as spare and lithe as a baby seal—and embarrassed by her almost total exposure. All the way to the lip of the pool, her hands fluttered behind her as she tried to hide her bottom. Our eyes and sympathy followed her to the concealing water, only to be drawn, when she slipped inside, to another bather barreling into our view, the Ridiculous nipping, as it will, at the heels of the Sublime. Battinged neck to feet in thick black hair, his girth gave his height a run for its money as he promenaded around the pool in a wee nylon sling that hung like a little smile beneath his belly. This guy had none of the perfect girl's misgivings about appearance; he strode the circumference of that pool like a landlord inspecting his acres. "Men," I sighed. "Yes" Anna replied, "men."

That casual dismissal of men aside, I can't really indulge in the sport of drafting them onto a single team with an eye to throttling the lot of them—though plenty of them seem determined to make it easy. Just pause on CNN when you're scrolling through channels and there is shameless Mitch McConnell baldly feigning principles like some discredited headmaster caught with his hand in the bursar's cashbox. And Donald Trump with his casinos and porn-stars and cheesy TV show and now this president-gig, spouting monosyllabic patriot-hate that seventh-graders can see through. And that presciently named desperado, Anthony Weiner, apparently addicted to teasing his penis out of his underpants and texting its tiny photo to the world like he was handing out school pictures. With material like that, it's tempting to paint *man*kind with broad strokes; which inevitably produces some very disturbing art, since so much darkness gets mixed into male enthusiasms.

"The taming of testosterone," I remarked cryptically to my husband Larry and our friend Mark during a commercial break in *Jeopardy* recently. We were sitting in front of the TV, waiting for the oven timer to ring in the glad news of salmon and roasted vegetables. "Remember to answer with a question."

"What are you talking about?" Mark asked.

"It's right there in Ken Wilber's book," I said, heading to the kitchen to move plates from the cupboard to the island and leaving a paperback copy of *A Brief History of Everything* splayed open on the couch. I returned with three glasses of wine. "Time's up! The answer is: What is the great task of civilization?" There was a moment of empty air in the room and then Mark asked, "Who's Ken *Wilber*?"

"Some early New Ager, I think—that was Fred's book." My friend Fred, who'd passed away the previous year, had been a classics scholar with a religious bent who'd read broadly about brokenness and redemption in people, in the world. He was a prayer and, despite my prickly apostate's mind, I am too. I'd found Wilber's book on Fred's bookshelf after he died and carried it home. Retrieving it, I glanced down at a page where a line was marked. "Wilber," I explained, "claims men have historically had two approaches to everything in the world. They could either 'fuck it or kill it.'" Reading it out loud, I felt a few dopamine neurons in my brain light up with pleasure at the pithiness of the claim—so like a slogan. It was something you could fit on the brim of a hat that let you stop thinking like, "Make America Great Again." I enjoy not thinking as well as the next person.

"That may be a *little* over-simplified," Mark observed dryly, nodding at Larry, and recalling me, just like that, to complexity and truth. Larry—the fact of him and his goodness—will never let me decamp to any shrill, general condemnation of men.

Stashed in my memory are a thousand examples of my husband's voluminous empathy and his kindness. The way he paid the babysitter at the end of our first date when I was a struggling single mom and would have had to dig into our grocery fund for the twenty precious bucks. The way he took me to a pretty boutique a few weeks later and insisted on buying me a dress, explaining, "Every woman should have a new dress in the spring." The way the very next week he showed up with a tricycle for Anna, who wasn't quite three.

"Is that for my big sister?" Anna had asked him in awe. But Maddie, at five, already had a bike.

"No, honey, this is for you," he explained, setting it down on the sidewalk and helping her climb aboard. But perhaps the most telling window into Larry's nature—and so, into the possibility of evolving goodness in humankind—opened a few years later when (married by then) we were volunteering at a dog-rescue event for our county's animal shelter.

No one seemed to know anyone else very well among the dozen or so of us who'd shown up to pitch tent canopies and set up card tables for the 24-hour "Adopt-a-Thon," but we worked congenially, pounding stakes into the ground to secure dog chains, dragging coolers, unspooling plastic mesh to make temporary animal pens. It was hot and we worked in shorts and tee shirts, except for a couple of men in the distance sweating in orange jumpsuits; the county jail abutted the shelter and they'd been recruited to lend a hand. They worked silently on the margins of our encampment, well away from the rest of us. After a couple of hours someone ordered pizzas, which we all—I thought—fell upon, chatting between mouthfuls. I was combing the cardboard boxes for another slice when I noticed Larry had disappeared and, looking around, I saw him bearing a large pizza to the men in orange who'd quietly kept working while we ate, accepting their exile, as if they understood that their human claim to community and its sustenance had been revoked. I'm not sure what physical thing actually happens in the chest when we say, "my heart swelled," but my rib cage got very crowded.

So no, I will never be able to write off *men*. Not even the aging white ones, all of them these days (in my liberal circles) with targets on their backs—at least until we confirm their credentials. Not even *Speedo*-Man who, for all I know, takes his aging mother to church and rubs her bunioned feet.

The Szechenyi Baths opened *Speedo*-free in 1913. Just a few years later, in the raucous heyday of Prohibition, the spectacular Buckingham Fountain was built in Chicago, where Anna now lives. This big, boisterous fountain has none of the reserve of Hungarian baths. It chortles. And then it laughs out loud. And then it erupts—like it can't get over the wonder of its own wet mischief, of its big green park spread along the shore of Lake Michigan, of the lake itself. I have no desire to live *near* it, as Anna does; I want to live *in* it. If there is an afterlife—if something of our individual spirit remains after our bodies break down into their various minerals, I want to inhabit, like a water nymph, those glorious, tiered fonts and bowls. I want to abide in that wild, sweet spray.

A few years before we went to Budapest, Anna moved into her first solo-apartment in Chicago. Solo: as in no roommates who might notice if she went missing one night. It was a classic *garden* (there is nothing new about spin) apartment, a few steps down from the street, with a front door concealed by the stairs to the apartment above it—in other words: a mugger's dream, a rapist's best-laid lair. I hated the arrangement and spent our first visit issuing warnings Anna didn't want to hear. Larry hated it too and would have set up his own, burlier version of the TSA by the unlocked gate to the yard if he could have. Instead, while I muttered, he drove to the nearest Home Depot, returned with an outdoor light kit, and while Anna and I sliced cucumbers and cheese for lunch, rigged up a light beneath the stairs that could only be turned on and off from inside the apartment. Seen from the sidewalk, a dark door would mean someone had removed or broken the bulb; it would say, "Run Anna run!" The only flaw I could find in the plan was that Anna might sometimes forget to turn the light on when she left in the morning, which could perhaps be covered under the broad daughter-safety-clause in my prayers. And as the late great bard Leonard Cohen noted, "There is a crack in everything." Driving back home to Michigan, we could at least take solace in agreeing we'd caulked up what cracks we could to keep her safe.

In Budapest, just about everything is cracked—literally. Dating from the Austro-Hungarian Empire, the city's great edifices resemble in grandeur her haughty sibling Vienna's, but like other co-opted Eastern European cities, Budapest shows evidence of having had the shit kicked out of it by the Soviet Union. In the world of 20th century political weddings, Budapest is a sister who married badly.

This being a broken world, there really is a crack in everything. Despite running at nearly 100% for confiscating my corkscrews, according to the more reliable voices online, TSA agents apparently manage to miss 70% of "test" weapons stashed in bags by Department of Homeland Security agents. Ironically, the corkscrew in my checked bag made it to Budapest, where we never used it. Anna and I sipped our wine in the cafes and "ruin-bars" of Pest, which are exactly what they sound like: small taverns homesteading in abandoned and graffitied buildings. And now, a couple of years after visiting Hungary, Anna is suddenly between jobs and Larry, who has lately been diagnosed with Parkinson's Disease, is working late at night, hours after his synthetic dopamine has worn off, to track down affordable health insurance for her. Nothing feels whole or strong right now.

This morning, as I was writing next to a window, a female cardinal hit the glass—that crack in things the human world creates for birds—and was deflected onto a vine climbing the fence that runs alongside our house. I jumped at the thud and turned to see her mate arrive heroically in full red regalia, like a Canadian Mountie, by her side. Cardinals mate for life. Following a courtship during which the male romances the female by feeding her beak-to-beak, they settle down like church deacons to lives of monogamy and routine. Year after year, sharing the responsibilities of raising their fledglings, they grow old together. I watched as the protective male, so like gentle, loving Larry, talked his shaken partner back into the air, watched as they flew together to the low limb of a red pine.

In New York, Maddie and I walked the High Line, that abandoned railroad-turned park—a sorely cracked and resurrected ruin, itself—and when we disembarked at its southern terminus, we wandered into the Chelsea Market where I bought a new corkscrew, which I used a time or two to open the cheapest bottles of Cabernet I could find in Manhattan. My weekend wine-budget, my weekend *whole*-budget had taken a blow on Broadway when Maddie and I each ordered a glass of wine at the theater before seeing *To Kill A Mockingbird*. Dismayed when the bartender handed us inelegant, plastic *Slurpee* cups with slotted caps and *Ticketmaster* imprinted on the bottoms, I was appalled when I signed my *Visa* receipt for 78 bucks, plus a tip. And in keeping with that old adage about insult and injury, the next day in DEPARTURES at LaGuardia, New York took my new corkscrew too.

The corkscrews confiscated on that trip to New York were neither the first nor the best and undoubtedly not the last I will lose to the TSA. That I persist in packing them in a carryon bag proves my memory isn't getting *better* by the year. And the traveling I do is closer to my nest these days, and often with Larry, a bona fide homebody who doesn't like to stray too far from his own time zone.

Boarding the plane at LaGuardia, I settled in next to a friendly kid named Mike who explained, while repeatedly diving for the wine-stained book that kept sliding off my lap, that he was a sophomore at the University of Toledo and had spent the previous week with his former high school Latin teacher who now lived in Brooklyn. His earnestness made him seem even younger than his nineteen years and it occurred to me that he was on course to grow into one of those very good men, like the one I'd married. They'd seen all the sights, he said, and told me about The Statue of Liberty, The Ground Zero Museum, The Metropolitan Museum of Art. I told him about my lost corkscrews and how I was profiled to disprove the rumor of profiling. When the plane began rolling toward the runway, he swallowed hard and admitted, "This is the first time I've ever flown—well, except for the trip out here." As the jet engines roared to life and the plane lunged toward the sky, he gripped the small crucifix hanging from a cord around his neck. "Just a little nervous," he gulped.

"I used to be afraid too," I told him in my most soothing teacher-voice, which is true. Until I'd watched my mother succumb to Alzheimer's Disease a decade earlier, I'd thought going down in a plane crash was a bad way to die, but the older I get, the more it looks like an escape hatch. None of that, of course, is helpful to a nervous nineteen-year-old. "It helps if you can embrace the theology of physics," I added, nodding at the crucifix and namedropping *lift* and *thrust* but not mentioning human error—that crack in aviation-related things. And I thought about the Leonard Cohen exhibit I'd gone to see, which was titled after Cohen's famous couplet: "There is a crack in everything. That's how the light gets in." And it never *hurts* to pray," I added, closing my eyes as my ruined book slid back to the floor.

JURY-RIGGED

Yesterday I jury-rigged a bird feeder out of a toy highchair and a flowerpot and planted it near the sidewalk in the front yard—three feet of highchair stabbed into four feet of snow. I would have preferred to place it near the house, by a window, but the blizzard that had come through the previous night had left tsunami-sized drifts for which my to-the-knee boots were no match. Outside our back door, my husband Larry had shoveled a path across the patio for our dog Scout, but there is no feeding the birds back there because skunks cannot resist seeds and Scout cannot resist skunks. We've tipped that domino before.

Nothing was jury-rigged in the house I grew up in. My own father was not a fix-it man and when things broke, we just stopped using them. Windows that got painted shut stayed shut. Pocket doors that jammed were consigned forever to their sleeves like something walled up in Poe. Faucet handles that froze stayed frozen and we lined up at taps in other rooms.

Larry, on the other hand, is a fix-it guy—willing to get in there with a pair of pliers and a roll of duct tape. But he's a jury-rigger rather than a journeyman, a truth to which our drawerful of chipped kitchen knives will attest. My sister married the real thing: an electrician, and lives in a house where everything hums. The first thing she told me when Kim asked her out was, "He has a tool belt." We both swooned at the sexiness of that and she has *never* looked back.

By far, the biggest and most ambitious jury-rigger in this broken house we call *the world* is love—it puts our inexpert hands on everything and has us mismatching the sparking ends of live wires and cutting against the bias at exactly the wrong time and walking under anvils like cartoon people all the livelong day. Let the universe shoot us up with a little of the good stuff and we *will* fix things for those who comprise, in my friend Jeanne's words, "our shitload of loved ones," if it kills us, which sometimes it does. Dogs see a lot of this coddling, cooing action because we love them, we do.

Scout's world is wholly rigged to maximize her pleasure. As I write, her belly is full of scrambled eggs and she's settled at the end of her favorite couch which is fading by a sunny window. This troubles me a bit, the fading, but that's where she likes it, the better to keep an eye on things, by which I mean on other dogs who walk by, whose presumption she does not approve at all. We have not been able to successfully trouble-shoot this fact of other dogs in the world, but we do commiserate with her when her fur gets up and the barking starts. "I *know*," we purr, "It's *terrible*. You are so *imposed* upon."

Scout was a rescue—returned goods—shunted back to the animal shelter when her first family swapped her out for a human baby. We don't fault them—she's not a completely easy dog and babies are hard enough to domesticate. But we are determined to make her rocky start on the planet up to her, which is easy enough to do. That's the thing with dogs—you can very nearly perfect their worlds, which is a deeply satisfying power to have, a god-like thing, that gets results you can never achieve for people, try as you might.

My non-fix-it father was at his best with the dogs I grew up with: his purest and most obvious expressions of love were for them. The rest of us, the humans in the house, registered his love in the way he executed his duty to us, by staying around instead of walking out, chronically unhappy for reasons that were at least partly traceable to his own father, a man I never met, who did prison time in the thirties, though my dad never talked about that, or anything else from his boyhood. For the most part, he was a self-isolating, behind-the-newspaper and ball-games-on-TV man—with dogs sleeping on his feet or draped all over him. He jury-rigged their world with too much food and endless praise and constant, gentle strokes. I loved the way he loved them and loved him, in part, for loving them so well.

He taught me how to travel, my father did. Specifically, he taught me proper travel-attitude, which is hugely important if you want to siphon joy from the work it takes to get anywhere. When I graduated from college, he took my mom and me to England, my first trip abroad. "There will be *lines*," he said, preparing me, "wherever we go. *Don't* be impatient. *Don't* complain. Just accept that that's how it *is*." I traveled a lot after that and travel still when I can. There are lines. I never complain.

I also never cut the lines and very seldom have paid the extra money to get around them, though as Jeanne says, throwing money, if you have any of that, at a lot of things can fix them. This is true. As my sister can confirm, money will remove the better part of a kitchen floor from the belly of your Great Pyrenees. It will put a generator in your backyard when the lights blink out and the heat vents choke out their last sweet breath. Even a little bit of it will get a daughter to Scotland and then get her out of Montenegro.

Because they are few enough to be had, it seems wise to savor the situations the world permits us to fix. So when our daughter Maddie, who was studying abroad, called crying from Heathrow because she'd missed her flight to Paris when a friend forgot her passport and she—Maddie—didn't even want to *go* to Paris, she *wanted* to take a train to Scotland with a group of pals from school but now her weekend money was gone, splat, down the drain and what was she going to do, I slipped a little cash into her account and told her to get on the train. She loved Edinburgh.

Montenegro was harder. Maddie and I were together this time in Dubrovnik, an old Croatian city on the Aegean Sea very near the Montenegrin border. Why not slip over and look around? Who wouldn't go to Montenegro when you could practically see it from Dubrovnik's ancient walls? There was a tour company eager enough to drive us there in a not very banged up minibus with a dozen other day-trippers. We signed up for a tour and met our guide and party at a curb just outside the city walls shortly before dawn. It was going to be hot—in the high nineties—that day.

"Is this van *air conditioned?*" I asked the driver.

"Oh yes!" he vowed.

"*Is* this van air conditioned?" I asked the guide.

"Oh yes!" he confirmed.

Maddie and I took a seat in the second row.

By the time we got to the Montenegrin border and stopped for gas, an hour or so into the trip, the sun was up and temperatures were well into the eighties. Most of the passengers were already showing signs of alarm: we had discovered the great air conditioning fallacy—let's call it a lie. After leaning forward and asking that it be turned up, be turned *on*, I had put my hands in our row's little canoe of an AC vent which was as hollow as an empty gravy bowl and pouring out exactly nothing. "No freon," the driver— let's call him the conman—finally admitted, shrugging. The windows, we had already discovered, were sealed, single panels of glass, never designed to open at all. The situation, which was feeling less fixable by the urgent second, presented as this: we were sealed in a glass and metal oven, headed for really who knew where without so much as a map among a people whose language we did not speak. I recalled terrible stories about human traffickers leaving their *cargo* to die of heat inside locked trucks and felt panic stir. This wasn't that, exactly; still, as the heat rose, so did the parallel in my mind, along with one all-compelling thought: my daughter must not die like *this*. I needed to calm down. I don't travel with Xanax but I do pack muscle relaxers. I took two.

When the van pulled into a gas station, which had a convenience store lobbed onto one side of it, we all poured out, some of us (me) with the dream of refuge in mind. But there was no town at all, it was just an outpost on a highway where cars were backed up in both directions, in and out of Montenegro. "We have to go back," I told Maddie. But there was no way back, beyond approaching strangers with our useless English and alarming body language, which didn't exactly promise results. Maddie found the bottled water in the store and we bought liters and liters of it, all we could lug. Then, with everyone else, we climbed back into the long, hot tube. When we got to an actual town, we would cobble together a plan; we would broker a way out.

Back on the bus, I tried to foment a revolution. At least half of the sweating passengers spoke some English. I leaned into the aisle, facing the rear. "Who wants to turn this van around?" I called. No one answered. "We could *die* in here," I prodded. A couple of people shook their heads but most demurred; they would stick it out. Across the aisle, another American, Amber-from-California, kept checking her phone for flights, ferries, buses out of Montenegro and we kept checking with her. "This is the last time we travel without an international data plan," Maddie, who was remaining composed enough to envision a future, remarked. Without WIFI, our phones were useless weight in our bags. An hour later, we disembarked the second time to ride a ferry across the Bay of Kotor; it was the only bit of Montenegro that we paid enough attention to admire. Though the mountains surrounding the bay were Bronte-esque with their wild peaks and gothic shadows, and worthy of awe, we were most enthralled by the wind. The wind on the deck of that ferry felt like life and we drank it in thirsty gulps.

To our acute disappointment, no town awaited us on the far side of the bay where we disembarked so with a huge, pulsing dread we climbed back into the van where everyone peeled off all the clothes they decently could. Sighing, Amber looked up from her phone and gave us the bad news: yes, an actual small city, Budva, was our next stop but there were no international flights out of it. No international trains or buses. Vaguely, I wondered what Montengrins had against their neighbors. "What about a ferry?" I asked. Budva was literally just down the coast from Croatia, right smack on the same sea.

She spent another five minutes scrolling. "No ferries," she sighed.

I closed my eyes and tried out my friend Lynn's calming mantra, the one she uses in MRI scanners. "I have everything I need," I murmured. But I didn't. I needed my daughter not to die in an Eastern European tourist-racket and I couldn't be sure I could pull that off. Maddie was still showing no signs of panic—in her twenties, she seemed more the adult than I was—as we rode deeper and deeper down the length of the baking Balkan peninsula.

Finally, after pulling into a grim, gravel parking lot surrounded by a chain link fence in the unpromising, promised land of Budva, we oozed out of the van for the last time. "There is a market," the criminal calling himself our guide announced and most people began trickling in the direction to which he pointed, though why anyone would believe him was beyond me. Maddie and I watched them slog off. "We'll get a hotel here, figure something out," I said. Around us, the bleak cityscape looked brutally industrial.

Then, "a taxi," Maddie murmured wonderingly, like she was dreaming dreams and seeing visions. She pointed and, rising to the reality of it, cried, "a taxi cab—over there!"

Eons passed as we crunched across the wastes of that parking lot, waving our arms; I was terrified the taxi, which might or might not be a mirage, would pull away before we could throw ourselves in front of it. But there it still was, in hard steel, alongside its driver, in real flesh, when we made it to the curb.

"Hello!" we panted to the middle-aged man who introduced himself as Meech, and whose English exceeded our Montenegrin by about a hundred happy words. "Can you drive us to Dubrovnik?"

"*Croatia?*" he replied, like he'd maybe heard of it once.

"Please!"

"Wait." He held up a hand, then he called a guy who seemed to know a guy who'd met the guy who owned the cab.

"A hundred euros," he finally said, pocketing his phone. We climbed into the cab and practiced running the windows up and down, up and down.

And two hours later, Meech—driver, deliverer, savior—who, besides another guy's cab, also had up his sleeve a road less traveled that came with a desolate, unmonitored, and probably illegal border crossing site, dropped us off in Dubrovnik, not far from our hotel. Pushing all of our cash at him—the hundred and a little more—we wished him a happy, *happy* life.

Throwing money at it did not, by itself, spring us from what I now think of as "The Montenegrin Affair," which has a very *Bond, James Bond* ring to it that is arguably out of proportion to its perils and thrills. Some fair amount of luck jury-rigged the events that placed Meech in our reach which, by contrast, sounds pleasingly Seussian. Luck is probably always the biggest link in the supply chain of salvation in this tumultuous world. It's how all of my dad's dogs came to him, and how Scout came to set up camp on our couch.

On our final day in Croatia, Maddie and I were sweltering over cold drinks in an outdoor cafe, next to a table of three local men and a white dog with black spots who was lapping water from a bowl by their feet. We always take great, noisy note of other people's dogs. "What breed is *he—or she?*" we squeal, and "how precious!" It's arguably intrusive and largely beyond our control. But we didn't need to inquire after this dog's lineage because he was the world's most recognizable canine, even slurping solo, without an entourage of 100 identical fellows. He was also an animal whose exotic, famous coat has been thoroughly jury-rigged by its breeders to stand out everywhere. But here in Croatia, he fit right in. "Look," I nudged Maddie, "on our last day here, a Dalmatian *Dalmatian!*" And to that redundant, random luck we raised a parting glass.

WHAT'S HAPPENING NOW

Despite a universe straining against the likelihood of it, one of my little poems brought home a bit of money the other day. Strange cash in hand, I went straight to Williams Sonoma and bought a copper tea kettle which now sits in queenly disdain next to my surly old steel kettle with a snubbed spout that hisses and spits all over the stovetop—there's a lot of upstairs-downstairs drama going on in the kitchen these days. Adorning the left, back burner is a copper saucepan that came home earlier this year after a three-Chardonnay lunch in a fancy mall I had no business being anywhere near. Together, as there are no jewels to be had, they constitute my daughters' inheritance—a copper pot apiece.

Their beauty aside, it's the elemental purity of saucepan and kettle I love, the fact that their matter is irreducible, that I can tuck them right into a slot in the periodic table as amenable as my kitchen cupboard: Cu, atomic number 29. In a complicated world where things keep changing—technologies, governments, my middle-aged body (shocking enough) into an old one, copper stays copper.

In a staggering alteration of things as they were, my friend Fred died last spring. Over a long winter of illness that tapered into a moment, he went from being a jovial sage in a sweater vest to a memory—not that any of it feels absolutely real. It seems he is merely off to Rome again, or watching live opera from the MET video-streamed at the nearby multiplex, soaking up the high culture the rest of us had no taste for. I still feel his intelligent weight around town. Sending him an email that won't ever be answered might set me straight about things, but I have nothing like that kind of courage.

When I woke up recently at four in the morning and went straight to weeping, I got out of bed and put a flame under the new kettle, medium-low, per instructions—the aristocracy's constitution being so compromised by purity. Imposter to the core, I try to turn a stoic face in death's direction, at least during the day. There is a whole routine where I encourage the students in my world religions class to think of themselves as *events*—as brief collaborations of atoms—rather than as separate *beings*. "What doesn't exist in the first place can hardly stop existing," I congratulate myself, casting about for that victory high-five and coming up empty every time.

When the new kettle whispered its steam, subtle as the royal wave (the old kettle howls like a fishwife) I filled a ceramic teapot and settled near a window to turn Fred's ballpoint pen around in my hand and waited for the birds to wake up.

I like these gaps that sometimes open early in the morning, well before sunrise, between sleep and work. I occupy them greedily—all mine each minute—to read or think or write. After sunrise the world clamors for a piece of you, but before dawn that same world leaves you alone. I have occupied these long mornings variously: baking, meditating, wringing poems from the silence.

Four A.M.: the hour of prayers and vandals. In an effort to fuse the two, on the Sunday before the 2018 midterm elections, I tried something new and, dressing silently so as not to wake my sleeping husband, crept out of the house.

Riding shotgun around town in the dark, a big bucket of sidewalk chalk rattled at each pothole. Like lots of subversives and defacers of public property, I was shrouded in black, from sneakers to gloves to wool cap—a portentous soundtrack playing in my head, heavy on the bass clarinet. My first stop was our town's big box store which sells everything from pine nuts to belt sanders. Easing into a space in the empty parking lot, I glanced furtively left and right, then slipped from the car, dashed to the doorway, and dropped to my knees. Gripping a chunk of chalk as thick as a bedpost, I scrawled "Protect Families! Vote BLUE!" on the sidewalk. Then I scrambled back to my car and shot out of Dodge with an eye on the rearview mirror.

It took an hour to hit a handful of targets around town: the multi-storied assisted living center ("Save Medicare! Vote BLUE!"), the library ("Facts Matter! Vote BLUE!"), the mall ("Protect Women's Healthcare: Vote BLUE!") and so on. Banksy, with no art or irony or, frankly, much of a plan, I left a trail of emphatic pleas in whatever last-minute language I hoped would persuade my neighbors to turn from the lies, the rancor, the march toward despotism.

Fred, who was not "political," would have liked my story of darting around town in the middle of the night, had he lived to hear it, though he preferred ruminating on ultimate things: deity, the possibility of grace, the dynamics of redemption. I do too, I would have told him but, from time to time, you have to clean out the gutters of your democracy; you have to sweep out its chimneys and hose down its decks.

Complicated as self-governance is, it's not nearly as complex as the contraption that creates the mind. Every once in a while, I google "elements in the human body" just to remind myself what, at our bare minimum, we really are, as if I can get to the bottom of things. The myriad science websites report that 99% of the human body is comprised of six elements: oxygen, carbon, hydrogen, nitrogen, calcium, and phosphorus. The negligible rest of us is a small handful of others including magnesium which I beef up every day with a supplement to keep my aging muscles from cramping.

Something in that elemental matrix and the bone and organ and connective tissue it produced, something in its unfathomable grid of axons and dendrites, had once produced the *Fred* of Fred. And when a rogue bacteria shut down the mechanism, he disappeared like a hologram when the power goes out.

The anatomy of consciousness, that sentient hologram, seems to be the great mystery of our time. Neurology certainly weighs in on it a lot these days. It is so robust, so convincing in its hour upon the stage, we script future, post-mortem scenes for it, where it breaks free of the world's grip like a helium balloon and floats off into eternity. Maybe it does; Fred hoped for as much.

The late, great poet-neurologist, Oliver Sacks, pictured consciousness not as a hologram, but as a river of overlapping moments which our brain tracks, allowing us to create a narrative with a past, present, and future that gives us "a thematic and personal continuity." Its genesis all but a miracle, this insistent *I* rises from the elemental soup to put on Easter hats and combat boots, to build its gods and demons. As to whether or not there is more to heaven and earth than that, Horatio—the jury is still out.

Fred taught a rigorous Latin curriculum for forty years with loads of panache and humor. I met him at our local Catholic high school where I was hired to teach in the liberal 90s despite my agnosticism. A scholar of theology as well as classics, his knack for moving agilely between the sacred and profane was legendary. I don't know how many times I watched him line up humbly during Mass, hands clasped, to confess his sins to a man lucky to have half his intellect during the Sacrament of Reconciliation, then return to class to blast some stammering kid for being out of dress code.

"Where are your socks, son?"

"I...I don't know..."

"You don't *know?* Someday, when you're a surgeon and I need you to save my life, *you won't be wearing socks.* Where will *I* be then?"

His students loved him—not fondly in any ordinary way, but in that rare way we love when some large spirit briefly sweeps us up.

Fred and I left the Catholic school the same year for positions in separate public schools—he to beef up his retirement, I to shore up my daughters' college savings accounts with infinitesimally higher wages. I knew at the time that I was also leaving because Fred was going; I couldn't face his empty classroom across the hall from my own. It wouldn't have been vacant in the literal sense, of course—some brainy classics scholar would have stepped in by the following September, but it would have been empty for me.

Now he was really gone. Live long enough and the world steadily empties itself of your friends: an irreducible, copper kettle truth.

"In Latin, you pronounce all of the vowels," Fred once explained when I hit him up for help with an Emily Dickinson poem we were reading in my American Lit class. In a shaken, newly Darwinian world, where many people, stripped of their old faith, still trundled to church out of habit or longing, Dickinson had written, "Better an ignis fatuus, than no illume at all": better a will-o-the-wisp, than no light at all.

"It's *fah-too-oose il-loo-may*," Fred had said slowly. Clearly.

"Better an ignis *fah-too-oose*," I repeated to my students, "than no *il-loo-may* at all." What do you think Dickinson meant by that?"

"It's better to at least pretend to have faith in a phony God than have no faith at all," Nora, who sits halfway back in the classroom and lives for this stuff, replied.

"How so?"

"It's comforting," Lee chimed in. "A godless world is terrifying." These kids are only high school sophomores, but they're smart.

They were appalled when I told them about Dickinson's only year of college at Mount Holyoke, about how, though she had longed for a saving Christian faith, she could not bend her mind to the creed or will her stubborn soul to give itself up to Christ. For this tortured refusal, her headmistress had labeled her a "No-Hoper," as in *no hope of Heaven for you, my pretty!* I always picture that terrible woman in a black and white world, riding a bicycle through a tornado.

A part of me wants to be a Roman Catholic in the way some grown women want to be cheerleaders. Sure, there's the degrading sexism, but there is also all that *unum corpus*-team camaraderie and hope eternal. All that delicious mysticism running through rituals: statues buried upside down and throats blessed against the common cold and socks that can't be changed during playoff week. All that collective ecstasy.

A few years before Fred died, a stone statue of the Virgin Mary turned up in the garden center of a nearby market. I'd been looking for one— something to do with my mother's death and, more vaguely, some eternal female principle. As I was struggling to lift this weighty Mary into my shopping cart, a very handsome, masculine-looking woman swept in. "Can I help you with that?" she offered, then hoisted her in. Her chivalry caught me off guard and as I gasped my thanks, I am sorry to report that my vanity, which forgets how jowly we've gotten, positively blossomed. "She's hitting on me!" I thought, shining in the way we do when we realize we're the object of someone's desire, until I watched her rejoin her beautiful partner among the geraniums and collided head-on with the brutal truth: *she was helping the elderly.*

Lying alongside a package of English muffins and a bottle of cheap *rioja* at the bottom of my cart, Mary completed a fairly eucharistic-looking tableau which I snapped a picture of and texted to a friend with the message, "Am I Catholic yet?"

A convert to Catholicism, Fred chose his faith. His wife Kathy said it was the Church's pageantry that drew him to it; he did love musical theater and interior decorating. Because I come up empty in home-rehabbing skills, Fred generously wallpapered our foyer one hot, summer afternoon, pressing grassy-looking vertical stripes to three walls in exchange for a Caesar salad; for the next dozen years, walking through the front door felt like striding into a veld. He'd dropped out of seminary in his twenties to marry, then practiced law before settling into teaching high school, which suited him. "Mr. Partlow," a burly boy complained one day, ambling down the hall as Fred and I loitered together between classes, "I'm about to bomb my history test."

"Side-Angle-Side!" Fred called. And another day, "Help, Mr. Partlow!" a panicked, future valedictorian wailed, rounding the bend and clutching her French notes, a tight ponytail pulling her eyebrows back, "I'm drowning in the past-subjunctive!"

"Angle-Side-Angle!" Fred advised.

As a teenager Fred had been a "soda-jerk"—his words—at a lunch counter in Lansing. "The owner of the shop had an actual indulgence *from the Pope*," he recalled when we were talking in a bookstore one day.

"How do you know?"

"He framed it and hung it over the milkshake machine."

I had just got home from school when I answered the phone to the news that Fred had died. For twenty minutes, I did nothing but gaze through the sliding glass doors at the pre-spring landscape. Watching squirrels scramble over the frozen world, foraging in the ivy for the old stores that sustained them, I felt a chasm open; nothing—not even the hard ground—seemed firm or steady. Eventually, I went into the kitchen and, dethroning the copper kettle, set a heavy, stainless steel pot on the front burner into which I poured rice and water, and turned the gas flame up high. Then I pulled a cutting board from a drawer and numbly began building a meal for Fred's family. The labor gave me something to put my hands on.

Though the calendar insisted it was April, winter had been unbudging and the impossibly green scallions I pulled from a vegetable bin, trucked in from some milder place beloved by God, lay like lily stems on the kitchen island. As I sliced them into short rounds and scraped them into a ceramic bowl, they released an alien spray of spring. Rummaging in the pantry, I pulled out dried cranberries and sunflower seeds; from the fridge I culled hothouse tomatoes, feta and Stilton cheeses. Toasting almonds in a cast iron skillet, I remembered the brownies Fred had loved and while the rice cooled in a colander, I dragged a slab of baking chocolate from the pantry and was soon stirring batter with a wooden spoon.

I also cooked on the last full day of my mother's life—doggedly, perversely. As my sweet, unconscious mom lay dying in her narrow hospital bed at my sister's house across town, I tore lettuce and pruned broccoli and scrubbed potatoes in the sink. I bought wine. A modest dinner gathering—a reprieve for my sister—was the excuse I invented for that vigorous, grief-ducking labor—a few hours release from the responsibilities of nursing. I had slept on the floor of our mother's bedroom for the previous two nights but Sue had been tenderly caring for her full-time since she climbed into bed after a fall a few days earlier and then never got out. I would spread a cloth on the patio table and transport us for a few hours to a less desolate place. About the time the oven had pre-heated, I fell apart and wept to Larry, who hadn't asked me to do anything at all, "I *can't do* this!" We stashed the food in the fridge, folded up the tablecloth, and I drove to Sue's and spread my blankets back out on my mother's floor. It was her last night. The next morning, between sliding ice chips into her mouth, I wrote her eulogy. By the time it was done, she had slipped away. Her absence left a cleft in the world.

My students and I talk a lot about the emptiness of such clefts, about the Buddhist concept of *sunyata,* that "fertile *void*" out of which everything emerges and to which everything returns, "a sort of cosmic blender," I tell them, putting a wry spin on it. Which is not brave, just behind-the-curtain humbuggery every time.

I recently toured the Catholic school where Fred and I used to teach with my friend Kathy, who was still fighting the good fight there every single day. There is a beautiful new chapel with stained glass windows reaching toward the student parking lot. The auditorium has been refitted with roomy, "business-class" sized seats and gleaming panels of buttons for high-tech sound and light systems. A giant football stadium now rolls out behind Fred's old classroom in a continent of artificial turf. So much was markedly different and so much was the same. Winding through the currents of past and present in Sack's river of consciousness, I was caught in the confluence of two worlds.

Traitorous as it looks—dispensing with us individually as it does—I have to concede that the natural world is really neither profligate nor unfaithful, which we recognize if we pay attention and can manage to give up our own stake in space and time, God help us. "If you got skin in the game, you stay in the game," I sing along with Lin-Manuel Miranda when I'm cooking dinner, but we *don't* get to stay in the game. My personal consciousness will flicker out when the atoms sustaining it finally trickle away in an ongoing process that will pick up speed in some critical moment. Nothing will be thrown away or lost, except what I know as *me*. "The body dies, but the Tao remains," the *Tao Te Ching* tells us of the permanence that underlies and choreographs all things. Small comfort—that. Which is not quite the same thing as no comfort at all.

In the meantime, while I'm still here in all of this confounding flux, it feels important to follow Fred's example by attending to what the comedian Flip Wilson once called, *The Church of What's Happening Now*. *What's Happening Now* is one tough church—Calvinist-tough, Appalachian snake-handling-tough—and I admit I've had to start lowering the bar in taking up its more exacting rituals. On my 63rd birthday, for example, I vowed simply to get my lipstick above my neck.

Fred never gave up on *What's Happening Now*—this mega-church of day-to-day living—not on understanding it or salvaging what could be saved. On his 70th birthday, he got his first tattoo. *LXX*, it read, and then in Latin: *Ne vetus homo scire potest:* "Even an old man must learn." In the final years of his life, he threw his muscle into supporting a school for Kenyan orphans. Over the months prior to his death, he lost most of his hearing and I saw him less frequently. The last few times I exchanged emails with him, he was studying Greek and reading the Egyptian author Naguib Mahfouz's book, *Palace Walk*, which he recommended. A few days after he died, I drove to the bookstore where we'd so often met and bought it; it was, in this way, the last book we would share.

Dreamland

Harvard edX wants me to be happy. I am on their email list. The persistent and probably shady Quick Fix company wants to sell me synthetic urine, which might make me happy if I had a drug habit and my job or rehab outfit required random drops. I am on their email list too. Delta Airlines wants to make me happy by giving me 90,000 free miles if I sign up for their credit card which is, sadly, an American Express card, and so feels too hoity-toity to me, like the Episcopal Church did to my mother and the Dow Chemical executive parties did to my cousin Mabel, and the whole town of Oxford does to every tourist who's ever swung through there to get a look at Hogwarts. I am on Delta's email list too.

I recently unsubscribed to Indiegogo; God knows who sold them my email address—probably the urine-people. I gave them a chance (read their spiel) because I'm a sixties girl and everything sounds like Downtown-Fun-With-Petula Clark when you lob on a *gogo*. Diet-A-Gogo, Fly-Standby-A-Gogo, Colonoscopy-A-Gogo: who wouldn't jump at any of those opportunities for dreamy happiness? But Indiegogo turned out to be a crowdfunding operation, which is really just panhandling online with a website instead of a cardboard sign and a more elaborate (if less urgent) agenda than Fund My Supper. As it was my good dumb luck to have supper and enough books to read too, I thumbed my nose at crowdfunding and unsubscribed.

Snooping around for the pleasure of a small retreat, I recently discovered a grotto below the arcing branches of an old redbud tree on the MSU campus, which is near my house, and to this sequestered place I sometimes take a lawn chair to read. All around me, a lot is happening. Straight ahead, a small fountain is happening: it shoots up a pretty column of water which falls gracefully back into its bowl. To my left, a boxwood hedge is happening—it runs for some number of feet—twenty or a hundred, I never know—and behind this hedge a white tail doe sometimes beds down at night. I accidentally flushed her out early one morning and her mattress of pressed pachysandra bore her shape. Happening when there is a breeze, the redbud tree wags its seed pods which resemble pea pods and are, in fact edible, as are the tree's blossoms. In this cloister, I meditate on the miracle of photosynthesis, which upstages everything else that's happening, that's *ever* happened on this living earth. I mean, water into wine—sure—why not? But sunshine into glucose, light into food? This is the First, the Ongoing Supper, on which everything else depends. The goddess's hand in the heart-shaped leaves leaves me limp with wonder.

There is also something going on with symmetry here that intimates rightness and quiets my noisy anxieties, which puts me a little in thrall but a little ashamed, as if I'm settling too soon for surfaces. You can fold each heart-shaped redbud leaf down the middle like a paper valentine and its sides achieve perfect congruence. The four mossy sidewalks that meet the fountain at right angles, the linear hedges that hem in their sides, the way gravity tugs each drop of water flung up by some hidden pump to earth, massage the knots out of my mind, at least for a little while. It's a happy idyll of order in a tumultuous world. "It's Dreamland," I think.

"It's Dreamland," I breathed when I stumbled into the new high school's courtyard as a child. I was eight, probably, and my mom had dropped off a bunch of us kids from the neighborhood at the swanky campus for summer swimming lessons. Unlike our blonde-brick elementary building, the new school was exotic: it was built *California-style*, I'd heard my mom tell my aunt on the phone, which meant it had *grounds* with not one but several buildings. My friends and I were sitting on our usual bench in front of a brick wall, waiting for the little kids in an earlier class to come out, dragging their wet beach towels—our signal to file into the *natatorium* that resembled, with its broad curved roof, one of the giant stingrays I'd seen pictures of in our *World Book Encyclopedia*. But on this day, I got tired of waiting and wandered down the sidewalk to a different wall. Peering around the edge, I felt a deep surge of pleasure. Before me lay a perfectly square garden, each side identical to the rest, each punctuated with two benches bolted in at precisely the same intervals. Between the benches, neat mounds of boxwood were packed into pebbles; in the center there lay a panel of lawn. This sudden world of parallels and right angles was like nothing I'd ever seen in our raw little suburb of dirt roads and scrub. Its geometry stirred the stem of my soul, which vibrated down through my feet to some seismic force I felt rumble and move. It was Eden revealed—God's own quad.

Looking back, I see in that small enclosure the courtyard of every hospital cafeteria and nursing home and Best Western motel. Even by the time I got to high school, it was nothing more than a prelude to the principal's office. But gaping there at eight, in my red elastic two-piece bathing suit with the white flippy skirt and twin white buttons sewn over my nipples, a thick rubber bathing cap strapped onto my head, I whispered, "Dreamland!" Then I launched myself into it. Around and around, from bench to bench, I flew shouting, "Dreamland! Dreamland!" Leaping in Beauty, twirling in Truth, I felt myself born into symmetry.

I'm not sure even today if that childhood flood of ecstasy was religious or aesthetic, nor can I point to where those two raptures intersect or diverge, and I suspect they're often the same thing with different labels. The noisy reductionist in me—that bore—clamors about surges of dopamine and serotonin like some people drone on about wines and golf. How clever and dull we become when we're grown, drawing our models, charting bliss.

The world's brain-mappers—scientists, neurologists, psychologists—have all chimed in on our human love of symmetry. Symmetry is a sign of good health, they say; its repetition is reliable which makes us feel safe. "Our own brain, "the physicist Alan Lightman writes, "was born from...the same pure mathematics that happens in flowers and jellyfish and Higgs particles." Symmetry, when we encounter it, feels like a happy family reunion because it feels like *us*.

But the conscious world is not a perfect anything—not a circle, not a square, not a tidy, folded heart. Outside much of the physical world, and the metaphors we draw from it, life is not symmetrical at all—it's a breaking, budding, horrific glorious mess—and something in us recognizes and responds to the truth of that too. Insisting on congruence where none exists and shoving each other into templates that conform to some idea of order, leads only and ever to cruelty. It's a specialty of purity ideologies. Ask the survivors of name-your-holocaust. Ask the refugees from name-your-theocracy. Ask the Uyghurs of China, the Rohinga from Myanmar, defectors from the Evangelical church. I caught a glimpse of Dreamland the other night—the real thing, all dented and busted up and revolving in place, because that's the way it looks in the actual world—like in a hospital emergency room.

"It's Grinder." That's what the enormous security guard said to the other enormous security guard outside the E. R. They were mountainous men, both of them well over six and a half feet tall, and they wore commanding blue uniforms with badass belts. One had a beard; the other had a man bun.

Gripping a tray with a plate of scrambled eggs and a rapidly cooling tea, I was on the last leg of a mission to the cafeteria to get breakfast for a friend who was a patient there—if possible before everything was stone cold, and I had to pass back through security to return to her room. Grinder was holding me up.

Grinder, clearly a regular, was a homeless man and he was in trouble. "Oh, this is bad," he muttered, turning slow tight circles in place. "This is bad, this is bad." He was small and thin and layered—black leggings under black shorts below a black jacket—and he was revolving like a grazed sparrow.

"It's okay, buddy we gotcha," the beard-man comforted him, while apologizing—"sorry, buddy, gotta do this"—the bun-man pawed through his filthy duffel bag. Grinder's cigarette-rolling machine and his manicure scissors had lit up the screen on the security scanner and needed to be confiscated before he could enter the emergency room, where his dream of salvation waited. "You're almost there, buddy," bun-man encouraged him. We'll take care of you."

By the time Grinder's contraband had been extracted and placed in a bin and I was waved through the body-scanner, my friend's eggs were, of course, cold. But this was a moot point since they were also diluted and salty with tears. Because, confronted with the tenderness of a couple of guys who were essentially bouncers, I'd started weeping and kept on crying all the way to the elevator. Grinder would be okay that day. In a beautiful busted wounded world, which is really the only kind there is, a pair of giants had his back, had delivered him to symmetry, to a plumb and stable dawn. "It's dreamland," I whispered to no one at all. It wouldn't last. It never will. You build it and build it and build it again, at least as far as I can tell.

Which is maybe what Harvard had in mind with their course, if I read their syllabus. I deleted it. Back in my grotto, a book splayed open on my lap and thinking about Grinder and giants and saviors and such, I realized what I really liked best about idling there, wasn't the grid I saw, glancing around, but the pleasure I felt looking up—where the sun glowed through each leaf and each leaf stirred in the breeze and patches of blue, irregular sky flashed with clerestory light.

ONSET

Early in March, in the fourth year of American occupation by the Trump cartel, I found myself grinding slowly to a stop—again: no reading, no writing, no exercise. By then, of course, I knew the political flavor of this paralysis, which had been resurfacing for thirty-nine long months like bouts of malaria: the fitful sleeping, the vise of fear on the ribcage, the slow leak in the bubble of optimism that buoys hope.

For weeks as I tried to write, mice (I hoped they were mice—and not something larger, bolder, toothier) assembled IKEA bookcases in the attic directly over my head and, when I threw in the writing-towel and crept down the hall to the solace of a warm shower, they tap danced on the ceiling vent in the bathroom. Besides all of this clatter and scraping, they had a lot to discuss, which they did in a flurry of chirps that sounded like the old British phone signals I ran into decades ago riding trains around Europe on no money and, of course, no Internet. Tracking down cheap rooms at each English station we pulled into, my friends and I would drop a few pence into an old steel phone bolted to a filthy wall, then crowd around the receiver to "wait for the rapid pips" which signaled, if memory serves, the moment to dial. Not that far over my head, mice (I hoped) conversed in torrents of rapid pips.

"We had mice in the attic," a neighbor told me when I was complaining about the noise. "They used to come down and sit on the ceiling fan blades in our bathroom. One day, without thinking, I flipped the switch and it threw two of them into the toilet."

"I *hope* they're mice," I said.

For a couple of weeks, my husband Larry and I had attempted a gentle relocation program, setting no-kill traps around the house, scouting out warm(ish), hay-filled barns as drop-off sites. "We have to take them over the county line," I told him. I'd read how mice, relocated, will find their way "home" from miles away, over rough country. Considering the flat, docile landscape of mid-Michigan, I insisted, "Mice will respect a county line." But all of this forethought yielded exactly nothing. Each night we baited the little trailers with cheese and peanut butter and propped their hinge-doors open and each morning the free meals were gone and the mice were sleeping it off in our walls. So finally, out of humane options, I put in calls to a few "animal removal" specialists, aka *assassins,* for chilling plans of action at equally chilling prices. "You are forcing my hand!" I called up to the ceiling one day when they were bowling. Then I closed the book I wasn't reading and stared at the blank screen on my laptop as thoughts of the cartel swelled in my head and my pulse began racing again.

On Super Tuesday of the 2020 Democratic Primary season, a few days after I called the pest-removal people, Larry and I were watching CNN and waiting for Dylan, our 19-year-old hired gun, to show up and set poisoned bait stations throughout our attic and basement and close what he could find of entry points into our house. We knew the death-by-poisoning was cruel, but the mouse droppings in the silverware drawer had whittled away most of our sympathy and the two little non-swimmers we'd found face-down in our dog's water bowl had solidified our resolve.

On TV, Democrats competed with the burgeoning coronavirus for celebrity and national relevance. I watched it all unfold—polling conjectures and global quarantines—with a gnawing anxiety and a bowl of blueberries in my lap. The dogging of cable news was for keeping abreast of a mounting international crisis; the blueberries were for fighting off dementia. I had recently read about a study that suggested a regular diet of blueberries might make a person less likely to succumb to Alzheimer's—as my mother had. So on Super Tuesday, in the micro-universe of our house, I sat on the couch and watched Democrats drop from the race like windfall apples and cruise ships, with their cargo of 21st-century lepers, languish in harbors and ate blueberry after blueberry while my thumbs grew blue

Meanwhile, as viruses flourished and aspiring tyrants chipped away at democracies in the macro-universe of late winter days outside our house, I sought a measure of beauty and moments of peace by continuing the protocol I'd put in place at the beginning of winter. I always take on a winter project, something to enrich the long nights and generate a little trophy of accomplishment when I pop out the other end of the tunnel into spring. As a result, I can make five kinds of North African stew, sketch a stack of books that discerning people might identify as a stack of books, and stammer several potentially essential phrases in German: 1. *Darf ich einen Korkenzieher haben, bitte?* (May I have a corkscrew, please?); 2. *Wo ist die nächste Toilette?* (Where is the nearest bathroom?) *Buchhandlung?* (bookstore) *bäckerei?* (bakery); 3. *Ich habe nicht für ihn gestimmt.* (I didn't vote for him.) Now, more than ever, it seemed important to develop and grow in new ways in spite of the cartel's stranglehold on goodness and truth—maybe to disprove its reach and powers. So I'd signed up for a weekly drawing class and practiced looking at light; I attended a French class and practiced liaisons and rolling my Rs. And, day by day, I deleted unread emails from most of the thousand do-good organizations that needed slices of my little teaching-pension-pie to save the world. "I'm with him," I got into the habit of saying in my head, pointing to philanthropic Michael Bloomberg, who had also moved in there, letting him pick up our check.

So that all this forward-and-improving action wouldn't collapse into a tangle of malaise, I'd wired my days to a structure, like training vines to a trellis. Mornings, following a slog on the treadmill, I settled down to tea in a cafe, spread out my note cards, and practiced French conjugations and short sentences. Gradually, favorite phrases distinguished themselves, like celebrities on the red carpet at the Oscars. *Aujourd'hui sur les escaliers* (today on the stairs) for musicality with no practical application. *Nous voudrions une table sur la terrasse* (We'd like a table on the terrace) for future utility. Then—damn it—coming in first, for conciseness and accuracy: *Trump trompe:* Trump lies.

Donald Trump was stuck in my mind like a boulder in a riverbed; not even a steady, sloshing current of French vowels seemed to rock him loose. Gradually, I began to understand I would have to work around him. I recalled the writer Lauren Slater, who suffers from OCD, explaining that she had learned to live in the silent moments outside her mind's noisy compulsions. If she could cohabitate with her mental illness in this way, I could surely find a way to live alongside Trump for as long as it took to expunge him.

Eventually Dylan, our mouse-man, arrived with his bag full of death slung over one shoulder, and we directed him to our basement and then to the attic, where he climbed a stepladder and disappeared through the ceiling. "It's mice," he confirmed half an hour later, then explained where he'd laid his packets of poison that down the road would turn our mice, he vowed, "to dust." Ashes to ashes.

Over the next few days, wrapped in a soft afghan because I'd come down with a cold, I read the poet, Jane Kenyon, who had lived with her poet-husband Donald Hall in New Hampshire. A translator of Russian poetry, Kenyon had an intellect far superior to my own, as do so many of the voices who live on my bookshelves, but I always liked hanging out with the smart kids in school and I still do. She was an enthusiastic gardener and in one of her short essays, written in winter, she goes on about seed catalogues. I've run into these intrepid poet-gardeners before: even inside, at their desks, they manage to do a lot with mulching and pruning—wringing them for metaphors, transubstantiating all that lower back pain into soulful resurrection.

For quite a few years, in bouts of hero-worship, I tried to love gardening—like I tried to love yoga; I wanted to *be* those mindful people with God's good dirt under their fingernails. I dug beds and sank shrubby perennials; I bought a mat and worked my creaky self into some lopsided version of a downward-facing dog in the last row of yoga class, but there were weeds, don't you know, and so many dogs—I'd no sooner get up when I was going back down, or trying to, which is, I suppose, the point of the thing. Eventually, I owned up to my hedonism and junked the gardening and the yoga and conceded that I was not so much a person of the ground as I was of the several feet above ground—and returned to my old routine of hanging a fern and reading in a chair on the patio, or in the winter, beside the fire—worn old shoes that fit.

I have a friend—let's call her Caitlin—who has been struggling with alcoholism for the past few of years and most fiercely for the past few months. She is a warrior-goddess. We non-addicts are all a heartbeat away from some form of addiction—this I firmly believe—and anyone who is not in thrall to some insidious, life-stealing cocktail or pill is just damn lucky. Recently Caitlin's AA sponsor encouraged her to find one beautiful thing to look at whenever she felt the compulsion to have a drink steal over her— this, of course, in addition to finding a meeting, calling a friend, going for a walk—the usual bag of tricks that help some people sometimes avoid throwing themselves over a cliff. So Caitlin was on the lookout for beauty, which is not so easy to be had in March in Michigan, the start of mud season. Nothing is blooming yet. The barren ground thaws and freezes, thaws and freezes. Old snowbanks gray and wither. If you're a woman on the far side of menopause, as I am, looking at this landscape is a lot like looking in the mirror—not much heartening is happening there. Nevertheless, I decided to take up the basic protocol of looking out for a bit of beauty each day. Though I didn't yet have a drinking problem of my own, I did have that specter of Donald Trump passing through the walls of my house, like Jacob Marley, rattling its chains, pointing to doom.

Passing through a room where Larry was watching CNN drove home how rapidly things were heating up with the virus. A couple of days before the Ides of March, our governor shut down the schools. The NCAA Playoffs were cancelled, making everyone's beloved brackets null and void and, judging from the acres of empty shelves in supermarkets, "March Madness" had acquired a whole new meaning. Back east in New York, the lights of Broadway blinked out and down in Orlando, Disney World's fireworks were cold in their cannons.

Meanwhile, our daughter Anna, who travels for work, got caught in the chaos of canceled meetings and came to stay with us for a few days because, in the airline industry's newly scrambled grid, for a handful of hours it was cheaper to fly into Lansing—a hub for nowhere—than into Chicago, where she lives. A savvy traveler, she passed out her own disinfectant wipes to the crew and together they wiped down their seats before settling into their nearly empty plane. We picked Anna up at the eerily vacant airport where I grabbed a cocoa from a snack shop—free because, though the refrigerators and shelves were amply stocked with sandwiches and chips and bottled drinks, there was no one to pay. Whoever had been there was gone. If this is the Rapture, I thought, the world's airport workers had done very well by it.

Back home, Larry flipped on the news. Redder and more bloated than usual, Trump spread into the TV screen like a batter finding the edge of its pan, as he lobbed blame for our country's slow response to the pandemic out into the world, trying to get it to stick somewhere, despite the fact that his administration had dismantled our pandemic response team two years earlier. But facts are gum wrappers to him, litter he kicks to the curb.

The day after Anna arrived, the day my classes were canceled, she and I tiptoed out of the house into a still partially open world that was growing tenser by the hour and went to a movie—a 10 A.M. showing of *Emma*. Observing the early, minimal restrictions of pandemic-protocol, we veered clear of the handful of other moist, respiring humans at the theater and settled as stiffly as Jane Austen's gentry into our seats without touching the armrests or cupholders. Afterward, we met my other daughter Maddie for lunch in a cafe, which was busier than we expected it to be with people like us taking fewer precautions than they should have been. The baristas handed us our tea in latex gloves—no one was onto masks yet—which we carried to a table in the corner, wondering how long it would be before we would enact this ritual again. We spent the rest of the afternoon at home working crossword puzzles by the fire while the still-robust mice rolled a roulette wheel and threw dice in the attic.

Gradually, shame had been growing in me for my blithe out-and-about-ness as better-minded people chimed in on social media (*les medias sociaux*, notecard #119—classless, I kept studying) with imperatives to self-isolate to whatever extent we could. So after Maddie returned to her home an hour down the road, after Anna's on-campus office hours were canceled and she was instructed to work online, we vowed not to leave the house except to walk outside in the chilly sun where we would imperil and be imperiled by exactly no one. We had been practicing a self-serving denial, giving a glance, at best, to the early facts about transmission. Finally, thanks to the persistent, wise advice of others, we began to wake up.

The day before St. Paddy's Day (*la veille de Saint Paddy*, notecard #67) Larry brought home a dozen chocolate cupcakes, frosted with electric green shamrocks. "On sale!" he sang—the man likes a bargain. "They're canceled-party cupcakes," I sighed, siphoning some of the joy from his full cup. Then I pried one out from its plastic caddy and headed upstairs to read in bed and scroll on my phone. My cold was getting worse.

In pandemic-stricken Italy, people remanded by law to their homes were singing together from their open windows; I watched on my phone as music tumbled along their streets and bounced off the hoods of their small cars pinned bumper to bumper along the curbs. In bed in America, I read about trees. Beech trees in an unspoiled forest, I learned from Peter Wohlleben, a German arborist, photosynthesize light at the same rate whether they are large or small, well or poorly positioned for sun and nutrients. In other words, they cooperate, so that all the beeches in their community succeed. Bravo for the socially progressive beeches of Germany, I thought, padding to the bathroom for another box of tissues, wondering if American trees were so high minded.

Around midnight, I began to feel my cold pull toward what I feared was pneumonia; it seemed like my coughing would shake down the house. Somehow Larry and our friend Mark, who was sheltering with us, making our soon-to-be-locked-down house-party four, had managed, through all that racket, to sleep, so Anna drove me to an urgent care clinic where I was given a chest Xray and forwarded to a hospital emergency room. By three A.M., I was sitting with a mask on my face in a nearly empty examining room with a man in his twenties, also masked. The beds from our wing of the ER were long gone to patients sicker than we were so we hunched on folding chairs in opposite corners and looked at each other and watched the hands of the big clock creep from hour to hour as exhausted people in scrubs drifted in and out of our room, checking our vitals and swabbing the high reaches of our nasal passages with what appeared to be chopsticks. Every few seconds one of us coughed into our mask.

Somewhere toward morning, another casualty was admitted to our room and deposited in the third corner. He was tall and thin and his big red eyes hung over his mask like setting suns and he leaned into his coughs; I could practically feel the tidal pull of the waters rising in his head. He'd been in the "quarantine tent" for the past couple of hours, he told us with more vigor than I thought he had in him, and was glad to be inside.

"There's a *tent?*" I said.

"Yeah—outside the back door." He pointed vaguely to the hall. "It was *so cold.*" He rubbed his hands together as I tried to picture *a tent* outside the door of a modern American hospital with a lobby that looked like a ski lodge. Eventually, *my guys* were taken away to where I didn't know, I was given a second chest x-ray and informed about the various influenzas and pneumonias that I did not have. "What about the coronavirus?" I asked, hating to inquire but knowing I owed it to everyone I'd coughed near, also knowing what the answer would be: that there were no tests available but that I should practice *social distancing*—still a new phrase, not quite yet a global habit—on the assumption that I'd been exposed and might be a carrier. Then I was handed a wad of prescriptions and turned out into the lobby where Larry was waiting. It was eleven in the morning. I never saw the tent, or learned why I hadn't been directed to it, but there it was on the local news later that day—a complex of tents by then, a tiny white town with zippers and flaps.

On Saint Patrick's Day I woke up, feeling noticeably better, to sunshine and birdsong coming through the cracked window. One irrepressible diva had stepped out of the chorus to belt out an aria. "I am *here!*—I am *there!*—I am *here!*—I am *there!*" she sang. Struck by her brash joy, I got dressed, put on a coat, and went outside. *Outside,* I realized, was going to be more than a daily winter walk; it was going to be the pressure-release valve to home-bound distancing. Unlike the mice still scrabbling in the small world of our attic, outside, I could be *here* and I could be *there!*

I like a garden out of season. I like peering down into ponds where reeds have collapsed and the flat leaves of lily pads floating on the surface have browned up like the age spots on my mottled hands. My people: the coming-apart denizens of a dormant pond. So to the pond Anna and I went—ponds, really—there are quite a few of them on the MSU campus nearby. We started with the Healing Garden behind the Radiology building where early irises were already blooming and even a few reckless columbines were out—way too early, like freshmen girls at a senior prom—and listened to water tumbling over rocks. Then we crossed the street and studied an Atlantis of sunken clay pots and tangled roots in a neat, rectangular pool in the English Garden. Farther south, mossy boulders surrounded a small basin in the Japanese Garden where, if you're inclined, you can rake out your fears and loathing in a gravel courtyard. There was no rake around so we crunched over the stones and headed to a spruce grove where not long before I'd found a lovely, delicate mandible, remnant of some small animal rolled back into the all-of-it as we all shall be. I always look for treasures where I've found them before, like our dog Scout, who revisits the regular places around the house into which we tuck her cookie-bones.

Shortly after schools closed, the governor shut down the gyms, forcing athletic Larry to exercise in the healthier air outdoors. Bars and restaurants were shuttered too, as well as most public institutions—museums, libraries, zoos—and most businesses suspended their services, including salons. When this virus has run its ragged course, I thought, battalions of ladies of a certain age will be mustached and gray at the roots—me included.

Late one afternoon, Larry and I took Scout to the Baker woodlot at MSU which, dense and mosquito-plagued in summer, was scrubbed clean by winter and full of light. Walking among the soaring trunks of oak and beech, whose high, leafless branches did not refuse the sun, reminded me of wandering among the great pillars and arches of the Hassan II Mosque in Casablanca, which Maddie and I explored one spring break a few years back. Like the mosque, which has a roof that can be opened to the sky, the winter woods in Michigan had lifted its lid.

But not for long. On a wet, gray (again) morning shortly after Saint Paddy's, an email from the National Parks Service announced it was the first day of spring, which couldn't be right, I thought. The decree felt like a mistake, not a portal from dormancy to stirring life. The American President had just declared, "People are dying today that have never died before" and you had to wonder if his initials didn't point to *delirium tremens*. As Mark observed wryly, putting down the *Times* in disgust, "Simpleton has the keys." That morning I left money under a rock on our porch bench for our intrepid friend-turned-dealer Julie, who dropped off a Costco cheese. We waved from a window.

Folksy old soap and water rocketed to sudden celebrity—it got half a page in *The Times* on the day after another handful of Democratic primaries were held, which was more than Bernie Sanders got. Here is how soap works, a mystery revealed: soap molecules have a head that bonds to water and a tail that avoids it. That tail wedges itself into the lipids of microbes and pries them apart. Proteins spill from the ruptured membranes into the water, killing the bacteria, which are rinsed down the drain. Soap and water don't so readily kill all the rogue players homesteading our skin—they're less effective against meningitis microbes, for example. But they are the kiss of death to the coronavirus, and that would do for the day.

Every few days, in what we were being told were still the early days of a churning global maelstrom, the little sparks of anxiety that mostly flickered, flared up and I grew fearful in a cart-ahead-of-the-horse way. There was nothing I could do about the endangered economy or our wee slice of it, nothing I could do about threats to our children's careers. Getting hopped up on caffeine and social media—easier than ever to do when you're confined to your house—did not help. I sometimes tried to peel off the crazy with a little trick of narration in which I imagined myself as an observer, merely, of what life gets up to on the planet Earth. There I am, among the envious on shore, waving my white hankie while well-heeled adventurers board the Titanic. There I am watching the Reichstag burn. Here I am watching a globalized world, traumatized by mass migrations and game-changing technologies that hatch by the hour, respond to a pandemic. How *interesting*, the caprices of human history.

Here I am fretting over my grocery list at 4 AM, strategizing.

As American cities began "locking down," getting what we'd need while the getting was good suddenly felt urgent. Sitting up in bed, I mapped out Meijer, the nearest big box store, in my head. What was the route of least contagion and should one or two of our little household go in? Two doubled our exposure but reduced the time spent inside by half. It seemed like a wash, and the next day Anna and I loaded up a cart with mostly root vegetables and beans and grains that would store well. Eggs. Vitamins. A few frilly greens. Extending from the pharmacy counter, an archipelago of black Xs were taped to the floor at six-foot intervals. I stood on my X and waited to retrieve Larry's prescription.

Pledging not to revisit the grocery store for at least a week at a time, we established the routine of eating perishables first—lovely, delicate lettuces and young spinach leaves (*les epinards*, notecard #33) which we would eventually divide into plastic sandwich bags and freeze for omelets. Each night Anna dressed our salads with delicious vinaigrettes of fresh cilantro and lime juice. How could we, in Michigan, in March, be dining on fresh cilantro and limes during a pandemic? Worry told me that the global economy was an agricultural and industrial house of cards, but it was not wobbling yet *for us*, though critical wobbling was predicted: hospitals would soon be out of ventilators and were already asking for donations of masks. Meanwhile, the supply chain of avocados held.

My friend Meri Anne called one afternoon after dropping off groceries at a food bank at the Catholic church she sometimes attends which, I am sorry to have to report, was a necessary wake-up for my crisis-crowded head. *Other people need things too.*

"Where is the grocery drop off?" I asked.

"Inside the front doors, by the propaganda table," she replied. So I filled a bag from the top layer of goods we'd laid in, drove to the church, and waited in the car while Anna—wrapped up to her eyes in a broad scarf—lugged our donation into the church lobby and left it next to the propaganda table.

In the third week of March, while the mice dragged patio furniture around over our heads, we woke up to spring-snow, ate our oatmeal, and listened to our governor initiate the anticipated mandatory shelter-at-home order, to last for three weeks, perhaps longer, depending on the rise or fall in COVID cases. Like the people in other states that were locked down, we were instructed to go out in public only for groceries, medicine, and gas. And we were encouraged to walk outside.

In the opening credits of every spring, I find lovely seed pods, slim and shiny as minnows, along the curbs in our neighborhood. Small brown seeds run the length of each one, like buttons on a high, satin glove. Occasionally, a seed is missing—torn loose by some incident at the midwestern winter ball that grows raucous in January and February—but most of them make it to spring in place, designed for utility as well as elegance. These are black locust seeds, fruit of the great American hardwoods that the colonizer William Strachey, who left one of the few surviving, eye-witness accounts of 17th-century Jamestown, described as surrounding "the dwellings of savages." These days, among mailboxes and power lines, they have gone native in the American suburbs. I pick them up when I walk and toss them into a wooden bowl I keep on a living room table.

One afternoon, ambling along the trails of a wooded nature preserve half-an-hour, by foot, from our home, I ran into several kindred, hike-by-the-hour types. In keeping with the skittish new rites of encounter, we all veered into the bracken to avoid any shared air and I wondered how long it might take for our everyday intimacies—handshakes, hugs, the avuncular backslap—to reassert themselves, and if they ever fully would. Maybe they'd go the way of sock-hops and Volkswagen beetles and we would become a more formal people, like cage-fighters and Oxford dons.

Other things were afoot in the forest. The purple tips of skunk cabbages (*Symplocarpus Foetidus*) had pushed up near a stream, curved and beaked as parrot-heads. These plants are always the first to awake in the woods because they can generate heat to 70 degrees, which melts the ground.

Architecturally interesting in the beginning, they are not nice for long; in a week they would put out broad, flabby leaves limp as shirttails that make the forest floor look dissolute, like it fell asleep in its clothes after a bender, and they emit a vicious smell if you happen to step on one. Also known as clumpfoot cabbage and polecat weed, their odor draws pollinating flies but puts them safely off the path of your more refined racoon and fox.

A rafter of wild turkeys that share, with IT execs and orthodontists, a woodsy arm of the suburbs adjacent to the park, which I walked through to get to the trailhead, let me infiltrate their tribe as long as I stepped quietly. Three big toms, their magnificent tails fanned open like headdresses, were courtly in their plays for the hens, who darted and fussed around them, and they were amiable rather than combative with each other, which surprised me. This being mating season, I expected bloody warfare and outright rape of the spoils, but they conducted themselves like Edwardian barons, three-abreast and talking Empire. I found myself thinking of them, very deferentially, as "the landlords."

Like many right-minded people, my sisters-in-law Jill and Jane were spending their lockdown sewing medical masks for local hospitals. Online patterns for these masks proliferated as more people pitched in, blogging about the benefits of ties versus elastic bands, stitching at their kitchen tables as the alarming numbers of new COVID cases scrolled by on TV. I imagined brightly colored masks piling up on their counters like Victory Garden carrots and beets.

For his part in the national effort, Trump bluntly told the country's governors to find their own emergency medical gear, including ventilators, which set states desperately *competing* for life-saving equipment. So *The Hunger Games* were on, brought to us by the American President.

In additional news, the International Olympic Committee suspended the 2020 Tokyo Games. A student in Kentucky was hospitalized after attending a distance-defying "coronavirus party." And, pandering to his Christian supporters, Trump declared he'd like to see churches full of people on Easter Sunday, in an effort to portray himself, I suppose, as Commander-in-Chief of the Resurrection.

Inside by the fire, I sipped tea and read Oliver Sacks's, *Oaxaca Journal,* which recounts his fern-finding trip to Mexico. Among the many things I learned, was that I had been: 1.) misusing the word *bracken* and 2.) growing bracken all over our yard. Maybe because the word itself makes a crunchy *brakbrakbrak* sound, I assumed it referred to the dry, dead understory that runs alongside every Michigan trail from mid-fall until mid-spring. The stuff into which I lately stepped (*brakbrakbrak*) to keep that prescribed six-foot distance from my fellow humans when we met in the woods. But bracken, it turns out, is no generic catch-all for dead plants; it is a very specific type of fern, prolific in these parts—for instance, in our yard. A lover of ferns, I have dug trenches and beds for the ones I've begged off of friends, and they have proliferated. Every spring when I am murdering dandelions, I move ambitious little fiddleheads with a careful trowel from the garden path to safer ground. I take individual photos of them, like they're kindergartners posing for school pictures, and I post those pictures online as if they were grandchildren. Who knew these fresh, green shoots were *bracken?*

In addition to his genius for ferns and neurology, Sacks also had a grand passion for the periodic table, classical music, cuttlefish, motorcycles, swimming, and botany in general, and he had an inexhaustible curiosity about perception which he explored in the 1960s with hallucinogenic drugs. In his journal, he describes grinding morning glory seeds, which contain lysergic acid derivatives similar to LSD, into a powder which he ate with vanilla ice cream.

Suddenly, we, the people of the pandemic, were all doing Zoom, an online platform for social gathering, just right for outbreaks of name-your-plague, which was springing up in conversation several times a day. Businesses, book groups, yoga classes, and AA meetings were all Zooming. And in a testament to the human love of camaraderie and a healthy preference for not drinking alone, people were zooming happy hours with friends next to their own ice buckets by their own fires.

On the antiquated medium that was television, CNN was flagrantly shopping for a Grammy with its pandemic graphics, while people on social media sites began voicing their suspicions that the President might work up a scheme to use the crisis to delay the elections in November. "Can he *do* that?" we asked. Maddeningly, after his deadly failures in policy and leadership, Trump's popularity was—inconceivably—on the rise in a world where the average memory seemed to fall just short of three minutes. Harnessing national fear and credulity, it seemed possible that he would ride the plague until he was king, and the American experiment would have come full circle.

Donald Hall, whose book, *Here at Eagle Pond,* I began reading after finishing Sacks, expresses concerns about our modern habit of living too much in "the thin, bare, accelerated moment," forgetful of the past, unable to anchor there anymore and draw from our fore-mothers and fathers' knowledge and values. Perhaps that is because there is so much present coming at us from every direction; it whistles by our ears and our heads spin like saucers on sticks. In any event, in his essay, "Rusticus," Hall argues that, like the rural poor of the American South, the rural poor of his New Hampshire maintain ties to the past the rest of us have severed and suggests that there is a psychological and sensible rightness to maintaining these connections. I wanted—and want—very much to sympathize with his rustics, but these are the same people who pour out of the shacks and trailers he describes to go to the polls and vote for tax breaks for billionaires. "It makes no sense!" I yell at the TV whenever I watch electoral votes come in from red states. And in the Trumpian dystopia, where up was down and down was up, it seemed especially futile to look for logic. The right wing manufactured "alternative facts" that blew around like free radicals, opening our national corpus to every kind of cancer.

April's first week broke open the sunshine and temps rose into the high 50s. On the suburban loop I often walk, I crossed paths with several runners and quite a few walkers. Even in recent, pre-pandemic times, I'd found that fewer people answered the *hellos* I called out, tuned in as they were to music from private playlists streaming through speakers that resembled small tusks sprouting near their ears. Attuned to wind in the trees and the colliding conversations of birds—there was a new guy in town singing "JeopardyJeopardyJeopardy!"—I marveled at anyone's preference for digital music over these songs, not to mention over the urgent mating trills of frogs which could drown out the music of most frat parties, whose own mating-rituals had been cancelled for the rest of the year. How strange that, in going about our day-to-day business, we people of a common landscape no longer shared an audioscape.

The ubiquitous Dr. Fauci, who was nipping at the heels of Soap as America's newest celebrity, finally began calling on Americans to wear masks. Not to be outdone, Trump began calling on people too. Specifically, he called on governors "to be appreciative," for whatever supplies he sent them, adding in a televised aside to his VP, "If they don't treat you right, I don't call." And regarding federal supplies of ventilators, his son-in-law and advisor, Jared Kushner, added, "The notion of the federal stockpile was it's supposed to be *our* stockpile. It's not supposed to be states' stockpiles that they then use." Which begged the question from any citizen paying taxes and also attention: Who are the people claiming *our* and who are the ones dismissed as *they?*

Ten million Americans applied for unemployment in late March. British Prime Minister Boris Johnson was hospitalized with COVID and the

Queen "invoked British resolve" according to *The Times*. Here in the American Midwest, I imagined—in black and white, like old WWII newsreels—members of the English working class straightening their spines and stiffening their famous lips. And all the women had stocking seams drawn up the backs of their legs.

If you crave being the topic of avid conversation, the latest thing—*an influencer*—stroll by a marsh where redwing blackbirds are nesting. Suddenly *you* are the only game in town and they are emphatically, militantly *not* happy to see you. Your press, all bad, goes out in shrieks from the battlements of nearby trees and the formations they fly in sweeping, dipping vectors are full of menace. Walking along a nearby pond, I pictured Donald Trump shaking his puny fist at them, crying, "Fake news!"

Ephemeral as lacey lingerie, our salad greens quickly disappeared, and we grew into sturdy sensible people of the potato.

It hailed. Actually, in the course of a single hour, during which I trotted around one of my usual routes: 1.) the sun blazed away in a blue sky 2.) that turned to handgun gray 3.) when the breeze curled into a fist of wind 4.) that pummeled the clouds 5.) that spat the sleet 6.) that turned to hail 7.) that broke the crocuses baring their crowns along empty streets in the chilling pandemic that Jack built. Let's just say there was a lot of cause and effect going on outside and you can swap Jack out for who-or-whatever you suspect is operating behind the curtain.

In hunkering down with us, Anna made an office out of our living room and a desk of its big library table which she shares with a bundle of bleached willow branches, a wooden bowl of stones, a bouquet of dried water lily pods, half a hive, and a big bracket mushroom attached to a rock the size of a catcher's mitt. An admissions counselor for an art college, she moves between troubleshooting the new landscape of distance-working with colleagues and advising the high school seniors who will comprise next fall's freshman class, *inshallah*. That's a thing Larry and I have taken up saying: *inshallah*. Arabic for, "if God wills it,' I've heard Muslims who use it criticized for being fatalistic but they're no different from Christians who claim to be "blessed" when their lotto card comes up a winner or murmur about "God's will" at funerals. Determinism comes in lots of flavors. Larry and I use it lightly because we're old now and have seen what the world can do to someone who merely goes out to get the mail. So "inshallah," I reply when Larry says, "I'll see you after tennis," and "inshallah," he answers when I ask, "Can you pick up Thai food on the way home?"

One afternoon, on another day of sudden, reckless weather, all of the iPhones in the house started shrieking in sync with urgent, incoming news, drowning out the lackluster bocce ball of what I imagined were the last, holdout mice. Tornado, I thought, as we all scrambled to check our screens. But no, it was the governor, extending her order to shelter at home through the end of the month, which we had expected. I put my phone down and looked out the window to watch snowflakes blanket the ivy. In the family room, Larry and Mark went back to watching a 15-year-old football game, re-televised for desperate sports-junkies, feeding America's addiction with Big Ten Network methadone. From what I could hear of their outbursts, it wasn't a bad high.

I had to give the pandemic this: it was teaching me how to stay home—a habit for which I'd shown no avocation. Teachers are wildly busy and you get used to twelve-hour days packed with classes, meetings, conferences, letters of recommendation to write, papers to grade, calls to return. A little panicked when I retired the previous June, and aspiring to the same familiar pace, I filled my days right back up with book-selling and sessions at the gym and appointments. I read to the blind, registered voters, attended political lunches, sat in cafes and conjugated French verbs. I was like one of those lab animals you read about that, finally set free, gives the outside world a sniff and then crawls back into its cage. Lockdown, which put the kibosh to all of that running around, was teaching me the tempo of staying in place.

The lockdown, customized by our daughters, was also *forcing* me to stay home—Maddie and Anna, who we suspected were in cahoots, insisted on 100% compliance. Lately fit out with a face mask to complement my big box of latex gloves, I itched to make *just a very short dash* to the store for wine, dogfood, chocolate—things you cannot run short on—but our daughters would have none of it and Anna upbraided me about responsible citizenship whenever I mentioned even a small, swift excursion. In all of this, I sensed an alarming, *custodial* concern for *aging parents* and suspected Larry and I were being *handled.* The smell of a future hostage situation was in the air.

When he wasn't cooking or baking bread or reading us crossword puzzle clues, Mark spent a lot of lock-down time talking with his Russian girlfriend Dilnoza, who lives in Moscow. Dilnoza works at a hospice where her primary responsibilities are fund-raising and coordinating volunteers but a lot of loose ends that need tying up fall to her, as well. Like us, she was mostly holed up at home, or she was until Fyodor Ioannovich needed to see his cardiologist, which sprang her from captivity. She sent a picture of hefty

Fyodor, the hospice's enormous pet rabbit, and his vet bill for 6,700 rubles.

Unlike Dilzona, I was free of professional responsibilities that might have spelled me from confinement. And unlike Dilnoza, I had no Muscovite hare.

The coronavirus hit the coasts earlier than it did the Midwest, so it seemed likely that the country's center would have to huddle in place longer before emerging into a new normal—already a cliche—whatever that might look like when it finally arrived. A month in, and our mice were finally gone, moldering silently below the rafters. Outside our windows, some hardy bird sang, "chim-in-y chim-in-y chim-in-y!" which I took it as a sign to go sit by the fire as the times implored me to do.

A Developing Situation

Writing in my study, which was adjacent to Anna's "office" and near-adjacent to the family room where Larry watched CNN when he ate lunch, I was consistently caught in an eddy of sound. Anna's voice, as she advised September's incoming art students mixed with Andrew Cuomo's as he updated the nation on COVID conditions in New York. Later, the governor would be discredited by many women's accounts of his sexual predation and he would be chased from office, but for a time he was thinking-America's sweetheart and that irony was on no one's radar. Larry had the same crush on him that I had on Adam Schiff during Trump's first impeachment trial.

Before she was locked down, Anna spent a lot of time traveling around the country, reviewing the art portfolios of her college's prospective students. As they discussed their work with her, she offered them critical advice and made notes that would be helpful to their submissions and future work. Then she would tear off the cover sheet and hand them a carbon copy. In droves, they were astonished—as if she had just disappeared a skyscraper or conjured a tiger. The wonder of finding this hidden tool from a past civilization *that was there all along* momentarily rocked them. Carbon paper was their Rosetta Stone.

In response to the world's rancor as we slid into the second month of pandemic, one afternoon I settled into a lawn chair in our driveway and began rereading the supremely civil E. B. White. Wrapped in a blanket with a beret pulled over my ears—there was a wind—I recalled my friend Fred's vision of paradise: the long, wide porch of a TB hospital where he might read with a blanket over his lap, unmolested by the world. He died (not of TB) two years before the pandemic broke out which is a tragedy for many reasons, one of them being how much he would have enjoyed his lockdown.

Like my lovely mother, E. B. White died of Alzheimer's disease, but his subject in the essay I was reading today was much less devastating; he was merely waiting for a hurricane that was hell-bent on hitting his coastal Maine town. He was droll as he walked me through his hurricane protocol, battening things down, locking away his sheep and geese, putting aside extra water, following the radio news in which broadcasters, thirty hours ahead of landfall, "were spending themselves at a reckless rate" as they augured the path of the storm and, it turns out, of the highly speculative 24-hour news cycle a few decades down the road.

I had the scantest experience with White's preparations, having lived for a very little while and many years ago in New England when there was, in fact, a hurricane. As a Midwesterner, I knew (and know) nothing about hurricanes; we specialize in tornadoes here, and wicked black ice, so the preamble to my first and only hurricane was at once exotic and prosaic. Living over a used records store in Providence with the man who would soon, for a short time, play the role of my first husband, I watched the coming storm ripple the laundry strung between second-story windows and listened as it stirred up conversations in the coffee shop on the corner. After the last hurricane flooded the city, Providence had installed a storm barrier that could be activated to close the river, but it hadn't been tested and no one knew if it would work. Walking down the chipped sidewalks, with infant-Maddie strapped to my chest in a *Snugli*, I watched big duct tape Xs appear on one window after another.

"To keep the glass from shattering," my future first husband, who was a New Englander, explained. Then we headed to a hardware store to buy spare batteries, which were sold out, and our own fat roll of duct tape, which we used to X the windows of our own tiny apartment. Eventually, the wind chased us inland to Massachusetts where we hunkered below the storm in a long, low house with my soon-to-be-in-laws. Outside, which I glimpsed whenever someone opened the door to take a peek, the trees bowed like penitents in the great howl. Maddie and I barnacled ourselves to an inner wall, as far away from windows as we could get, under the sanctified gaze of President John F. Kennedy whose portrait was framed and hanging on a wall. We were sheltering in Boston Irish land.

Rhode Island *was* hit by that storm, but the river barricade held and Providence, as I recall, was not much the worse for wear when we returned the next day. The duct tape was gone from its plate glass windows; the Portuguese housewives, who spoke little English, were hanging their husbands' shirts and socks back out on their clotheslines; and the corner store, with its chourico and sweetbread and plaster-cast saints, was open for business. In nearby Narragansett, which was south of us, I later read in the *Times,* "Three hundred people sheltered in a high school and were treated to a lunch of clam chowder and lobster donated by local restaurants." We had clearly evac-ed in the wrong direction.

It took E. B. White's hurricane even longer than the estimated thirty hours to materialize and he mentions the "telling effects of such sustained emotional living" that made his familiar world, as it waited for the worst, "assume a sort of unreality."

There had been, for several weeks, a sort of unreality to our world too, paired with the sense that something was coming for us. The ceaseless news was flush with the real crises in New York and Detroit and other large cities but for most of us, who did not live in those places, the streets were eerie not for their sirens but for their silence. We followed new protocols as the CDC unloaded them. Like White, we stocked extra water. We shuttered our businesses, closed our schools. To that we added stockpiling enough canned beans to see us through Christmas. Masked, gloved, sequestered, from one day of "sustained emotional living" to the next, we waited for the coming storm. The neighbors walking their dogs by flashlight at two AM told me I wasn't the only one lying awake at night.

In late April, we played croquet. To be more specific, my friend Jan met Larry and Anna and me on the grounds of a nearby school in the early evening and we played two rousing games of PSDC: Pandemic Socially-Distanced Croquet. Wine was BYOB, in keeping with distancing, and though we had no proper PPE, we all wore disposable gloves, though not masks, as tippling was as central to our purpose as the croquet itself. There was some doubt about the rules and Anna had to google the game a few times—none of us had played in years—but eventually she and Jan came away winners—twice.

Because there was nothing to distinguish one from the next, we eventually found ourselves losing track of the days. It was a relief to learn we were not alone in this. A radio station in some town mentioned in an issue of the newspaper I sometimes read added a new shtick to its morning lineup: *What Day Is It?* I was not ashamed to admit it was nice having company aboard our foundering ship.

One morning, as if there'd been a rupture in the strange bubble of all-things-suspended, a bit of news that got through my filters included this: Canada had sustained the worst mass-shooting in its history. In peaceable Nova Scotia, where wharves are painted apple-red and small boats rock at their moorings. By a denture-fitter in a cop suit. Nineteen people were dead.

Though I'd retired from teaching high school nearly a year before, my school's bossy electronic calendar refused to delete my contact information and continued to send me chatty messages. I called her Gladys Kravitz. "Fuck you, Gladys," I mostly said when she interrupted my reading or cooking or meditations. "Don't forget to wear your *Be Nice* shirt tomorrow," she texted shortly after the Canadian shooting. Helpless against the cash and vitriol of the NRA, showing up at school once a week in t-shirts that urged students to "Be Nice" was one of the steps teachers were taking to defuse the murder in the heart of future denture-fitters.

Demonstrating how spectacularly, glitteringly, neonly nuts she was, the mayor of Las Vegas announced her plans to reopen the strip. "Every flight there should be one-way," Larry said disgustedly.

"And that bit about things happening in Vegas staying in Vegas will need to be whoever goes to Vegas stays in Vegas," I sneered, picturing too-tan people from every city and borough and town in America flying off for a discount binge and returning to their homes with fevers and dry coughs.

My friend Jeanne, who is a much greater news junkie than I am, called to say, "They may tell people over sixty-five to completely stay home," adding, "I guess that's fair—we don't want to overwhelm the hospitals."

More selfish, and counting the months to my sixty-fifth birthday, I snarled, "We'll have to get fake IDs—like we did in high school." Shaving off the years we added at sixteen, the baby-boomers would come full-cycle.

A headline in the *Times*, which Larry had left it on the kitchen island, read, "135 Million Face Starvation. That Could Double." Hungry people in Kenya's largest slum, I read, stampeded a distribution site for flour and oil, leaving two dead. A red cloth hanging in a window in Columbia meant the people living there needed food. In India, workers laid off by COVID were waiting in lines for bread and lentils. I regretted that the previous day, as heads of state around the world were declaring "War on COVID," I'd let myself have a little pout about the weather. It was war, alright. But we are not all in the same bunker. We are not all playing croquet. Those of us who walked out on the other side of the pandemic would not all be carrying the same weight.

After late April dropped us back into winter for a few days, it finally stopped rain-snowing and temps shot into the balmy forties, so I went out walking with the goal of churning out a few endorphins. I was feeling glum about the suffering in the world, which I couldn't do anything to fix. Starting down the driveway, I noticed the newspaper had not been delivered, which felt like a reprieve and a blessing. My route was an uninteresting suburban loop that did nothing to raise my spirits. I should have gone to the woods, but I was too committed to orneriness to help myself in that way.

It was bagpipes that pulled me out of that funk, on the return leg of my loop. A few blocks from home, I turned a corner and ran smack into their plaintive strains; I might have collided with a camel for the jolt of it. I followed the eerie, lurching dirge to where a neighbor—white-haired and, from the looks of things, well into his eighties—was piping in his driveway and I applauded wildly when he finished. He was new to the pipes and still learning, he said, pointing to a book of sheet music propped on the raised ledge of an empty flower bed. Not wanting to crowd his practice, I soon continued toward home. When the music stopped, I assumed he'd finished, but when I stepped onto our porch, there it was again—softer for the distance—but insistent in that pining way of pipes.

Suddenly, it was gratitude I felt—gratitude for all sudden and unexpected beauty, for the spirit that pushes old bodies along new paths, for neighbors and neighborliness. Then, remembering a small but not completely futile thing I could do to help the world for which I'd been grieving, I went to the Red Cross website and made an appointment to give blood. As I was logging out, my phone dinged and I glanced at its screen. "Fuck you, Gladys," I said.

All at once, there were goslings at our neighborhood pond. They were easy to spot a few feet from the water's edge because six months earlier, on the hunkering-downside of winter, someone had commissioned a landscaper to mow down the dense thickets that surrounded the water. As a result, our pond had a bald, mortified look to it, like it had just had its first Brazilian wax, that made me want to glance away. "Someone should put pants on that thing," I muttered to no one the first time I rounded the bend where it comes into view. One afternoon I paused to watch the interplay of generations. Over the course of a few minutes, in twos and threes, the goslings toddled away from their hyper-vigilant parents to the water's edge until they all clustered there, like preschoolers at swim class, with their big, goose-defining decision. Then, as one, they turned and hightailed it back to terra firma. Not today, thanks.

Donald Trump, who even in the rare public moments when he was not dissembling, struggled to string syllables together, disgorged some nonsense about the salutary effects of ingesting disinfectant in the fight against COVID, an invention so egregious that Even Fox News had to ask, "What the hell?"

Scientists, doctors, and reporters exploded in a frenzy of media blasts to counter the President's lethal suggestion. An article in the *Times* featured American Sign Language interpreter, Rorri Burton, who'd become something of a pandemic celebrity for keeping deaf and hard-of-hearing people in the loop of the Real-and-the-True. Sign language was having a lot to keep up with, I learned from Shawn Hubler's article. The term *coronavirus*, itself, is expressed with "one fist nestled against and behind the other, like a sunburst." Suddenly, to "social distancing" and "bend the curve" and "personal protective equipment," Burton had to add "Don't drink Clorox."

In one of the rare, beautiful consequences of global lockdown, jellyfish were swimming through the canals of Venice. We watched them on television, where they look like negligees billowing in the slow current. In another upturn of events, our local bookstore was back up and running curbside service. I ordered a mystery and a couple of foodie memoirs and picked them up from plastic Tub #6, which was placed outside the store's front door.

On the last day of April, hundreds of Trump-supporters, many dolled up in assault weapons, laid siege to the Michigan Capitol. The state police, forming a human barrier between these "patriots" and our governor, whose shelter-at-home edict the radical right was using as an excuse to erupt, stood shoulder-to-shoulder as unmasked belligerents in MAGA hats breathed into their faces. Watching this ugly occupation unfold on TV, I tried, with absolutely no success, to shove my emotions inside some intellectual framework and refine my remarks with a little highbrow irony, but my feelings were too simple for that: all I felt was a bilious hate.

Here is what I know (dating to the hard days when my first husband was transitioning to my ex-husband) about hate: hauling it around is exhausting and poisonous. Also, as has been illuminated so often, it is easier to hate strangers en masse than it is to hate individuals we know. So, because I didn't (and don't) want to be tired and sick all the time, I tried to separate that mob at the Capitol into individuals by writing them little biographies. They couldn't *all* be wife-beaters who bet on dog fights and buried Spam and ammo in their sad little bunkers.

If, like me, you have a limited imagination, you can only get so far with a project of this magnitude. Scrolling through online images of the protest, I pushed myself to picture Baseball-Cap-in-Baggy-Jeans-Man taking his kids trick-or-treating. I conjured up a family camper for Yellow-Vest-Man and invented a three-legged dog for Fu-Manchu-in a Gray-Hoodie, but then I pictured him shooting that dog, so I gave him going fishing with an aging father instead. There was nothing I could do with Skinhead-in-a-Flak-Vest or anyone garlanded in guns or, frankly, any of the women whose support for "grab 'em by the pussy" man was too great a mystery and a betrayal for me to fathom. Still, it worked a little—it really did—trying to see individual people in this way, and I got to sleep by two AM with a bit more space in my ribcage to breathe.

By morning, all that ribcage room was gone. Waking up to warm, sweet sunshine, I felt my fears reset and the hate click back in place and saw how humanizing that mob would have to be a daily practice, something maybe even more rigorous than AA or dialysis. And I balked. Halloween and family camping? I could have played that game at every Nuremberg rally. How many Seig-heilers built kites for their kids? But there they still were with their arms in the air, stirred on by a small man who affirmed their outrage and their great white right to rule the world. Later, looking back on their lives, those people who swarmed the Capitol, shouting their poison into the faces of state troopers, would have to search for or invent their own virtue in *leurs histoires*. As would I. Finally, I understood why the French have a single word for *story* and *history*. I headed out early to walk off the hate, or some portion of it, if I possibly could.

"You get to cry," a voice in my head urged.

"Of course I don't—other people have it harder; they've lost family, friends, jobs. I'm an egoist, a narcissist, a privileged piece of shit."

"You still get to cry." And I did.

Lots of people I spoke with were intermittently, randomly weeping. Reading the paper, we cried for the selflessness of healthcare workers and for those among them who had died trying to save the rest of us. Organizing the pantry or scrubbing the shower, we broke into tears about old people trapped in nursing homes and patients dying in hospitals without the solace of families nearby. Down on my knees, prying thistles from the fiddleheads in our fern bed, I wept before the monolithic Unknown rearing up before us all. Not one of us has ever really known what the next minute will bring—I recall the game-changing second I fell down and broke both wrists a few years back— but we had the comforting illusion that we did, and you can do a lot with an illusion. *I will start college this fall. I will pay the mortgage on Monday. I will get the kids new shoes in June.* A person can fall asleep at night with plans like these. Suddenly, all that faith that makes a life hum rather than stutter had nowhere to go and it was running down our faces in tears, soaking our sleeves, our pillows, our good, mute earth. I wiped my trowel on the grass and went inside to blow my nose.

When Anna finally returned to Chicago in the warm sun of real spring, I felt a new stab of sadness which the moist-with-our-tears earth did not mirror. It was singing "One Hundred Bottles of Beer on the Wall!" It was shrieking, "Bottle of Wine, Fruit of the Vine!" It was belting out, "Why Don't We Get

Drunk and Screw!" Cherry trees shimmied with birds; watusi-ing tulips ground against each other when the wind blew and, surfing the water lilies swelling in small ponds, frogs bellowed their raw, amphibian need—oh baby, *I got* what you want!

Strolling through this bacchanal one day, I found a downy finch nest right smack in the middle of my trail and a few minutes later, a robin's nest left on a curb, like a cup on a counter. As if that were not miracle enough, a muskrat made a slight commotion that caught my eye and she let me watch her slip into a small lake and cut a neat path through the reeds. It was as if, in the middle of a global calamity, the world was throwing money at me. I stooped and stooped to pick it up.

In the midst of the natural world's profligate spending, on television Dr. Fauci warned us to keep a close purse, to budget our time spent in public places, and to continue to tuck our lean and hungry social selves behind masks. He knew the loosening pull of a warm sun; however, the intoxicating weather was not to be gulped but sipped unless we wanted cases of COVID to rocket like lupines. He plied us with data. He predicted a resurgence in the fall if we gave the virus a new foothold. In the out of joint times, I wondered what life *would* look like ahead of us. Would businesses simply open and close, as the Globe Theatre had, between bouts of plague? Would children, shut out of their schools, make songs out of what remained: *ashes, ashes, we all fall down?*

Less philosophically, in an effort to get the most bang for my lockdown buck, I started corralling all of my errands into a single day each week. One Wednesday that meant giving blood at MSU, followed by a grocery store run, plus drive-through banking, which I still do on site rather than through an app because I have hacker-phobia exacerbated by being-poor-again-phobia. Those memories of the lean days of being a single mother have never left me.

The blood drive, held in the university's empty International Center, was solemn and perfunctory. Distancing between donors was maintained but distancing between donors and Red Cross staff was compromised by the length of the human arm. The whole thing took less than an hour and then I was at the grocery store, masked and steering my cart down one-way aisles according to arrows taped on the floor, on my shiniest, good-shopper behavior.

That was not everyone's story. Due to shortages resulting from widespread illness in meatpacking plants, there was suddenly a rush on red meat. "People have been awful," the cashier checking out my groceries confided when I asked how she was holding up behind her plexiglass shield. "When I told one man with a cartful of steaks that they were two-per-customer, he told me he'd buy as much damn meat as he wanted."

In order to feed As-Much-Damn-Meat-As-I-Want-Man and keep his vote, Trump ordered meat processing plants to remain open, despite the fact that more than 1,600 workers at four meatpacking plants in Iowa alone had been infected with the coronavirus, according to the *Des Moines Register.*

Sitting at my desk one afternoon, screening short essays that had been submitted to the online platform of a literary journal, I came across a lovely piece in which a woman sits with her father as he grieves the death of her mother. Though he speaks in only a few, blunt monosyllables of a trip he and his vanished wife made to Italy, his daughter understands the depth of his devastation. Acknowledging the long history of the moment at hand, she gives his grief its rightful weight. "Pompeii," she says.

A moment is so much more than a moment—each one comes with an un-collapsible past. I hold a finch nest in my hand and I'm six years old, traipsing behind my Aunt Bea as she strides through ferns in some northern woods. A breath of lilac and I'm back at my Aunt Aud's open window, the linoleum floor of her kitchen sloping behind me, and every beach summons my mother, picking her way over rocks. Not until we human beings—the rememberers—complete our strange quest for extinction, will a moment be only a moment again. I suppose, when we are finally gone, every unmeasured second will have an immaculate austerity to it, like Bauhaus furniture, which no one will sprawl in or record. For now, I know the M&Ms I binge on are bringing down the rainforest but, like As-Much-Damn-Meat-As-I-Want-Man, I keep restocking my private horde.

In a personal, developing situation that tense spring, I named and gendered the tiny knob that had sprouted on my nose. Roberta, I called her. Every morning I peered at her from the cheap seats of my bathroom counter, bent over the sink for a better view. For her part, Roberta seemed to gain confidence, boisterously playing the stage of my face, enlarging herself on my largesse. When non-essential medical practices reopened, I introduced her to my dermatologist, who was not a fan. He pulled down my mask and squinted.

"It's a squamous cell carcinoma."

"Not a cyst?" I replied. "Not a boil?" I felt the icy waters of *carcinoma* run over me, as the "plague of boils" one-liners I'd assembled—a natural fit to the year—washed away.

"Not a boil," he said. "Cancer."

Then he sent me straight to a plastic surgeon's office across the hall for a biopsy, which struck me as awfully good service. Roberta's show was about to close. Her reviews had not been good and, anyway, I had started to suspect her of being a Trumper.

The plastic surgeon was tall, fortyish, and in keeping with his specialty, rom-com handsome—I suppose you'd wonder if he wasn't. "Will there be a scar?" I asked rhetorically—I mean, no scarring is *why* you hire a plastic surgeon.

"Oh, there *will* be a scar," he said matter-of-factly. Then he pulled a magic marker out of his pocket and drew a triangle on my nose to show what part of it he'd eventually be carving away—which looked enormous: picture New York City without Manhattan. I swallowed, then drew back against my chair when he produced a hefty needle with which to anesthetize me for the biopsy.

"Will this hurt?" I asked, rhetorical again—no quick study am I.

"Oh it *will* hurt," he replied. Damn, the man was honest. "Noses and toes: the two worst places for a needle." Then way too slowly, he turned my nose numb, and soon after that Roberta was on her way to the pathology lab and I was back in my mask and on my way to the grocery store. There would be another surgery down the road but, for the time being, it was Wednesday and my weekly shopping day again.

Ad Hoc

The gardens—my own mainly neglected one as well as the others I often loitered or trespassed in—were going to bits, going to seed, possibly going to God. Their stalks were bowed like supplicants. The hostas were the exception: their rigid spines, too stubborn to bend, kept the suburbs mildly apostate.

"The gardens are going to shit," I complained to my husband Larry, for I am not one of those compliant lives that go down with no drama or watch anyone else do so. My people rage and weep at the end of our season, and we see our finitude in every arrested life around us. Skeptical of its goodness, we do not go gentle into that unknowable night.

A couple of weeks earlier, I was ogling the fomes on the trunk of a maple tree outside the house we were staying in during a writing residency in northern Michigan. Fomes are a type of polypore mushroom, gargoyles that finish off dying trees. They look like they're made of stone or corroded metal, like spigots on old fountains in Tuscany. "Hoof fungus," they are sometimes called, because they also, in fact, resemble the hooves of very decrepit donkeys. They are tenacious dismantlers and I am fascinated by the way things come apart. It's a perverse sort of narcissism.

Larry and I and, of course, so many of our friends have entered the dismantling years, which is probably what calls me to autumn gardens, where I rumple the desiccated disks of fennel like the ears of old dogs and pat the dry bouffant on hydrangea bushes like I am combing out ladies in a nursing home. I recall that some intrepid optimist, whose name I've lost, said we find the teachers we need which, however pretty, seems unlikely to be true; nevertheless, I can sit by a pond full of reeds collapsed like straw hats below the water's surface and be still with a strange peace. I sense some kind of instructing going on, if only on conceding to the inevitable with a modicum of dignity. Not that I'm likely to take it up.

Because the pandemic had swept away the readings and workshops that usually went with the writing program, Larry and I were free to explore new trails and beaches along the Lake Michigan shore and loiter among the graves of an old Odawa burial ground. All around us, fall's fall*ing* was making a racket, most of which was identifiable during the day—surf hitting the rocks just *there*, *that* squirrel chittering on *that* stump, *this* woodpecker boring through *that* beech. Nighttime was another thing. The first salvo of nuts that hit our metal roof in the chilly predawn, sounding like artillery, sprang us from bed. Raccoons? Bobcats? Bears? Not bears: we shook our groggy heads. "Acorns," Larry finally allowed, yawning, "they're dropping from the trees." The morning brought confirmation: squirrels ransacking the breakfast buffet in our woodsy front yard. Rushing to stuff their larders like the hoarders we'd all become in 2020, they ignored me when I ploughed through their ruckus and headed down our dirt road to St. Ignatius, the white-framed Jesuit church surrounded by the Native graveyard. The mile of damp road to the church was a gallery of fallen leaves: pentimenti—silhouettes just visible beneath tire treads in the thin mud, insistent reminders of the one-way street we all walk toward our inevitable reunion with the earth.

Outside St. Ignatius, a sign explained that, after burning down in the late 19th century, the church had been rebuilt by the local Odawa people who had converted to Roman Catholicism. That it had burned on their watch, invited me to wonder about their motivation for so promptly restoring it—preservation of body being at least as compelling for most of us as is preservation of soul. And there are, after all, so many options to choose among for saving a soul, which may not extend to the flesh.

Lots of the Odawa graves in that cemetery are older than the big trees that were lobbing nuts at us. Their white, wooden crosses, erected in the 1970s by an Odawan caretaker over generations of unmarked tombs, trail from the main graveyard into the woods where they flickered like spring trillium in the autumn light. Some of them bore name plates but most were as anonymous as the beeches and oaks that rose over them, which made the return of those bones to the orthodox bedrock seem so much more seamless. On the days I wandered among them, I took good writer-in-residence notes and scratched out the beginnings of poems to the ambient shushing of the nearby lake, but for all that presence and mood-music, I mostly fretted about things back home, which beckoned. The 2020 presidential election was weeks away and I'd signed up with the Democrats to do whatever was needed to help shore up the battered American democracy, whose death rattle was keeping me up at night. I would do triage. I would roll bandages. I would stock storerooms with the tenacity of those relentless squirrels rattling the understory. My anxiety needed a JOB. And patient Larry needed me to have one; the little spikes I'd been growing over the previous four years were starting to throw sparks.

When we finally got home, Larry discovered a bit of uptick in the falling-apart situation on our own roof, which had been sloughing off for some time, and he went to work finding a house triage-r and bandager while I trained online to be a poll-observer during the weeks of early voting that preceded Election Day. When I wasn't madly taking notes in front of a screen, I chauffeured yard signs to their new homes and rolled leaflets into little scrolls and slipped them through the handles of front doors all over town, and I layered up to help staff a campaign table at the farmer's market on chilly Saturday mornings.

In my off-hours—because pausing too long in the gnat-hatch of panic was *not an option*—I plied the wooded trails near our house and explored all the less-traveled corners of the vast, deserted MSU campus, tossing peanuts I swiped from Larry's nightstand to the squirrels who snubbed them for the meatier acorns crunching under all our feet. And amid all that walking, I tried to deflect the more bellicose thoughts that sometimes broke through my firewall about the collapse of previous invincible civilizations which, in no special order, lined themselves up in my mind: Incan, Minoan, Sumerian, Roman, *Odawan*. Somewhere, in the high, thin atmosphere of intellect, I knew that America, on whose works the mighty had looked and despaired for a couple of hundred years now, would one day succumb to brutal or entropic forces, but it was inconceivable that it could happen here and now—torn down from the *inside*—on my watch. *"Hubris,"* I thought, with a nod to the long-gone Golden Age of Greece for that hard truth. Then I'd go home and take a hot shower, pointedly noting the working spigot and appreciating that we still had dependable infrastructure, unlike Syria and Iraq, nations ruined by civil wars—an unthinkable crisis to which even mainstream media was starting to suggest we might be heading. And finally, having washed off what I could of the day, I'd tear into that box of Merlot we keep on a shelf in the laundry room, our elegant *cave a vin*.

Shortly after Larry and I returned from the north, and eager to start all that good, necessary work, I met my friend Meri Anne for coffee in an airy cafe with socially distanced protocols in place because—not to be overlooked in the election frenzy—there was still a plague going on. We climbed into high chairs at a tall table in order to rise over the respirations of other patrons and brooded together about the volatile state of things.

Meri Anne has many qualities I admire; she is a brilliant lawyer, a luminous poet, an accomplished cook—but what I *envy* about her is her status as a lapsed Catholic—my term. Meri Anne says she's an ACO—an *Angry Catholic Outlier*, jonesing for John Lewis's good trouble to get into where the church is concerned. I am a lapsed Presbyterian and there is absolutely no comparison between these traditions, mainly because, even minus the doctrines she's dispensed with, she has kept so much of the lush upholstery of her faith tradition. Presbyterianism is unupholstered to begin with—thank you John Calvin—so there is not much to take with you when you leave—only memories of that cheap communion grape juice and a couple of verses of "We Gather Together," definitions of *chasten* and *hasten* included. Even after rejecting the weighty patriarchy and authoritarianism of her church, Meri Anne is loaded down with vast archives of culture and language and ritual that are hers to keep. In the catalogue of religious institutions, if I could be anything, I would be a lapsed Catholic.

"I am just chafing to do something!" Meri Anne wailed, burying her face in her hands. The various campaign organizations we'd both approached, ad hoc affairs bivouacking online and sometimes in rent-by-the-month offices, seemed to be shifting around and overlapping like shards in a kaleidoscope. Which was doing what, and where? Their emails and texts came in torrents and tracing any message back to its source demanded an Ariadne's thread. Still, we messaged and called and texted them all, gnashing the crowns on our teeth.

"The polls," she began, and I put up my hands.

"I can't hear about the polls," I said.

"Nate Silver,"

"I can't hear about Nate Silver either." Nate Silver is a data-prophet and poll-interpreter, a hometown boy who made it big in online augury, who we like around here. Still.

In the interest of self-preservation, I was two days off the news, but she was still quaffing it in reckless draughts. Up on the latest stats or not, we both heard planks splitting in our heads, felt the tremors of our composure coming apart. "I've contacted *Catholics for Biden*," she said, reaching both back and forward to her old tradition, "and Michigan Dems. What about you?"

I counted off the half a dozen organizations I'd approached on my fingers. "It feels like chaos," I said. We brooded over our paper cups—the civility of even cheap porcelain long gone to COVID—as we chatted about the few topics I would permit, then went home to, in her case absorb and in my case avoid, the news.

Chaotic as it felt to us, dangling at the end of our phones, the scramble of local politicos to build an army of volunteers that would push the Biden ticket forward gradually took shape and eventually we had assignments. And like the frantic, autumn squirrels, the Dems seemed to have some idea where to put their nuts, after all. Comparing notes most nights, Meri Anne and I showed up for the jobs they asked us to do. And when not on assignment, I can testify that she spent a lot of time cooking, as every few days another one of her excellent chowders or pastries or cakes turned up on our porch. And when I wasn't on assignment or eating, I kept walking.

It wasn't just politics that had repurposed my daily cardio-walks; poetry had actually gotten to them first. A few months earlier, I'd learned about the poet Ted Kooser's ad hoc ritual of correspondence with the writer Jim Harrison. Following treatment for cancer, which had left him sun-sensitive and depressed, Kooser, who had, in his own words, "all but given up on reading and writing," began walking every day before dawn near his home in Nebraska. And to his surprise, from what he observed during these walks, he began writing again—one short, vital poem a day which he mailed on a postcard to Harrison.

Well, if there was a literary regimen better suited to a pandemic, I couldn't fathom what it would be: local, solitary, outdoor ramblings that might each produce a small draught of wonder or hope—something to nourish not just myself but a *receiver*. My mind went straight to my friend Julie in Seattle—a teacher, an artisan, a kind, and above all, forgiving person—because, at the rate of one-a-day, not all of the short poems I immediately committed to writing were going to be top shelf. Some of them were bound to be poured straight from the well, but Julie and I had waited tables together in college and we'd sloshed a lot of booze in our day. We could wade through practically anything. So it was the work of a moment to sell another piece of my stripped-down soul to Amazon for the convenience of next-day delivery, and order a box of 100 postcards.

And the bright, new challenge of my daily walking regimen became paying better—much better—attention to things.

My inaugural peering and listening excursion, which wound through a serene botanical garden in the midst of the tense and locked-down world, yielded this, which I scrawled on the first postcard I pulled from the box:

What Worked

Today it was
an iridescent damselfly,
stick-pin thin
and luminous blue
who lit up the lapel
of a peony leaf.
Her black wings,
velvet opera gloves
folded narrow,
neat.

When I wrote it out in longhand, I was pleased to see how perfectly the poem fit the template in the narrow, neat world of postcards. I mailed it. Falling into a sort of wash-rinse-repeat rhythm, I walked and wrote and mailed my way through the fraught summer and well into fall as COVID cases spiked and fell and spiked again. The postcards arrived, Julie reported, in an unpredictable rhythm of downpours and droughts—she sent me a screenshot of four that turned up the same day—as the beleaguered postal system, itself under attack by the Trump machine, labored to deliver the mail. So while too-kind-to-mention-it Julie might have wearied at the windfalls, the daily joy on my end of the operation was absolute.

A couple of weeks before Election Day, I began slipping not just poems but my whole person inside a template, which turned out to be as narrow and neat as the back of a postcard.

My responsibilities as a poll observer for the Democratic Party, when they came, were circumscribed and black and white. I was to arrive at and depart from the Early-Voting site to which I was assigned on time. I would check in online via my phone when I got there and report conditions as I found them: *Was the site open and easily accessible to voters? How long was the wait to vote? Was everyone who applied there able to vote? If not, why not?* I was to respect social distancing policies and not to initiate conversations with voters. I would report any irregularities through a special crisis-app (snuggling like a puppy on my phone with all of the regular apps) to "The Boiler Room"—a badass mission control bunker of commandos (I imagined)—probably (in reality) a lawyer and a couple of poli-sci majors. My first gig was at a city clerk's office in South Lansing, where it took me all of an hour to start weeping.

I suspected that crying was not the response the Dems were hoping for in their agent, their eyes, their citizen-on-site. But there was absolutely nothing I could do to hold back the tears, which fogged up my glasses and soaked the top of my mask. I was just so *grateful.*

From a folding chair along one wall of the narrow lobby—a very easy to find lobby because a thousand arrowed signs outside pulled people from the street and led them straight there, making it impossible to get lost— I watched my fellow citizens arrive: timid, first-time, 18-year-old voters; newly naturalized voters—some with no or little English and a fluent grandchild in tow; bent and gnarled born-in-the-USA voters who were old hands at it. In ones and twos and threes, they lined up (though there was "never a long wait," I thumbed in to the standing-by Dems) and approached, in their turn, a half door with a plexiglass window. Where they were greeted by exactly who you hoped would be there if you had ever recited, with feeling, "and liberty and justice for all."

I wondered if anyone else noticed that Honest Abe Lincoln was in the room with us, that to address the national crisis—to serve justice and maintain unity—he had managed to push through death itself and was handing out voter registration forms and ballots, patiently taking people through the instructions: "And don't forget the propositions on the back. And make sure to sign the envelope here." Because that's who this tall, dignified man seemed to be, such was his gravitas and courtesy, this hero of a civil servant in a mid-sized town in America's flyover zone. Day after day, I watched his kindly and immaculate enactment of the democratic process and dabbed at my eyes with a soggy tissue. After the election was over, I realized it was he and people just like him who had saved us.

I was sent to two other polling sites in the days preceding the third of November, where physical conditions were variable but where the one constant was the poll workers' scrupulous adherence to election protocols and a huge, pulsating generosity of spirit while doing so. In the too-cramped-for furniture foyer of one clerk's office, I lugged in a lawn chair and sat in the draft of the front door to give voters enough space for whatever private time they needed with their ballots. In another, I was directed to a seat along the side of the bustling annex of a township hall where thirty people voted at a time as a team of election officials and volunteers circulated among them. Few of the voters paid me any attention, but at one site a small, panicked woman about my age blew through the door and halted at my chair. "I heard they were stuffing the ballots!" she panted, "ten and fifteen at a time!"

"Not. Here. They. Aren't." I met her glazed, Breitbart-glare.

The next day, a thirtyish woman in a trim coat and high heels, looking alarmingly like Trump's newest press secretary, paused to ask what I was doing. "I'm a poll observer for the Democratic Party," I replied succinctly, as I'd been trained to do. She turned, voted, and left. Fifteen minutes later, she was back, dropping a Starbucks gift card in my lap. "Thank you," she said, weeping herself, and was gone. Day after day, amid this river of people and their wildly varying ideas of what America was and should be, what emerged was the integrity of the process, the inexhaustible and uncompromising commitment to a fair election by the people who actually ran the machine.

I mailed my last postcard poem a few days after the 2020 presidential election. With the leaves gone, the landscape had turned inward and, like it, the poetry project had moved beyond its florid, ad hoc season. It was only the Hosta stalks, looking ridiculous near our front porch—brown and brittle and *finished*—that refused to throw in the towel. For weeks, every time I pulled into the driveway, they reminded me of those ruined Republican lawmakers who, a dozen days before Christmas, were still refusing to concede the Biden win. So I finally cut them down—in flesh and in effigy—while Larry hung holiday lights along the windows and eaves, in time for the darkest night of the year. Then we went inside and ate soup with more cheer than we'd eaten soup the harrowing year before, knowing the solstice would soon flip a switch and sure there was light enough for the day.

CAPER

On my 65th birthday, I got a Medihaircut. I was eight months into the great Pandemic-Grow-Out-Your-Gray movement and my tired old highlights weren't moving on fast enough, on top of which all the TV footage of crowded hospitals got me picturing myself laid out on a gurney with my limp locks hanging to my jawline—or what used to be my jawline. So much is open to interpretation these days. But a girl likes to look good even on a ventilator, so I strapped on a mask, walked into the salon I hadn't seen in nearly a year and said, "Cut. It. Off."

Medihaircut is a *portmanteau*, but not in the suitcase-way most of us are familiar with. A *portmanteau*, I'd recently learned in a Tuesday *Times* crossword puzzle, is also the term for a word that blends the sounds and meanings of two other words. The dictionary on my phone gives the examples, Motor + Hotel = *Motel* and Breakfast + Lunch = *Brunch*. *Webinar* is another and so is my personal favorite, a product of the global lockdown: *carbosexual*. It's a game that's too fun not to play, which brings us to Medihaircut. On November 2nd, as hair made a little pre-holiday wreath on the floor around my swivel-chair, my Medicare number clicked on in the national grid.

Once the Medicare card arrives, you pretty much have to stop claiming middle age—in the event that you've had a death grip on it. It breaks free of your formerly "freckled" now "liver-spotted" clutch and flies off to live with someone who, having just hit the bulkhead of 40, must find the staggering depth of character to accept they are no longer young. And God help you if you happen to have emigrated here from China and are waiting for the revering to start.

"I am old," I told our daughter Anna, who was working from our couch, pandemic-style. She did not disagree.

"How does it feel?"

"Interesting." And it did, actually. In fact, it felt a little exhilarating, like a new gate had opened. And yes, I knew where the path through that gate led, but I didn't know its route, precisely. Might it not pass by giraffes? Might it not swing through a caper or two?

Because, though my nature certainly can run stodgy and timid—I would never paint myself silver and stand in a subway station or dance like no one is watching in a rented parking space, as a performance artist I met had—I was definitely still up for the odd caper. "Old people do whatever they want," my mother told me when she was in her seventies, and I recall the happy glint of defiance in her tone when she'd passed that jewel, from the life's transitions box, on to me. So much lighter and brighter than the period talk, which was weighted with responsibility.

A little norms-veering wasn't *entirely* new to me, and there had been outbreaks of mild, local havoc that might have been traceable to my door. Poems scrawled over the white boards of poli-sci classrooms at nearby MSU might have coincided with some of my walks there. Sidewalk invectives ("Facts Matter!") chalked around town in the middle of the night might have mimicked the slant of my hand. And the trespassing footprints near this nest or that pond in a private garden might have fit the soles of my shoes—but the first incident I would describe as a personal *caper* went down in Marrakech and was filed in my head as, "The Great Moroccan Lizard Caper." Unlike the mild flaunting of conventions, capers require equipment and merit titles.

Agatha Christian as it may sound without context, the Lizard Caper was really an animal rescue. Poking around Marrakech one spring break, my daughter Madeline and I came to a cage of medium-sized (we supposed) lizards in Jemaa el Fna, that square famous for its snake charmers and magicians and other exotica left over from the Middle Ages. Surrounded by lantern and leather venders, whose wares were laid out on the ground, and not far from an actual hawker of human teeth (individual molars in a mound on a tray, hand-fashioned dentures fanned out for display), the cage sat on a broad Berber rug. Inside, its reptiles were piled on each other as densely as the dusty bricks in the nearby Koutoubia Mosque. We pitied them.

You can't save everyone, as they say. Some of these lizards, we later learned, would almost certainly get lucky and bask away their days in private gardens. Some, on the other hand, were probably headed for the chopping block, where their bits would be ground into powders and sold in local apothecaries as cures for hemorrhoids and rheumatism and some folksy version of Viagra. Either way, there seemed to be too much square inch of animal to too little square inch of cage, even for the meager ambitions of lizards. We stepped up to the rug and ventured a "Hello," which was the beginning and end of our direct exchange.

The lizard monger had no English and no French, Morocco's second language—a dividend France left behind when it cleared out of its African colony—and, beyond *shukran* and *la shukran* (thanks and no thanks), we had no Arabic. On top of which Maddie and I were totally winging it. We had zero reptile-rescue experience to fall back on even on our own continent. All we had was the flickering picture of a grand(ish) gesture that was trying to assemble itself in our heads, utterly devoid of the particulars. Like, should we manage to procure one, what were we going to *do* with a lizard? How would we even *carry it away* and where exactly would we *carry it to?* As we gestured and sputtered at the bemused reptile huckster, luck struck.

"Can I help you?" We turned. He was young and handsome and Moroccan-born: "Rihyad," he said, "but I studied in Canada. What do you want to do?" Which was an excellent question.

"We want to buy a lizard," I heard myself say. I looked at Maddie, who shook her head, still trying to draw in the lines of our plan—a half-filled Etch-A-Sketch screen. But we had a translator to whom I'd stated our intentions, such as they were, and only a moment to decide.

As luck (still ours) would have it, in North Africa, in Marrakech, in the Jemaa el Fna, lizards come "Buy One Get One Almost Free," at least they did with the Sudanese (it turned out) merchant we took our business to that day. With the help of our kindly agent—God bless study abroad, I thought—it took all of five minutes for us to hand over a few bucks in Moroccan dirhams and receive our charges: two Bell's Dabb Lizards, each the length of a miniature dachshund, in a wooden birdcage, in what was (later research would reveal) a completely illegal sale.

"We need a park," Maddie said, as we stood in the square, feeling awkward and conspicuous with our lizards. Our caper had developed a hazy protocol: capture and release. But we hadn't seen a park tucked anywhere among the narrow, walled streets of the medina.

"We need a ride," I said. There were also no cars inside the old city's walls. Donkeys there were in spades. And a fleet of caleches—horse-drawn carriages—some of them just over there, Maddie pointed.

A few minutes later, we were bumping behind an affable driver and clipping along Marrakech's modern streets beyond the medina, our horses deftly weaving in and out of traffic, two lizards napping in my lap. Our English was happily working again. Approaching the driver, I had lined up what French I could manage in my head: *"Nous voudrions un parc aller"*: "We would like a park to go," as if I were placing a takeout order, but he had greeted us in our own tongue and we'd made our request. Half an hour later, we pulled up to the curb at the city's Cyber Park, a popular botanical garden to which free WIFI had been grafted.

Because we didn't know what Moroccan law had to say about freelance reptile dispersal, the idea was to slip inside the garden, stroll insouciantly to a private corner, discreetly open the cage's gate, and watch two exuberant lizards spring out and start celebrating their freedom. (There was precisely nothing we knew about lizards.) But first there was the uniformed security guard at the gate eyeing our weirdly square, plastic bag, which I had pulled up to cover all but the top of the cage, the better to sneak in outsider-animals. The cage's sharp wood corners had perforated the bag and were sticking through it like spikes. "This garden is closing," the guard— very tall, very imperious—informed us, staring at the parcel that may or may not have resembled a bomb.

"Oh, well, thank you!" we gushed, smiling those ingratiating smiles Americans take on the road, and returning to the street, where one iron-fenced side of the park ran for at least a city block. Our carriage-driver, who had agreed to wait for us, watched as we sauntered—very casual: nothing to see here—down the sidewalk and looked at the park between the rails. Our better ideas, such as they were, were gone. I shrugged. "Let's tip 'em in." So we stooped near the ground and Maddie peeled off the bag and I tilted the cage forward and held it as flush to the iron bars as I could, leaving just enough room for Maddie to slip in a hand and lift the door and—nothing. No rush for the embracing palms, the warm stones, the low shrubs. No stirring of any kind at all; we might as well have been freeing bowling pins. We thumped on the cage, shook it, thumped again. Eventually the lizards spilled indifferently into the garden, landed with soft thuds, and lay there like house-slippers for some time, before inching toward the bushes, oblivious to the close call they'd almost certainly had with human erectile dysfunction.

The second caper (equipment, title) went down closer to home. The Great Pandemic Hive-Heist was born not of pity, but of greed. This time, Anna, who'd been visiting when Lockdown dropped a net on us in March, was pulled in. Suddenly, the known world was closed; with a flick of a switch, it seemed, its cafes and bars, its movie theaters and museums, were shuttered; streets were bereft of traffic, airports deserted. One night I crawled into bed with my laptop, vaguely intending to pull up maps of cities I'd explored over the years, testing the reach and reality, I suppose, of this new beast, pandemic, but a first glance at Paris broke my heart and I stopped there. Every pointy icon I clicked—site markers—flashed "Fermé." The Louvre: "Fermé." The Musée d'Orsay: "Fermé." Impossibly, The Eiffel Tower: "Fermé."

There are tiers of knowing.

There is what-I-read-online-in-a-coffee-queue knowing. There is reciting-the-French-conjugations-of-"to be"-verbs knowing. There is how-to-get-across-town-without-making-a-left-turn knowing. Then there is deep-knowing, when something abstract and spectral takes on weight and settles inside you. Paris was occupied, Paris had fallen, it was 1944 and my father would have to invade Normandy again. I closed my laptop and lay back on my pillow as this thing that had come to us crawled up and sat on my chest. It wasn't just here; you couldn't outrun it. The planet Earth was closed.

But wait. The indoor world was closed, but the outside world was open, and outside quickly became the only game in town at the gray, drenched end of March. And Anna and I launched ourselves into that drizzle and chill, with long walks every single day, and coming home wet, and in my case with sore (because old) ankles. One day, as Anna and my friend Jan and I were walking, at wary six-foot distances, on a paved bike trail that was new to us and took us along a high wall separating our path from a housing development, a shadow on the pavement made me look up. Dangling just beyond the wall, wed tightly to the leafless branch of some soon-to-be flowering tree, was a wasp nest the size of a Japanese lantern. It was exquisite. I knew how stubbornly that hive was secured to its twig because I had been hiving before. This was an architecture that had survived winter; wind and snow and hail had done their best to bring it down, but there it hung—as intact and as graceful and textured as a sonnet.

Like some people covet a Birkin bag (I'm told) or a Lamborghini (I've heard), I wanted that hive. "Send me a screenshot when you get it," Jan said when we returned to our cars. She was familiar with the loot laying around our house: the rocks and nests and seed pods, the polypores and bits of bone.

"We'll have to take the branch as well," I told Anna, pulling her in as we drove home. And for that, the narrator who commandeered my head pointed out, we'd need cover of darkness and tools (a caper!) which were limited to what could be found in our garage. A quick survey after we pulled into the driveway gave us a stepladder and a pair of 3-foot hedge clippers— imprecise instruments but all we had with which to infiltrate private property and nab a hive that appeared to be 15 feet in the air. Crossing the front porch, I didn't hate that little surge of adrenaline.

When I laid out our plan to him, Larry, who has a knack for cutting straight to the heart of a thing, suggested we might simply ask the family on whose property we'd be trespassing if we could have the hive. His is a civilized, caper-killing heart. I shook my head and shot him a piteous look, while Anna accurately pointed out that doorbell ringing was anathema to the times. She was *in* and we were resolute.

The caper went down at nine P.M. It was (in fact) a dark and stormy night and, wrapping ourselves up like commandos in black coats and hats and gloves as we gathered supplies, we tuned into our own badness; I had the delicious sense that we were *becoming* the night. Stashing our tools in the back of the car, and keeping religiously to the speed limit, we crept across town, a steady vector approaching its target. Stealth was our game. The deserted streets, eerie in their emptiness, however, took on a desolation that magnified our sense of exposure. We were most certainly *not* the night; seat-belted into a bright, white SUV, baldly breaking with the lock-down, we were the only show in town for anyone who glanced out their window.

It took us twenty minutes to get vaguely *there*, where, squinting into the dark between swipes of the windshield wipers, we rolled down a street, searching for the right house from the front, based on what we'd seen through a chink in the fence in the back. Each place looked unremarkably like the next. But we had counted the number of homes from a particular crosswalk to the property of interest, so we eased to the curb near that. Then, slipping from the car, we grabbed the clippers and stepladder and plastic trash bag (in case it turned out to be a *live* hive, contradicting all of the intelligence online) and legged it for a gray two-story with a very soggy yard—a lot of rain had come down that day. Moving furtively along the side of the house, past its empty screen porch, through the entanglements of a swing set, with sod sucking at our boots, we spotted the tree by the silhouette of the hive against the dusky sky. Pointing and whispering, we squished our way to it.

Anna placed the stepladder on stand-by against the fence as I gripped the hedge clippers with two hands and hoisted them awkwardly into the darkness over our heads where those unwieldy blades took on a life of their own, like a divining fork. Finally, I wrestled them around the slim branch we were after, which I pulled down for Anna to grab just north of the nest itself. Then I snipped the limb free, she cradled the branch, I retrieved the stepladder, and we scrambled—*sucksucksuck*—back to the car, bagged our hive, tossed in our tools, and tore out, hellbent for home. The whole heist, house to hive and back again, took less than an hour.

It was almost disappointing   how easy our caper turned out to be. It went off without motion lights, barking dogs, or some child's NRA-dues-paying dad watching us through a scope with his night goggles on. At home, we laid our limb and hive on the front porch bench to dry—and to give whatever of last season's layabouts who might remain in it an opportunity to jump ship—then went inside and ate two kinds of quiche, like any hardened criminals. The next morning the hive found its new home on top of a hutch full of books overlooking our living room, its ruffled layers fanned out like the shelled roof of the Sydney Opera House. The spindly branches of its narrow limb were covered with dainty red buds that I hoped would hang on.

Hanging on was certainly the name of the game that spring, when lots of us were having our groceries delivered and wiping down our cantaloupes with Lysol. The crowded markets of fall suggested that not many of us were doing that anymore and my Equinox once again blended right in with all the other cars on the busy roads. And when Britain pulled ahead of the rest of the world by a nose and started vaccinating its people against COVID, I think it's fair to say that most of us in the stands cheered. We who had been lucky enough to make it that far into the pandemic, into the decades themselves, were hanging on a little less frantically, our white knuckles not quite the wintry Alps they once were. Still.

Still, the holidays were upon us and we were not over the river and through the woods yet, the ubiquitous Dr. Fauci kept telling us. The pandemic had made superstars of the unlikeliest people.

As for my own path, whether it runs through another caper or two, there is no disputing where it really does go, and from what I've seen, there will be a lot of shedding along the way: income, agility, dignity. Independence. And finally, breath.

Every August, when the water is warm enough to feel like a caress rather than a slap, I walk into Lake Michigan and lie down and float. "I'm Getting Buoyant," I call to Larry as I surrender to weightlessness with the sense of shedding gravity itself. Larry, who has no interest in getting wet, monitors my drift from the beach, as attentive as a Newfoundland dog, ready if needs must, to launch himself in—he knows I'm not a strong swimmer. But I'm an A+ floater and, resting there in the lap of the lake with nothing but sky overhead, my desires for the world sink away like silt. It's a trick that springs me from the years. It's as close to free as I've ever felt, as near nonbeing as I have been, as least as I have been for now.

THE C WORD

I was up at 3 AM, sleepless because 48% of Americans believed that Fox News was *Actual News*. No, that's not true; they didn't all believe it; some of them merely feigned belief to whip up mania in the Republican Party's credulous base as they mainlined Sean Hannity's hate-porn like heroin.

Forty-eight percent was no reckless hyperbole; it was the hefty slice of people—almost half of the American pie—who voted for Donald Trump in the 2020 election. And they did this knowing him for the braggart, the serial liar, the charity swindler, the tax cheat, the environmental ransacker, and the rickety Romeo to Stormy Daniels' shy Juliet that he is. There seemed to be nothing I could do about this vast American defection to a terrible darkness, except work my teeth steadily through my bite guard at night. If I ran my tongue over its formerly smooth surface, I could feel two tiny Tetons my incisors had pushed up in the tectonics of insomnia.

So I put on my mom's old soft cardigan and shuffled down to the kitchen and sliced up an apple, a *Sweet* something-or-other Larry had picked up. And I poured a glass of red wine from a spigot on the box in the laundry room ("gracious-living-in-the-Midwest," my friend Jeanne says) into a short glass with a flat bottom and, balancing these on my laptop, climbed upstairs and back into my bed next to an open window. After an astonishing week of Indian Summer (can you say that anymore?), November was roaring in through the screen. I pulled the covers over my knees and breathed it in. Then I took a bite of my apple, tasted nearly nothing, and wondered what sort of decline taste-ageusia foretold.

It's probably all blather, but I tell myself fairly often that I am ready to die. Not eager but prepared enough if needs must. Aging is an unpromising business, or rather, it's darkly promising. That shadow in the road ahead might only be Online Bingo or Mortifying Incontinence or A Condo In The Villages—manageable atrocities—but it might just as easily be Alzheimer's, which came for my mother and might be waiting around.

After a Costco run a few days before Christmas—with COVID cases rising again, it seemed prudent to lay in a supply of Chocolate Kisses and a few cinder blocks of cheese—I stopped by my sister's house for a cup of tea and a chat. Her sweet, ancient black Lab, Lucy (a sack of ribs with a dowager's hump), and her young white Lab, Sugar (Renee Zellweger in a cashmere sweater) met me at the door and escorted me to the living room where Sue and her husband Kim and my niece Sydney were watching the (real) news. Crying foul over the election and refusing to concede defeat, like the despot he dearly wanted to be, Trump had just fired his fourth Secretary of Defense and his corrupted Secretary of State was declaring four more years of a Trump presidency. "I'll go into the streets if he refuses to leave," Sue said, raising her mug over her elevated bad knee. "I'll be right in the streets!"

"I'll go with you," I declared. "We're old. We've lived our lives. If they shoot us, they shoot us"—*they*, of course, meaning the MAGA camp, who had all the guns. "But not you"—I pointed to Sydney, who was in nursing school. "You do not go into the streets. You have important work to do." I dropped a tea bag into my cup. "But right now, I need you to help me find a birch tree." I'd seen a pretty little artificial birch at Costco a couple of weeks earlier that seemed better suited to the pared-down Christmas ahead than a big fat fir. Letting go of old fixtures that didn't fit a pandemic was a lesson I was slowly learning. (Cc to the people who would bring us the depressing Macy's Parade a couple of weeks later.) But Costco was sold out. So we muted the news and while Syd was getting her iPad, Kim showed me a picture he'd taken of a spider on their deck ("*Where* did you see that?" Sue gasped) and asked if I knew exactly what type of beast it was. People think I know these things, but really I just have an app. I took out my phone.

"It's called *iNaturalist*," I told Kim, showing him the icon. "It identifies animals, insects, flowers, trees—anything. Watch." I took a picture of Lucy, sleeping on the carpet by my feet.

The app spun its little wheel. "Domestic Water Buffalo," it reported. I sighed.

iNaturalist did know its spiders though, and eventually we identified Kim's specimen as a type of Jumping Spider ("a *what* kind of spider? Sue gasped) and Sydney ordered my birch tree from Kohl's and the water buffalo climbed up on the couch and I went home to shower before heading over to my friend Lauri's house to sit around her fire pit with a few other pals. The days had turned warm again, but the weather-prophets warned that this really would be the last balmy night of fall.

It is a singular, confounding, tragic fact about Donald Trump that, despite whatever joys the world is showering on you—in this case Joe Biden's popular and electoral win—your mind and conversation always return to him. It's a perverse magnetism the press has never been able to resist and what probably got him elected in the first place; he is that proverbial train wreck no one can wrest their eyes from. If God reached out of a cumulus cloud and dropped lottery tickets like manna, if Jesus came back in spectacular drag, if Buddha and Elvis walked into a bar and bought a round for the house, Trump would still be the story, despite having the global cachet of Caligula and the courtly charm of Jabba the Hutt. Just over half the country sees his horns, the others (setting a match to his resume) manage to see a halo. All of this is to say that, as soon as Lauri lit up our bonfire, as soon as we filled our glasses and settled into our chairs, our celebratory talk took a turn to the unholy elephant in the backyard.

"He won't *leave*."

"He'll shred every bit that he can of this democracy before he *does* leave."

"Whose job is it to *make* him leave?"

We had our invasive theme. But we also had that resistance-grit that had helped us beat out a path through the previous four years and we had 60 degrees in November and several open bottles of wine. So, despite this newest wave of anxiety, we danced. We shouted. We raised our glasses to Biden and Harris and especially to new First Dogs, Major and Champ. We celebrated; we did.

The next day I walked into our family room where Larry, who was taking a break from a Griswoldian knot of Christmas lights on the front porch, was watching CNN. The latest White House press secretary, a bony blond whose lies had recently tipped the scales to so shocking an extent that even Fox had cut away, was firing off some brazen new fiction. I paused and thought about shamelessness, which you didn't use to run into so often and so publicly. And I felt the velar stop of the hard letter C form at the back of my mouth, heard the soft U coming, felt my tongue touch the ridge behind my front teeth for the alveolar NT. "Cunt." As slurs go, the big one.

"Cunt," I said to the woman on TV. But the word glanced off, it wouldn't stick, and not just because televisions don't work that way. The slur wouldn't land because it was linguistically disingenuous, because I have a problem with that edgiest expletive and that problem is this: "cunt," a bullet, a missile, a bomb to most people I know, feels as soft and warm and cuddly as a puppy to me. Its effect in my ear mimics the moment someone brings a Golden Retriever into a Home Depot and everyone in the middle of a roof or basement crisis suddenly relaxes. Doesn't it then follow that we each should be, if we possibly can, a cunt? The term simply hasn't been a pistol-whip for me since I read *Lady Chatterley's Lover* decades ago and Mellors, the sex-worshipping gamekeeper, purred it so reverently. I have never been called a cunt myself—at least not to my face—but if I were, I think my response would be, "how splendid!" So Trump's little press secretary could never be a cunt. *In her scheming dreams.* I turned from her tirade and went to the kitchen to make soup.

Picking up the mail Larry had left on the kitchen island to make way for the big, copper-bottom pot, I took a moment to thumb the letters into separate stacks. Underneath the appeals for money and a couple of medical bills, lay a big, manilla envelope. I eyed my hand-written name, then the return address, and the truly alarming C-word flashed a warning in my head: *cousin. Cousin:* the insidious family-splintering animal that had been plaguing holiday dinners for the past few politically divided years. Nearly everyone I knew had a cousin in the Trump camp.

I hadn't seen this woman in years. She was a gentle person who lived inside a soft fog inside a hard religion who had given away all her money and would have swallowed Hitler hook, line, and sinker if her pastor had endorsed him. As it happened, her pastor was also my cousin. Earlier in life, he'd been that most benign and superfluous of creatures, a male stripper, but he'd eventually found Bible college—the dangerous kind with all the Answers. I have rationalized and blundered my way into more sins of co and omission than I want to count, but these cousins—both *nicer* than me—are two people on the narrow road to Nuremberg, nice people in love with the fiction of easy answers and looking for someone to blame for all of life's pretty little terrors. Nicer than me in a hundred ways. And yet.

When I retired from teaching high school English, I left completely. I'd had a good run: joyful, I would call my career. I was not like some retired colleagues who maintained concerns about curriculum, who worried about the continuation of their hard-wrought programs. Legacy-shmegacy; it was someone else's turn. But as I watched my cousin's—let's call her Betty—as I watched Cousin Betty's blindered devotion to Trump unfold on social media, my mind returned to my old classroom, and a conversation my students and I always had about *Huck Finn* which, because I manipulated it, went pretty much like this:

"What do the Widow Douglas and Tom's Aunt Sally have in common?"

Inevitably someone would offer, "They're really nice."

"And what else?"

"They have better manners than Huck. They care about Huck. They have stuff Huck doesn't—houses and farms and—slaves." And there it was—the segue.

"What do you think average Nazi mothers did with their days? And sweet Nazi grandmas?" The turn always surprised them, but they were adept scramblers.

"I don't know. They cooked? And took care of their kids."

"And baked strudel?" I'd ask.

"Yeah."

"And went to church?"

"Yeah."

"And supported Hitler?" I'd press.

"Yeah."

Then—the big moment: "How does evil spread?" This was the clincher. This was why I kept teaching the book year after year, though there were persuasive reasons not to.

"Through regular people? *Nice* people?" And we were home.

"There aren't enough monsters in the world," I'd cut back in—big shiny finish—"to orchestrate a Holocaust. Or slavery. Evil can't spread unless what kind of people take it up?

"*Nice* people."

"Exactly." Then we'd look around at each other; we were nice people, right? Would we ever be tempted to go down such a sinister road? And then the bell would ring or someone would spill their *Red Bull* or latte or the Homecoming court would be announced over the intercom and we'd move on. And though few of us remember many conversations from our high school days, I always counted that one as time well spent. You never know.

My insomnia didn't arrive with the defection of the 48%. In the weeks before the election, my cousin Betty's Facebook posts wedged themselves into my head and kept me awake at night. "Daryl" (we'll call her husband) "and I always vote Republican because we don't like name-calling."

"Did you *see* what she wrote!" I shouted at my sister the next day on the phone. "And Trump just called Kamala Harris a *monster!*"

"You *have* to unfriend her," Sue sighed, calm and centered. She had made a pool of peace in her head where she let Betty float, out of love for our sweet, deceased aunt. I marveled at her Sufi-like detachment, and envied it, but I couldn't get there. I was a terrier at one end of a very ratty sock. Because *it didn't make sense.* This cousin was, by all accounts, poor; she lived in a trailer, far beneath the contempt of her reality-TV President and his congressional toadies who would not have sat down at her tiny kitchen table to save their gilded lives. And she knew suffering. As a teenager in the 60s, she had slipped away from home to ride a Greyhound bus from Michigan to Mexico for an abortion in some accommodating Tijuana slum; then she'd ridden all the way home bleeding. Now she was decrying other women's access to safe abortions inside the U.S. *It didn't make sense.* I couldn't see that this insistence on *sense* was the sock I needed to let go, that of logic, there would never be a lick. So back and forth we went, posting our blistering condemnations of each other's candidates: mine a reasonable, empathetic, capable man, hers a ravening narcissist with ambitions of world dominion—which I might have mentioned—and I stewed in my bed at night.

And then one day Cousin Betty texted me directly. She had been sorting out old family pictures and had come across some of me and my family. Could she send them? "Love you, sweetie" she signed off. I thanked her and sent her my address. "Love you too, Betty!" I wrote. Which I do—and I saw that that was the hook in my obsession with her views, the tooth caught in the logic-sock.

The next day, I officially, electronically unfriended her. The picture she'd posted of Melania and Ivanka Trump and that hapless, never-to-be-a-cunt, Kayleigh Something as exemplary women we should all aspire to be, was the last brittle straw. I cut her picture out of my online family album and began sleeping a little better.

The family photos Betty sent were mostly of my daughters when they were toddlers and of my first husband. In fact, they reminded me of another picture, taken in what must have been the same year, which had led to a prescient moment, and which I still have somewhere around our house. That photo, taken by that early husband just after he'd returned from a covert morning run to the liquor store, insisting he'd gone out to get groceries—which turned out to be the last lie I let him tell me—showed Madeline at three and Anna at one and me sitting together on a picnic table. I had developed the film the next day and, studying that picture, I'd felt the stir of a sudden conviction: "Now we are three." And I knew, in a deep calm place, like the pool my sister lets Betty float in, that this was true. I filed for divorce.

Clarity like that is rare, I have found. And, except for the moment when I fell in love with Larry a couple of years later, I don't think I've known it since. "I am never going to understand the 48%, am I?" I asked him after reading that, while they were few, more minority voters had supported Trump than in the previous election. It was exactly the kind of ironic little pea that could get under a thinking person's mattress and keep her blinking at the ceiling at three AM; I let it go. Like my wise sister, I would be in the streets if that's where America needed me to be—and would hope for nice weather and damn few guns.

It turns out the term "Indian summer" for those lovely late warm days, does ring wrong in a few ears. Among alternatives suggested by one website I visited was the European, "old woman's summer." I like its fit. And as the world doesn't often toss sweets to old women, I've happily taken it up.

I mailed my cousin Betty a thank you note. It's unlikely I'll ever see her again. But I can feel her weight and force out there, and from here in my parallel world, I go on pushing back; we are two old women locking horns. And here's the impossible grace of the thing: I'm bound to go on loving her—not because we're *cousins* and not because I'm good or even because I want to—but just because I do.

Nest

This morning the good angels at eBay declined my bid on a twenty-volume *Oxford English Dictionary*, published in 1989. It was, I consoled myself, for the best; I had no actual money to back up that bid and storing it would probably have meant ceding to those weighty tomes the whole bottom shelf in our wall of fiction—Voltaire, Vonnegut, Walker, Waugh, and Wodehouse might have been wiped out in an afternoon. Still.

It was an impulse-offer I made, sitting by the fire with a cup of tea and an unclaimed hour, and it didn't fit our life at all. My husband Larry and I had been in the gradual process of unloading the heavy fixtures of our home, after all. We'd gotten the half-empty paint cans out of our basement the previous summer, and the hollow dressers, and were down to the old cross-country skis—relics of livelier times, resting against the wall of the furnace room like bones in a catacomb.

And, working from the other direction, there were the heavy things we were making a deliberate choice not to bring into our home, like a Labrador Retriever. Down to only one dog, there was way too much room in our beds—well, mine is a single bed these days, but I could have managed a Lab. We simply both noticed pockets of planet and air in our daily routines where a second dog should be. But we also grudgingly allowed that we aren't getting any nimbler or stronger and even a young dog would only age into dependency along with us and how, we asked, would we get her to the vet when she lay down sick, lay down in pain, lay down to die, as our string of big dogs have always eventually done. We agreed that, should we take on a second dog at all during the denouement of our lives, she should certainly not outweigh our toaster, which we could still hoist without help.

Then, on a Sunday morning, in the ninth month of a pandemic, as COVID cases soared again: the sudden craving for 137 pounds of an outdated dictionary. (I looked up its weight on the Internet, which is another place you can go for information, that weighs precisely nothing.) But it really wasn't sudden or new at all, the desire to house and infrequently dust this repository of knowledge and culture; it was merely latent and had been riding around in my head for decades, keeping such a low profile that I didn't even realize it was there. Heaven knows what woke it up—the times, perhaps.

I met my first *OED* in the flesh over thirty years ago when I accompanied a man I was dating to visit elderly friends who had recently sold their well-appointed (I was told) country estate, and most of its appointments, to move into a condo. Their new home was sleek as a mink, white and silver, and so minimalist that our slight disturbance might have echoed were it not for the thick carpet that captured our footsteps and half of our syllables. But there, running across a broad shelf in a starkly filled bookcase was the *OED*, in all its grandeur. It had a pageantry about it that made me feel like the Queen's Guard might at any moment materialize and change right there in their living room. I'd previously seen it, and only a time or two, in bookstores, which were the only places I'd ever see it again after that day. It was like sighting a giant rare bird, a mythic creature: a griffin. These frail-looking octogenarians had sold off just about everything to lighten their last years, but they'd lugged along this beast. Clearly, they would drag it to their graves. And I knew that, if I could ever afford one, I would too.

Thirty-plus years later, after everyone with enough disposable income to enjoy shopping privileges on the planet had already done so, I created an account on eBay. And made my bid.

It wasn't strictly age that was redrawing the patterns of daily life for Larry and me, although the decades will line right up to do that for you. A couple of years earlier, Larry, who was always a formidable tennis player (but unwaveringly gracious: "Saint Larry," I'd heard him called by other players), had started complaining that his forehand was off—it was baffling. It took a few months for us to find the neurologist who would diagnose Parkinson's disease. Larry took the apocalypse gracefully, as he takes all things.

There had been signs that some rogue agent had arrived with a wedge that would widen and split open our lives—in hindsight there are always signs—but we'd lacked the Rosetta Stone to read them. It had been the better part of a decade since Larry had been able to smell anything—not our Thursday night Thai food, not the flowering fruit trees we passed beneath on evening walks, not the easily rattled and highly reactive skunks that fed on the mulberries in our backyard, nor our undeterrable dog Scout whenever she managed to mix it up with them.

And there was the sleep combat, not an official term but one that explained my migration to a bedroom down the hall. Parkinson's disease is a motor disorder, the result of dopamine neurons dying off in the brain. Besides whittling away at his tennis game, Larry's increasingly chaotic motor cortex began driving him to flail and strike out in his sleep, as if he were in a bar brawl. He actually made fists, this gentlest of men. For years, I clung to the far side of our bed, elbows and knees cantilevered over the edge, took a few punches to my back, and hoped for the best. Then, shortly before the pandemic broke out, I started making furtive, middle-of-the-night forays down the chilly hall to an empty bedroom. The relief of lying down without vigilance—and the fear I'd wake up with a broken nose—was delicious. After about a month of this creeping away in the night, and with Larry's understanding help, I moved a few things permanently into my mother's old bedroom, the one she'd stayed in while Alzheimer's had unraveled her a dozen years earlier. Beneath the plain jute rug there was still a bright red stain where her blood had soaked into the hardwood—a fresco left from one her falls.

In a poem he wrote after beating a tunnel through his own catastrophe, which came as cancer, the poet Ted Kooser describes the pastures surrounding his Nebraska home. He notes

> that awful February gray
> that goes to the heart,
> the gray of single mattresses
> and the hair of forgotten old men.

A Midwesterner myself, I know that winter gray, but my mom's single mattress, which had belonged to one of our daughters in an earlier world when our girls parked their twin beds in a shared room, seemed anything but grim. It felt like family to me. So I bought it a dust ruffle and dressed it in an old quilt with a torn patch where a child's toe had caught a loose seam. Smoothing out its wrinkles, I stroked that tear like the wounded ear of a kitten. Then I bought it a new dresser, for company, and for beauty, I hung a friend's painting—branches hanging over a pond like a veil—on the wall. And finally, it was mine. Plain and chaste as a nun's cell, the room was everything I needed it to be for a future I imagined of contemplation and— there is no disputing it—loss.

Drifting through the bedrooms upstairs, wandering downstairs from the living room, where most of our fossils and hives and bird's nests are stashed, through my study with its framed ordnance map of the Cotswolds, where Larry and I once hiked *to the stile and across the pasture*, through the kitchen cramped by its old claw-foot table, to the fireplace in the family room, I tried to envision what I wanted our house to be during the years that lay ahead, which promised to hold some bright but also very dark moments. And I wondered how I could prepare for whatever was slouching toward us, wondered how to be *ready*.

"You can't do it," Chauncy, Larry's affable young neurologist at the

University of Michigan said, spinning around on the stool in front of his computer monitor to talk with us. Larry likes his boy-doctor, who always exuded optimism and told him that no matter what happened to his game, he should keep playing tennis. Larry has the slowing and stiffening version of the disease, rather than the wild tremors for which it is better known, and exercise and synthetic dopamine are the imperfect sticks he has with which to beat it back. "Parkinson's affects every person differently—you can't really *prepare.*"

But I persisted. "Should we sell our house?"

"I wouldn't."

"And get something smaller?"

"I wouldn't rush to do that."

"Should we at least take out a wall and enlarge the bathroom downstairs, maybe put in a shower in case..."

"I'd let things sit for a while. You have no idea what's going to happen."

I am not good with *laissez-faire* living. I am definitely not friends with *No Idea.* Which is why I wasn't patient and tender enough with my mom— rushing in to control the uncontrollable chaos of her decline with corrections ("that isn't a *car;* it's a *pill*") that were futile and so only cruel, when I should have been simply loving her. I wanted to do better by Larry. I needed to make peace with that loose cannon, *No Idea,* in order to do better *This Time.* The chances to serve love were not, after all, infinite.

You could tell at a glance by the loom on the living room table that Anna was with us again, as she had been on and off through the months of pandemic, camping out in her old bedroom and working remotely. Her new car, which Larry helped her buy with a loan in order to spring her from the shared air of mass transit, was parked at the curb because I am a notorious backer-into-things. It's not failsafe, the curb. The tree I've skidded into three times on ice is only a block away. Larry never mentions the nicked and dented things of the world that have carried the paint of my cars during the decades we've been married, though the fact that I'd taken over all of our driving must have given him pause. Our daughters were not so demure. "There's your tree," Anna noted when we passed it on our way to pick up ingredients for the samosas she'd offered to make for dinner. An expat from crowded Chicago, she planned to be with us at least through Thanksgiving.

A couple of days earlier, Anna and I had turned our attention to a different tree than the one I keep driving into. As I culled birds' nests from living room shelves, Anna pulled six feet of trunk and flexible limbs from a long cardboard box and tucked them into a corner of the family room. The new arrival came from the Land of Online—dropped on our front porch, like everything those days—and even up-close looked passably like a live, leafless birch, albeit one fitted out in LED lights. "Only choose nests that are sturdy and light," Anna called, which left the mud and twig work of robins, heavy as Victorian sideboards, on their tabletops and shelves. As he was leaving, Larry wandered into our project with his tennis bag.

"What do we have here?"

"It's our Christmas tree!" I called from a stepladder. He gave it an affable nod then headed out the door. The limited reopening of his tennis club had been a boon.

From the twiggy, leafy candidates I submitted, we settled on several goldfinch nests—little teacups made of grass and down, and a horsehair nest from the rafters of a friend's barn, and the deep mitten of a vireo hanging from its own twig and Anna, who has the artist's eye and hand, carefully placed them among the tree's acetate branches. Finally, we stepped back and surveyed the lithe, little stand-in that would supplant the traditional blue spruce Larry and I had always trudged into the weather and dragged home for the fat, gay gatherings of Christmases past. But 2020 had whittled the extravagance out of everything and the labors of a real tree seemed too much for the winnowed holiday ahead. Our slim new sapling, decked out in intricate nests—little miracles, every one of them—seemed to coo, "lean times *can* be lovely too," and felt exactly right.

The second lockdown in Michigan was scheduled to begin in three days and everyone was talking about Thanksgiving, wondering how we'd pull it off that year. How much risk was responsible? Answer: none, and governors were pleading with people to celebrate only within individual households. But we are complicated creatures—stubborn and perverse, and we were hungry for the old rituals, plenty of which we'd once complained about: the dishes, the cooking, the *cousins*. But we were all sick of exile. Everyone wanted to go *home* on the homiest of holidays. "We are going to fuck this up," I told Anna.

"We'd better get our groceries soon," she replied. "Then. Stay. Home." I'd noticed how protective she had been of us, even stern at times, and I suspected half the reason she'd been turning up so often was to place herself squarely between the world and Larry. Dr. Chauncy had assured us that Parkinson's disease did not make a person more susceptible to COVID. Nevertheless.

I handed Anna a cookbook and began making a list. An hour later, we drove across town to Horrocks, a sprawling, noisy farm market where six kinds of yams and five types of eggplants towered in peaks beneath a menagerie of hanging pinatas, and where an exotica of produce—Buddha's fingers and dragon fruits and tamarinds—were heaped in bins near cheese wheels the size of spare tires. The place was packed and jostling with the sort of ruckus we usually liked, but this time the commotion felt perilous. Too many bodies, too many breaths. We piled golden beets and avocados in our cart, tracked down the curry paste we needed for soup, threw in the licorice Larry loves, did a quick, happy dance at the discovery of coriander (which has been AWOL for weeks in the usual stores), then made for the car. It was time to stay home. Again.

Though we hadn't met it personally, COVID had come to us like a contractor the previous spring, walling off some of our best-loved rooms—my favorite bookstore cafe and Larry's tennis club. But it had also built an addition on our notion of home, which now encompassed the whole outdoors. It followed that the narrow discipline of staying home was more expansive than it had originally sounded and included anywhere walkable in a ten-mile radius—farther if you were feeling plucky. So after we dropped the groceries on the kitchen island and the candy into Larry's lap, Anna and I stayed home by heading outside on separate paths. She chose a route that passed below a very tall oak tree dangling actual violins like date palms—the work of a visionary neighbor—and I headed for a bike trail that ran through a corridor of woods and past a low field of willows and wildflowers that each March became a vernal pond.

My own walk was pokey and investigatory, rather than rigorous, and it brought us three new nests, offerings extended by November's bare limbs that reached out and practically dropped them in my pockets. Once they were abandoned, I couldn't resist these nests, placed just so like exquisite small poems in the trees—it was as if Emily Dickinson had tippled a path through her agoraphobia (and that death business) and decorated the whole woods. On my best days, I had nothing like their eloquence, and I carried them home reverently to tuck into bookshelves, now that our Inn of Curiosities—a cabinet we bought to get the detritus off our end tables—was full. I placed a cardinal's nest near Anna's loom: inspiration for the rug she was weaving.

Though she also marvels at these small revelations, there for the taking, the naturalist Helen Macdonald does not collect nests. I was reading her book, *Vesper Flights*. The process of their construction is as mysterious, she allows, as that of any human painter who knows *somehow* that a particular brushstroke will create "a sense of balance or conflict" and she wonders how much, in the making of a nest, is imagined and planned, how much the mere instinctual placing of twigs. Somehow, amid all that consideration, she manages to leave these mysteries alone. "They were secrets," she says of the nests she discovered as a child, from which she felt she "should look away." Still, these secrets were instructive. "I think differently of home now," she states, which for her has become "a place you carry within you." And, though I suspected she had more of the nomad in her than I did, it seemed like language I could work with, and a view I hoped might help me reimagine our home to resemble my better heart—not my bossy, middle-management heart that likes a tidy room, but a heart wide open to mess and ruin because that's what comes with love. I was keeping Macdonald's book next to a finch nest near my narrow bed and reaching for it whenever I woke up in the night. Which was a lot.

Much as Helen Macdonald and I enjoyed making comparisons, a bird's nest, I learned, is not a house at all, merely a cradle; no one grows old in a nest. Once the eggs hatch and the young birds are fledged, while lovely to behold and hold, these little cups of twig and earth have no more use than an old shoebox.

Built for the long haul, our human "nests" are more complicated, and their elements—their location and function and furnishings—are radically open to revision these days. The usual chatter about moving to Canada during Republican presidencies, in my half of a divided America, crescendoed during the cruel years of the Trump regime. For starters, the shame of living in a home whose doors had been slammed in the ravaged faces of refugees was too much. Who the hell lives in a house like that, we asked ourselves, as talk of expatriation grew serious in a way it hadn't done before. But there were hard points to settle. Who would stay and who would or could go—and what would become of our kids and their kids? It was a lot to think about at three in the morning.

But that wasn't all. To the tumult in my taxed imagination, I added a world where more and more of the well-wired young were choosing to be homeless, living in rooms they rented by the week, then flying off to work from new perches like actual starlings and jays and wrens. A world—and no one could overlook this—where fires and storms on steroids were wiping out the upright planks of whole human colonies. And to bring it on home to our own little nest, there were the demands of aging and decline that had begun slipping inside our door.

And it finally dawned on me one morning, as I brooded over page forty-six of a book I wasn't reading, that maybe this was what had been waking me up in the night. This—the rioting all of it—was what sent me prowling online for a grande dame of a dictionary too *landed* for the upheavals of the wildly changing times, too steady for ephemera like *clickbait* and *bot*. What promised stability, however doomed that notion is, more convincingly than the *OED*?

Dropping onto the couch, I ran the little tale of my failed eBay bid by Anna, as she worked from her current perch at her loom. Frugal Larry, who would have been horrified by such a close call with profligacy, had just run out to fill his prescription for dopamine, that stabilizer of disorderly neurons. "Was it a just grab for stability?" I asked. "Was it all about the fall of Rome?"

"Maybe," she replied, weaving a purple strand through a warp of gray. "The *OED* was the dictionary of Empire—written in the language of power." And there it was—my tough-to-budge need to right our roost at any cost in a tumbling world where nothing is ever secure, where the best we can do is fall together and fall together in love. And I considered how long I'd let this stone block a valve in my heart, and wondered if, having found it, I'd find a way to let it go.

A Mystery

Here is proof that I am a *retired* person. Yesterday, through the window by my desk, I could see the front half of a big, red truck. Oil rig big. Flashing lights. Blocking the driveway two doors down. There appeared to be a ladder and some sort of tank. But this would not do; the intelligence was insufficient; one *had* to know. I finally dispatched Larry on a mission of surveillance, in the guise of walking the dog (okay, he was walking the dog). "Find out what's up!" I called as they stepped off the porch. He and Scout would be my team on the scene.

Our next-door neighbor George is also retired and I knew his window would give a better view of the unfolding situation though he, being a man of action, a former pipe-fitter, would have been out in the street if he'd been home, chatting it up with the truck-guys, who were milling around in *DayGlo* hoodies and *Carhartt* overalls. But George's truck was not in his driveway so there would be no INTEL coming from him. His wife Debbie is also retired, as of last week, a milestone we acknowledged by leaving a bottle of Baileys on their front porch, pandemic-style. She may have been home but, as she always parked in the garage, her whereabouts could not be confirmed. So I was left to the vagaries of theory in my warm house, which I didn't want to leave.

It has been just over a year since I stopped teaching high school—a year that, disfigured by a rogue virus, still perplexes me. Are Nowhere-To-Go and Never-Running-Late and Not-Buying-New-Clothes retirement things or COVID things? Maybe they are both. Maybe they are each, in fact, "a floor wax and a dessert topping" and we are all living inside the archives of old *SNL* sketches, which might explain why the days feel so off-kilter and why we harbor the sense that Something is coming for us: "Landshark."

"To withdraw to a place of shelter or seclusion," is the definition for "retire" that I get from my phone which is not only a *phone*, but a key to all knowledge. Here in my place of shelter, strings of early, colored Christmas lights draped over bookcases and wound around windows boil through the gloom of high noon in late November. Winters are gray in Michigan.

Once a week or so, a few rays of sun pierce the gloom and I have to stop whatever I'm doing to go outside and walk in the light. But those are rare days; the fickle sun does not become dependable here until May, then hightails it to *wherever* in November, like one of those slippery men with a secret second family in Nevada, and we are left in the semi-dark.

"It's Lake Michigan," I tell myself—picturing that long, svelte freshwater sea I never tire of walking beside from spring through fall—"which you *love*." This is true. Our weather comes from the west, crossing that big lake and skimming its water up into clouds that roll over us and hunker down for the winter. For a good six months, we literally live below the lake-in-the-sky. Sunshine glitters away on its surface, which we cannot see but remember from things we once called *flights* that were related to a thing we once called *travel*. From below, we study the lake's underbelly, which occasionally splits open to douse us.

I try—I do—to find the adventure in this dark occupation, thinking this is maybe how the French felt every time the English or Germans rolled in. Below the leaky lake, where we live an amphibian life, I squish through groves of maple and oak and keep to the drier sides of mucky trails that wind through osier and willow and swamp. I note simple beauties—the stiletto marks deer leave in the snow, the house slipper tracks of rabbits, the squirrel nests like big Russian hats in the trees, and the rough black twigs covered with lichen. It's a thin beauty, a broth that leaves me hungry.

"I can do a pandemic *or* clouds," I told Larry when he got home from his newly reopened tennis club one day, like he was my agent in charge of meteorological and viral negotiations, like this could be settled by reasonable people. Hadn't we, after all, negotiated realms of influence early in our marriage? "You can choose the house and schools and furniture," he'd said. "I'll take care of our policy with China." Which worked. But he had nothing this time. "It's grim," he allowed. As I already knew.

Some people are born secluded, some people achieve seclusion, but most of us had it thrust upon us nine months ago. Whole humans have been conceived and built and birthed since lockdown last spring: Generation C. In a world tilting more heavily than ever toward virtual, they will probably have cyber-bits installed in their lobes by the time they register for kindergarten, a new and improved species, brilliant and utterly controllable, and the rest of us will shuffle desultorily to our ends, hard to herd as cats and nearly as stupid, discontinued models, obsolete.

"Okay, come back!" I called to Dark Mind, which gets off the leash once in a while. "It's time to bake a souffle!" There are days when you have to put down your foot and stop yearning for the lost land of libraries and theaters and sunny cafes and make your own joy in your own house.

In the prime time of the 1960s that I was raised on, someone always had a souffle in the oven and an apron around her wrist-sized waist. And she was usually blonde. "If I've only one life to live, let me live it as a blonde!" was the profoundest bit of philosophy I absorbed (kudos to Clairol), which edged out even, "Ask not what your country can do for you, but what you can do for your country" and "take all that you have and give it to the poor"—contenders, but not finishers, it would turn out. Donna Reed, Barbara Eden, and Elizabeth Montgomery would cost me a fortune in highlights.

It wasn't until retirement collided with a pandemic that I finally put away childish things, married myself to the gray revolution, and let my roots grow out. But the romance of a souffle persisted. So finally, in a Thanksgiving scaled down to suit the times, I sent Jeff Bezos a little cash to help him put his kids through college and let him drop off a proper souffle dish at my door—free delivery. Then I googled *souffle*.

Not much goes into a souffle, it turns out. Some eggs, some wheat, a lot of wind. And maybe it was beginner's luck or being just the right distance from the winter solstice or the stubborn *esprit* of the hens who laid its eggs, but my first souffle was—there is no other word for it—brilliant. The prime-time ladies had always made such a fuss about creeping around softly as their souffles baked, panicking when their phones rang and flinching like they'd been slapped when their lumbering husbands, dumb as dinosaurs, let the door slam when they came home from work.

My souffle baked to the soundtrack of *The Marvelous Mrs. Maisel*, while I danced around the kitchen in Birkenstocks, an apron that pinched a flannel shirt to my waist-sized waist, and oven mitts to, thematically on the money, "I Enjoy Being a Girl." And through all that stomp and racket, my egg whites rose like the Himalayas; when I pulled it from the oven, that souffle would have made a sherpa shrink. I served it at Thanksgiving dinner—a modest spread for four: Anna, our friend Mark, Larry, and me. When I scooped great clouds of it onto our plates, it chummed right up to Anna's salmon chowder and my leafy salad and Mark's homemade loaves. Larry asked for seconds, as he was sharing with Scout, who homesteaded her usual plot under the table.

So my first souffle not only nourished us, but temporarily lit up the dual-darknesses of early winter and pandemic. Scooping the last of it into Tupperware, I felt a little tug of that old Thanksgiving gratitude stir for those blonde beacons of my youth.

A few weeks later, Anna and I went looking for a different kind of light. There had been a lot of Internet buzz about a "Christmas Star," about how you could lay eyes on a lantern very like the one that brought the Magi to the baby Jesus if, on the off chance, any of that lovely story really occurred. Regardless of the fact to fiction ratio of the Nativity, there was to be something showy hanging in the southwestern sky, outshining everything else. "It's a conjunction," Shannon Schmoll, who is the director of Abrams Planetarium at Michigan State University, explained online to throngs inflated by more folks than were reliably tuned in to astronomy. A conjunction, she went on, occurs when one planet passes by another as they orbit the sun. On December 21st of 2020—a year that arguably owed us a gesture—poetically the date of the solstice, Saturn and Jupiter would draw close enough to snuggle, galactically speaking, in the night sky, and might even appear as one bright light, visible to the naked earthling eye.

The Michigan sky on the solstice was, per usual, obscured by clouds; I scowled at it from our driveway. But by the next night—and NASA was promising the spectacle would last for a couple of weeks—the clouds had drifted apart and there were whole swaths where you could see straight into the solar system. So an hour after sunset, Anna and I put on our identical, to-the-ankle, puffy coats (purchased a year earlier because when would be ever wear them together?), double-wrapped ourselves in hats and scarves, and headed down a dark street bedazzled with holiday lights.

"Be grateful it's dark," I said. "We look like a pair of sister-wives. I'm the old, bossy one nobody loves, but your lot is way worse—you have to sleep with the Prophet."

"I'm in my thirties," Anna reminded me. ("When did *that* happen?" I thought.) "I'm way too old for the Prophet." I love the way she hops on board with my inventions.

"True—we're neither of us fourteen anymore."

We were headed for the parking lot of a nearby middle school, the idea being to get clear the trees blocking our view, but found, when we got there, that its blazing lights eclipsed the more delicate glimmers beyond, so we moved into the soccer field and kept walking until we were dead center in its swaddling dark. And there, hanging in the southwest sky, just as promised, high over the takeout-only Applebee's and takeout-only Cracker Barrel and business-as-usual Shell station, accompanied by the thrumming carol of the expressway, was the Christmas Star. It wasn't precisely the same conjunction of planets that occurred in 2 B. C. E. (That Jesus was actually born some years "Before Christ" is one of the quirks of Christianity.) That interstellar marvel, which got itself immortalized in scripture, astronomers tell us, involved a flirtation of Jupiter with Venus, in addition to which, during the same year, Jupiter twice passed by Regulus. Both planet and star, Schmoll posted, "were associated with kings and might have had special meaning for the Magi."

Stories evolve, and myths can be fictions or actual histories that grow to mythic proportions because they embed our lives in a larger narrative that *means* something. In other words, a myth can be both a floor wax *and* a dessert topping. Maybe "three kings"—arguably Zoroastrian priests, possibly astrologers, eventually rendered wise—did take off by foot or camel or caravan toward a bright light in the sky. The world, thank God, has no shortage of mystics, eccentrics, and explorers. Maybe they were three retired guys with time on their hands, having handed over their kingdoms or star charts or apothecaries to their sons—ready for the next adventure, possibly a caper, at least something less redundant than golf. And maybe they stopped by a stable crowded with animals and shepherds and God knows who else.

"There is a *bagpiper* in your Nativity scene," I called to my friend Connie last year when, in the blessedness of days before the coronavirus tore away from some poor creature's exhalations and bore down on the rest of us, she was hosting our book group. I had wandered away from the others with a glass of wine, the better to browse her mantle, which was singing all of December's songs. Tucked amid the candles and trims, a small creche was filled with the usual characters, but wait a minute: who was *that?*

"*What?*" she called back from the kitchen.

"Right there, behind the donkey, a bagpiper."

"Nooo!"

"Yesss!" She came into the room and squinted inside.

"I had no idea!" Had he been able to see, the little bagpiper would have registered two big cat-eyes, peering in at his tiny, mouse-like self. Connie reached in a paw and plucked him out, which took a bit of pulling; he was taped to the floor. "Jim got this Nativity scene at a garage sale."

"This year?"

"Ten, a dozen, fifteen years ago."

"And you never…"

"Never."

The next day, after doing a bit of research, Connie texted me that bagpipers in creches are actually pretty common. She was running defense for her little interloper, who was back in his corner. Pipers, she'd learned, are no strangers to Italian creches, where shepherds traditionally played some Apennine version of the pipes to entertain passersby wherever Nativity scenes were constructed.

I asked about *this* year's little stable and its residents recently when she and I were social-distance-walking together on separate sides of the street. "So did you retire the bagpiper?"

"Absolutely not!" she said. "In fact, he's in the front now, right out in the light." In a "be not forgetful to entertain strangers" sort of way, she had promoted him to kneeling Joseph's wingman.

This Christmas, in our iteration of a story repeating around the world, most of our family stayed away, locked down in their separate homes and, in the strange quiet, I retired our more excessive holiday traditions and made no plans to resurrect them. Anna and I prepared fewer dishes but what we made was special and good—cheese fondue on Christmas Eve, which she and Mark and Larry and I scooped up on crusty bread as we stood around the kitchen island, and a seafood risotto—for which we sat down at the kitchen table—on Christmas day. Waiting to be stirred into the rice, threads of saffron, exotic in a Pyrex measuring cup, turned the white wine in which they floated a smoldering orange. But the sanest change occurred when I put a cap on gifts and, to all our relief, we spent less money.

George, who finally did get home late on Big Truck Day, opened the door when I walked over to drop off a tardy holiday basket, but by the time he'd returned, the First Big Truck and the Six Other Big Trucks that had joined it had rumbled off and he had no clue as to what had gone down. All that remained of the spectacle, which drew in so many players, was a patch in the road the size of a pup tent saying something happened here, which was still more than enough for us to wonder about. George and I studied it and shrugged. For his part, Larry, whose nature is tragically unintrusive—we did not bring identical gifts to the marriage—had returned with precisely nada. "It's a mystery," he concluded, hanging up his coat, then retired with Scout to the couch to read.

Pavlova

Here are some things you can do while walking around with an enlarged spleen as you wait for the results of your MRI during a pandemic. You can shiver in the wind while standing in line outside a filled-to-capacity supermarket on New Year's Eve Day and think about how nice a face mask is, after all; you can tramp through the woods and guess at the names of leafless trees based on striations of bark; if you're very desperate, you can clean out the cupboard under the sink. You can read about rising COVID cases. You can make a pavlova.

A pavlova, as anyone who watches *The Great British Baking Show* religiously while slogging along on the treadmill will tell you, is a cumulus cloud, a fresh drift of snow, a light, white angel you can dismember and eat and never regret a thing. It only wants a bit of your time. Our daughter Anna and I made one on New Year's morning—our first on the 1st day of a whole new year.

The holidays were hard to gauge in the year of our Lord 2020. What was too little, what too much in times of such excess and restraint? Christmas morning saw just over 100,000 *new* cases of Covid: how full should a stocking be for that? (I asked around; answers varied.) Destruction in American cities had followed the unremitting destruction of Black lives. And in a deplorable effort to overturn democracy itself, the nearly spent Trump cartel was refusing to budge despite those pesky, sizable margins by which it was defeated in both popular and electoral votes. Meanwhile, Anna and I had barely put away the German Shepherd cookie cutters we'd used to tailor our holiday to the times—stacks of new First Dogs Champ and Major Biden cookies still filled a deep casserole dish on the kitchen counter—when we turned our minds to meringue. Like most people we knew, we had sheltered at home for the holidays and January 1st was the last of them. There was a lightness in turning toward the new year. Whipping up egg whites felt just right.

The previous year, pre-pandemic and (more personally) pre-uppity-spleen, I'd thrown a big, splashy Christmas Eve party following a big, ashy chimney fire which had brought firemen scrambling over our holiday lights to get to the roof. While appreciating the *A Child's Christmas in Wales* tone the smoke and commotion contributed to the season, after feeding our heroes a platter of prosaic frosted bells and stars and trees, after getting the dogs and documents and family photos back inside the house and closing the windows and doors, Larry and I sat on the couch and looked at the cold, dark maw where so many fires had been. The word *condemned* is hard to hear. A few days later, for our Christmas Eve fete, artist Anna rigged up a centerpiece of twinkling lights inside the empty grate, eye-catching but cold. No one drew up a chair to the hearth and most people crowded the kitchen—but then, they always do.

Looking back from the early days of lockdown in March, I would wonder if that fire, an inconvenience nipped before it became a disaster, had carried an omen and wondered if everyone who looked back would find a sign pointing, like the bony finger of the Ghost of Christmas Future, to dark days ahead. And I concluded they almost certainly would, for we are a species determined to wrest from chaos a meaningful narrative with all the bells and whistles, foreshadowing included.

Despite the joy and relief that came with the imminence of a new president, I spent the very early hours of 2021 quietly weeping about losses in the narrow genre of Tonys. I'd been rereading Tony Hoagland's poems, which are wry and sad and funny and loving, with the awareness that he was two years gone, swiped from the living world by pancreatic cancer, that bastard, and his name put me in mind Toni Morrison, who we lost the previous summer. A world without the weight and eloquence of her witness seemed bereft of light and heat, as desolate as our empty fireplace. And because I am superstitious and know that disasters come in threes, I was wondering who the next indispensable Tony to fall would be. It was a private indulgence, that pooling grief for people I had admired, taken instruction from, but hadn't personally known. How many Tonys and their like the world would shed in the following months, how many howling families they would leave behind, God maybe knew. On the first day of 2021, when the global COVID death count was creeping toward 2 million, Anna and I made a pavlova.

Here is how you make one. There isn't much you need: egg whites (which will apparently get on board with your vision sooner if they are at room temperature), sugar (superfine, if your grocer's ravaged shelves can still manage it—ours could not), vanilla extract, corn starch, and cream of tartar which, it turns out, is meant for something other than gathering dust at the back of your spice cabinet. (And regarding that cream of tartar, pavlova enthusiasts far and wide maintain it isn't *necessary* to use, but among their numbers are a few who concede it's *helpful,* an encouraging element, a cheerleader for egg whites struggling to rise and so, I would argue, why be a hero—and maybe a fallen one—if you don't have to?)

Once you've assembled the above, it's all about beating. I used my little Sunbeam hand-mixer, "my Beamer," I think of it whenever I take it out for a spin, as Anna read the instructions which, for five to ten redundant minutes, are simply, "While beating, add…" When your egg whites reach their ideal form in the stiff, glossy peaks for which they are celebrated, philosophy turns to art, so I handed the adventure over to Anna who has a BFA. (An artist in the house is on absolutely no one's list of ingredients for a successful pavlova, but I had one so why not?) Using my old chewed up plastic spatula, Anna spooned the egg whites onto parchment paper covering a cookie sheet, sculpted them into a full moon with a shallow crater, teased up a few pretty peaks around the crater's periphery, and slipped it in the oven, where it was to bake at 200' for 90 minutes. Then, while we waited for the big reveal, she worked at her loom and I arranged grass and twig birds' nests into a "January tableau" on the library table and googled the proper punctuation for *bird nest, bird's nest, birds' nest*—which turned out to be a much more complicated thing than making a pavlova.

A pavlova takes a while to cool because it prefers to do so in the oven it was baked in; it likes a slow transition, a little coffee-date, if you will, before jumping into dinner and a movie. When the oven finally registered room temperature, we removed it and set it on the counter for inspection. Shiny as a seashell, its exterior was a delicate crust we could tap with our fingers and all its little peaks pointed to heaven. A few hours later, its crater filled with whipped cream and fresh raspberries, we served it up in big wedges to Larry and our friend Mark and dug in ourselves. And that pavlova *performed*—with just the right resistance, just the right give, just the right sweetness. She (there's no resisting the personification) was an easy diva, and she was spectacular.

The results of my MRI, confirming a CT scan's pronouncement of *stupid, giant spleen*—not the official terminology—arrived in my inbox a few days after we'd devoured the last of the pavlova, via the hospital portal. I scheduled a doctor appointment for a few weeks down the road where more, perhaps, would be revealed. As cream of tartar isn't absolutely required to exalt a bowl of egg whites, a spleen isn't necessary to the rising and exuberance and glory of a human life. But, like cream of tartar, it helps.

I was not the only one, by a long shot, who developed a superstitious contempt for 2020 which, there was no denying it, put on a persuasive show. Break a window, break the bank, break your quintessential back, and someone within earshot was bound to mumble, "2020"—an explanation for every grim thing in four, fatalistic syllables. The pugnacious year—grammatically a thing, a noun—had even bludgeoned its way into the prancing chorus line of the world's verbs. "I got 2020-ed" had become a global refrain.

On December 31st, the day before Anna and I built our magnificent pavlova, I felt wary about going for a walk on the slippery-in-places roads outside. It was a classic fear of the narrative. Because the world loves irony better than anything ("Then, at the last minute…") and manufactures it in spades (move over Voltaire, give it up Sophocles, get in line Twain and Parker and Swift), I could feel 2020 lying in wait with one last shot. If I summoned the hubris to walk outdoors, I just knew I'd fall down on the ice. So I put in my time on the treadmill with the British bakers, who *will* put prunes in their puddings, then I timidly ventured out to buy groceries (tiptoeing from parking lot to store, easy does it!) which I delivered to a sick friend (car door to front door, careful, careful), then drove home and sheltered inside, with an eye out for throw rugs and stairs.

The new year was a dark horse during its first few days; no one yet knew what 2021 would bring, but it did get busy right out of the gate. Every scientist worth her weight in carbon warned that the post-holiday COVID count would rise, which it did, and we even had ourselves a coup d'état at the Capitol, as some of us—not the police (see *irony* above)—had expected, on day six of the wildly welcomed whole new year. Everyone I knew was either still tense or tense all over again. But if spring and all its new green life was still a long way off, the news was fragrant with fresh vaccines. So while I allowed the heavy world might never meet pavlova heights, the weight of this early hour was leavening, light.

Vaccination

"Could you open these bandages?" Doug (we all had nametags) asked, pulling on latex gloves and grabbing a syringe. He pointed to a little plastic basket on his rolling cart which was full of still-wrapped, nickel-sized discs, just big enough to cover a needle puncture. A dozen of their unwrapped cousins adhered by a sticky bit of their backs to the basket's rim, easy to pluck. "I'm sorry, what?" I asked, then raced off to greet the next six vehicles which were streaming into our lane.

"Hi!" I chimed, beaming into the window of the first car—I was irrepressible in my bit part, backing up the actual medical people who were doing the important work. "Who's being vaccinated today?"

"We all are," the driver replied, pointing to herself, the man next to her, and the woman behind her own seat.

"Wonderful! And is this the first or second vaccine for each of you?"

"This is our first."

"Great!" I scrawled three number 1s on their windshield with my magic window-marker, remembering to circle each little 1 as the campus police had instructed those of us entrusted with pens to do, then called, "Happy Vaccination Day!" to them before darting off to the next car. Strapping on our *DayGlo* vests at the volunteer check-in table, we'd been told we would be vaccinating 1,600 people against COVID-19 that day—there would be no pause in the five-hour shift that had just begun—which I'd found completely undaunting because, though I was getting ricketier by the minute, I was buzzing on whatever peppy chemicals teamwork, choreography, and good shoes pump out.

A few weeks earlier, I'd been vaccinated at this same drive-through clinic on the MSU campus, where I'd wept over my steering wheel with gratitude for the people making me safe—a hodgepodge of county health workers, fatigue-clad men and women of the National Guard, and volunteers. Now I was on the other side, percolating with common cause, thinking this must be what growing a victory garden had felt like—well, maybe growing a cabbage in a victory garden, half a cabbage, a cabbage leaf. I wasn't saving lives myself; I was merely Lane Four's lowly scribe—a tad euphoric with a mild-to-mad gleam.

The protocol at MSU's Pavilion, a vast, lidded structure that sees a lot of agricultural demonstrations and home-remodeling orgies ($50,000 *outdoor* kitchens in wintry Michigan are a thing), and an annual "Lama-Fest," which had been commandeered by the county to dispense its COVID vaccines, was this: upon entering, cars that had lined up outside were funneled into one of seven lanes. Each lane held about a dozen cars. Each *vaccinee* interacted with (in order) the recorder (in my lane, me), the registrar, the vaccinator, the recorder again (yippee!)—who jotted the time of vaccination next to the little 1 or 2 on the windshield, and the patient-observer, who checked for side effects during the 15-minute, post-vaccination wait. Generally cars were admitted and released in groups of six, so there were always people to attend to who were arriving, waiting, or leaving.

"I just checked in a guy in a Mini-Cooper," I informed Doug when I dashed back to the cart for one of the cheap, county pens people were struggling to fill out their forms with. "It was like writing on a Barbie car." One of Barbie's vehicles, anyway. In the several decades since I was eight, Barbie (I later learned) had acquired a plane, a helicopter, a camper, a boat, an SUV, a tractor, a food truck, a snowmobile, a scooter, and a dune buggy. Additionally, prescient Barbie had picked up a Mobile Care Clinic—in case she was ever called to respond to some modern plague, apparently—an item which could only have sold out during the previous year. And naturally she'd held on to her signature pink convertible. She's not stupid, Barbie.

"My circles look like dinner plates on that tiny Cooper-windshield." I added, rummaging for a pen.

"If you could just unwrap some bandages," Doug, who seemed to be very nice, if a little single-minded, answered. During our day together, I would learn that he was a retired dentist, which explained, I reasoned, why he was used to having his world arranged on a tray and handed to him. Briefly imagining him in a tidy office, reaching for a proffered and sterilized metal pick, I glimpsed a pretty, prelapsarian element in dentistry—at least on the doctor's side of the drill. Nurses, who did the bulk of the vaccinating, are old hands in a fallen world; used to being up to their necks in it, they never asked for a thing. But I was already sprinting away to drop off the pen and greet the rest of the drivers who had pulled into our lane.

Wherever it is we think we're going, we all show up with our peculiar expectations. This isn't so noticeable when they're met, which feels like business as usual. But let the world throw us a curve—whether it's a jackpot or a shakedown—and we sit right up and look around. Evolution, I read somewhere, has primed our minds to amplify the jar of that missing, last step—right after we stumble. Poor Doug must have felt flummoxed among his confetti of Band-Aids, I thought, and probably abandoned until he resigned himself, if he ever did, to scrambling like the rest of the world.

Because my neurons had taken up the bad habit of waking me at four A.M. over the previous year, I'd had a lot of predawn hours to churn out my own expectations which the times had chiseled to something pushing dire. Not *avalanche*-dire, as they were during the harrowing years of the previous presidency, more like *glacier-melting* dire, but picking up speed.

That spring, a poet I admired published a *New and Collected* volume of poems. I am no fan of "new and collected" publications, which always sound like someone is sneaking one by on the world and on me—a little new work propped up on stuff I already have on my shelves, which I am expected to pay for and lodge all over again. Were *I* ever invited to publish a "new and collected" anything, my mind might change on this matter, like coming into money can change people's ideas about gentrification and marital fidelity and their carbon footprint. I had, however, collated in my restless mind, a lively "new and collected" list of anxieties, which were mouthier and more strident than you really like your ruminations to be.

The merely *collected* fears I'd been schlepping around forever were mostly prosaic: fear of the dark, fear of pain, fear that my kids would be injured or worse. Perhaps more idiosyncratic were fear of being stranded on a high ledge—specifically on Angels Landing in Zion National Park—a terror I acquired by looking not down but *up,* and fear of getting stuck in the Chunnel, 250 feet below the seabed, which is itself some terrifying number of feet below the water's surface where all that delicious Anglo-French air and space live, and fear of being buried alive in Mammoth Cave. The obvious measures I could take that would 100% prevent those horrors from happening helped slightly less than you'd think.

The *new* material had to do with the rogue antics of aging lying in wait for Larry and me. I saw in the shadows on my bedroom ceiling—the work of streetlights and maple limbs—a dark parade of trips on the stairs, broken hips, and worst of all, dementia. I imagined our house collapsing around us, the spigot of our savings trickling dry, the Republican Party finally putting that bullet in Social Security and calling it Fiscal Freedom or Financial Freedom or Free To Be You (not mentioned, "and destitute")—their sophistry wrapped up in its usual *freedom* burrito. Finally, I saw myself alone and wondering if I fed the cat, wondering if I *had* a cat. My lovely mother languished in dementia, dependent on the gods to free her at their leisure. They played a lot of golf before they did. I didn't want to wait, down the road, for the gods.

All of that fretting made me keen to grab the wheel of the runaway bus we were banging around in. As a result, every time I got bad news from a bone scan or Larry forgot to put in his hearing aids and answered me with an amiable non sequitur ("Did you pick up the wine?" "I had a pretty good time!"), I discarded something, cleaned something, bought something new. Or hired someone to shore up our shaky enterprise—which was how Pauline very nearly came into our lives. As it turned out, she was merely a drive-by, and she kept on going down the road.

Pauline briefly flickered into our world as a result of my asking a neighbor to recommend a painter. Despite the actual plywood planks we had placed under the cushions of our ancient couches, a spring had pushed through and grazed my hand when I was groping for a breakaway *M&M*. While ransacking our travel account allowed me to nab a couple of new sofas (to avoid choosing chairs, I always ordered them in pairs, like glasses of Chardonnay on long flights), that purchase led, as it only could, to my total and vehement contempt for the color of our family room walls. Introducing any new element to a home is tipping one dangerous domino; suddenly the fixtures you've been affectionately dwelling with become shabby, impossible to live with—what were you thinking all those years—and the need for myriad other updates becomes urgent. Add this to the alarm that you may be losing steam, that the very vessel of your*self* may soon be foundering—and that it might in the too near future *show*—and there goes that airfare to Iceland. There are people who have cultivated the wisdom to sidestep this pitfall, but I am not of their tribe. I belong to the demented crew of the SS Shipshape. So, a painter.

Pauline showed up on our front porch, a few days after I called her— slim, graying, and as agile-looking as a cat. Quiet as a cat too, and almost purring as she prowled around our room, running her hands over the walls. She wasn't wearing a mask in this, the second spring of pandemic, but Larry and I were weeks past our second vaccinations, so I let it go for a few minutes. Then curiosity—no, irritation—moved me to ask, "Have you been vaccinated?" Scratching at a nail hole in the drywall, she calmly allowed that no, she hadn't been, then gently went on to explain.

"I don't live in four dimensions anymore," she said dreamily. "I live entirely in the fifth dimension now."

I let that sit for a minute. It was no deal-breaker; I really hate painting and didn't want to do the job myself—this was no time to cultivate a prejudice against dimensions.

"Really?" I finally replied, forcing my voice to sound interested rather than judgy. "This will definitely take two coats," she observed, standing back to appraise the turquoise wall surrounding the fireplace. Then she made an offhand (or not) remark about "the Illuminati"—I don't recall if she feared or revered our counted herself among them—or if they, too, by rights of mysticism and long mythology, inhabited another dimension, or were resigned to the narrow four most of us squeezed into. I was, in fact, too busy composing hilarious, snarky remarks in my head, and deciding who to text them to when she left, to follow anything else she said closely, except for her, "Call me once you buy the paint," and then she was gone. In the end, I only got one text—not that funny—out before shame overcame me. I knew nothing of Pauline's story. I mean, how battered did a person have to be by life in space-time as most of us knew it to have to pack up and move to another dimension?

I let a week go by before calling Pauline to tell her that I had purchased the paint, the kind she preferred that allegedly (meaning never) goes on in one coat. "Oh, honey," she sighed, clearly trying to spare my feelings. "Have you been vaccinated?"

"Of course!" I heard the robustness in my reply, the zeal, even.

"Honey, I am *so* sorry, but I've been doing *a lot* of reading, and I just can't risk being around vaccinated people. It isn't *safe*." There was a longish pause as I ransacked my brain for a reply to *that*; then she freed us both. "You take *care* of yourself."

"You take care, too, Pauline," I stammered. Then I went to the basement and foraged for the old rollers and brushes we'd stashed under the stairs.

There had been a lot of talk about things getting back to normal that spring, as more people were vaccinated, an expectation—heightened by politicians and the media—of returning to the old life we knew *Before COVID*—the fondly remembered new BC. But I wondered if we could really go back—no one ever had, and I suspected no one ever would. Those Great Depression survivors balling up bits of string and tin foil came to mind. The soldiers of every war there ever was came to mind. The survivors of Hiroshima, of heartbreak, of high school came to mind—no one passed a day in this world, or an hour, or a minute, without being altered by it. Dimensions one through four left dents on our tender flesh and on our tenderer minds, and there was no vaccination for that.

Working at the Pavilion one afternoon sans Doug, who volunteered, I learned, several days a week, I was admiring the panache of the traffic-director performing at the end of my lane and I noticed other people pausing to watch him too. You couldn't not. He had *moves*. The other traffic guys pawed their glowing batons like construction workers, made heavy, rote gestures that got the job done but never suggested art. Our man ascended. He was Michael Jackson in a Jedi suit. He sky-walked his lightsaber. He could have been waving in Concordes at JFK.

"You should be in air traffic control!" I called, walking down to share his stage. But he was already busy being a fulltime physicist, it turned out. Like Doug, he had been volunteering at the vaccine clinic from the day it had opened several months earlier. And like so many other MSU instructors, who'd flocked to staff the site in return for receiving the world's first, priceless Pfizer vaccine, he had donned his vest and accepted his baton. When others had put in their time and drifted away, there he still was.

"In the beginning, it seemed like it was all PhDs in here," he said. "Everyone you talked to had a doctorate in something." I imagined all that gratuitous knowledge of vectors and cosines and Elizabethan sonnets rising and roiling in the rafters of the Pavilion and pictured Van Gogh's *Starry Night*. But mostly I thought, here was a man who knew his dimensions, who understood the edges of space and time and how they fit (or didn't) together. I almost led with Pauline, but at the last minute swapped her out for a question of my own. Pushing boundaries, I reached for his hand in that bluff way we'd once used to greet people, before COVID killed off the handshake. It was probably muscle memory that made him reach back and meet my grip.

"Why don't we merge?" I asked.

"What?"

"Our hands are plenty roomy, right? Just atoms and lots of empty space. What keeps them separate?" He didn't pause.

"The electrostatic field," he said automatically, like he was ordering soup in a campus lunchroom—chicken noodle, what else? "The atoms repel each other," he added, which was the last thing he said because he'd resumed his dance, had locked eyes with a new driver and was moonwalking over the concrete floor. *Aha!* I thought—a force field—I'd heard of *those*—driving the action in hidden ways beyond what we could see or hear. How fascinating, our difficult world. How full of turns and mystery.

Had Pauline stuck around, I would have happily carried *The Tale of The Electrostatic Field* back to her as she was, after all, a disciple of hidden and ultimate things. But, I had to consider, maybe she already knew her force fields; maybe it was in one of them that the fifth dimension resided: in the closed palms of our open hands.

I saw Doug working his lane across the Pavilion a couple more times, but we were never again assigned to the same team—and I regretted having dismissed his life as easy and neat; no life was ever that and appalling things happened to us all, dentists included. He and I were of an age and still both standing, our feet conventionally planted in dimensions one through four—but that could change on the blithe world's dime and you never knew who would have to jump to the fifth. I hoped Pauline was the greeter there, for everyone who made the leap.

Soon enough, our walls were a new color and ready to receive the couches I bought which, like so many things in pandemic space-time, had been placed on back-order. In an article called, "Why the World Has Run Short of Everything," *The New York Times* pointed a finger at Toyota, for inventing what they called *Just in Time* manufacturing—a sort of print-on-demand system for, in their case, cars. Apparently this method caught on and, with the sudden demands of vaccinated people ready to restart their lives, lots of companies' inventories ran from slim to nothing. And, of course, there was human error—that constant element that defies all trends. "I just know my refrigerator is on that damn boat," my sister complained, after a container ship the length of four soccer fields managed to wedge itself across the Suez Canal, preventing at least a hundred other *very big boats* full of *all new stuff* from getting through. Throw in the COVID wrench, which closed factories and quarantined workers, and it was no wonder we were all living out of coolers and watching TV from kitchen chairs.

But Larry and I were unperturbed by delays—Larry because he was satisfied to sit with the ghosts of sofas past. And I was content to have tipped the first domino down a path I meant to take, figuring a handful of things would probably fall in place largely as I intended them to, and that soon enough we'd have sturdy seats again in the tilt-a-whirl world. It was a faith in probability, in the physics of how things usually go, enough to almost hang a hat on and buy a priceless bit of sleep.

Story

Here is a story.

Eons ago, when I was in college at Michigan State University, I began every new term in the Pit. In this, I was the farthest thing from alone. From the packed and steamy looks of it, the Pit was the only place in town. When it was up and running, businesses may as well have shuttered their doors—except for the bars. The Pit, an arm of the ancient world—fast on the heels of fire and alphabets—was a colosseum of Drops and Adds.

There is much I have forgotten about the Pit. For instance, there must have been some criteria for entry (though never departure), something along the lines of: "Juniors Who Say *Pajamas*: 12:37" and "Sophomores Who Say *Pajahmas*: 3:09," but the place always felt like everyone was there at once. I recall the line to get into the arena, how it snaked along the corridors of the Intramural Sports building, wound its way up and down stairwells, passed by the pool. We moved without agency—a word that was still decades from enjoying its moment—like cattle in a shute, toward doom or deliverance.

Inside, over a sea of varnished wood planks, a fleet of chipped folding tables, flagged by course numbers—ENG 370, PSY 280, TRIG 321—held sway. Held, in fact, the line between those employees the university had deputized to be gatekeepers of our futures, the dispensers and withholders of limited class seats, and us, the hordes of desperate undergrads who had changed majors, found courage, lost courage, vowed to rise early, vowed to sleep late or had, for countless other reasons, screwed up our registrations.

The most memorable thing about the Pit, besides the eternal shifting of your weight in the endless queues at individual tables, antenna up for the miracle of someone in front of you dropping the course you needed, was that there was absolutely no guarantee of coming away a winner. Hours logged there, individual genius, dire circumstances—none of it made a lick of difference to your outcome. The whole thing ran on antique punch cards—when the deputies had dispensed the last of them, a class was full and the wait for someone to return one began—and on the inscrutable will of God or that flap of a butterfly's wing, depending on your school of thought.

It was exquisitely grim and exquisitely joyful precisely because we were all in it together. Afterward, sitting around pitchers of beer downtown, everyone shared a more barbarous *Tale from the Pit* than the person before, in a perversely gleeful game of one-upmanship.

Drops and adds are different today; all you need is a laptop and a latte and the whole thing can be done in a bathing suit while you simultaneously shop for shoes. These improvements can be defended persuasively, if they have to be defended at all, and even I, with my happy twisted memories, would never send anyone back to the Pit. What sane person clamors for the good old days before Novocain? Who covets the downtime of an iron lung? Still, I found myself recently wondering, what happens on campuses these days that whips up the same sweet neurochemical froth that comes from all being *in it* together?

Here is another story. My friend Beckie, who grew up among the Finger Lakes of New York, told this one when, into our third week of temps that flirted with both sides of zero degrees, I was grousing about winter.

"We had tons of snow when I was young," she said, "four and five feet were normal. It was common for houses to have second-story doors with stairs so people could get out. After one really bad blizzard, when helicopters were lowering rescuers onto people's roofs, one of those dangling men tapped and tapped at the attic window of a buried house and a woman finally appeared and yelled through the glass, "We can't help you!"

Here is a third story, really two stories, one tucked inside the other like a pair of nesting dolls, which happened near the end of my mother's life.

Because my smart, curious, generous mother was stripped to dependency by Alzheimer's, she lived with us part-time during the last disoriented years of her life where sequences made no sense at all, where cause and effect done flew the coop. But often even in chaos, stories will out.

One afternoon, I walked into our family room to find my mom standing in front of the television with a concerned look on her face. On TV, a young woman was brushing her teeth. In the mirror over her sink, a galaxy of little stars sparkled, showing us how the light glanced off her blinding incisors, promising that our smiles too would become little suns if we switched to whatever toothpaste was being hawked. "Where is that girl's husband?" my mom asked.

A few minutes later another commercial filled the screen. This time a burly man in a plaid shirt was eating soup, spooning it in over his beard and nodding happily as he filled up on chunks of beef, showing us what a manly thing soup was, in case anyone had any doubt about that. "There he is!" my mother beamed, relieved at how things had turned out. The toothpaste lady was not alone; her husband was in the other room, eating his can of lunch. Who doesn't love a happy ending?

The first story—"The Pit"—is a nostalgic rendering of the "good old days" of moderate, privileged, middle-class struggle. It overlooks the glaring fact that struggle is not evenly experienced and the very notion of "good old days," is anathema to many people's histories. The second story—"The Rescue"—is about individual gumption and self-reliance, one of those true accounts that fuels the great American myth of bootstrapping, which, however entertaining, is a fiction every time. No one goes it alone, and if you've used a road or a bridge or any flavor phone, you're as beholden to the commune as the rest of us. And the third story—"The Happy Ending"—is about threshing meaning from randomness, about coaxing a narrative fire from a pile of broken sticks strewn by strong winds. It omits the fact that many times no fire ignites at all. But stories are always exclusive; like sculptures, they comprise what remains when the clotted earth is carved away, or like songs, they persist when the world's clashing notes are peeled off. And interpretations change. We are story-builders, all of us, and we work within the confines of what we see and know.

In his travel narrative, *The Log from the Sea of Cortez*, the great American story-sculptor John Steinbeck talks about the human ability to hope that drives so many, maybe most, stories, which he calls "a shock-absorber" that balances our "projection of a future" with the memories of a blasted past and assures us that better roads lie ahead, rather than more of the miserable same. Hope, he argues, evolved by necessity; without it our ancestors would have all jumped into volcanoes ice ages ago. And from hope, he says, "we build our iron teleologies and twist the tide pools and the stars into the pattern." *In The Beginning…*

The tide pools, of course, don't need our narratives; their denizens are fixtures in their own story, with all the drama and conflict and character development a mollusk can stand built right in. But Steinbeck is right. Since the seminal day we noticed our nakedness and were shunted out of Eden, self-consciousness being incompatible with innocence, and paradise henceforth out of reach, we've been rigging up stories to explain the pain and confoundedness and wonder of it all. And we drag everybody in.

By any thinking person's estimate, our actual 3.5-billion-year-old story is not headed for a happy ending—not for humans or starfish or the beautiful Sally lightfoot crabs Steinbeck tried and failed to surprise. Billionaire global overlords and their apparatchiks aside, I think lots of us will concede that we are approaching the conclusion of what's turning out to be a tragedy. And guiltily, bemusedly, anxiously, we wonder who, if anyone, can write the twist that will turn the plot around. There's long been a buzz among editors, who've been scribbling for decades, "Don't shit where you eat." I drag my recyclables to the curb, overcome with the feeling of being small, smaller than I've ever felt before. From the dread of staring ahead, I turn back and look behind, and wonder about the narrative arc that landed us where we are. Did the engine of evolution, our author writ large, leave any wiggle room in our decisions at all?

It's not a useful question to ask and my smart, resolute, hopeful friends don't like to hear it. It's deterministic and defeatist and in challenging the comfortable concept of free will itself, it's better suited to the musings of undergrads drinking beer after drops and adds. You ought to move on.

Still, I schlepp it around with me, this question of choice, like I carry fear of the dark and the illogical sense that what I think (not do) might alter events in the world. Sometimes I lug it to the beach to brood, where Lake Michigan gulls rather than the Mexican cormorants Steinbeck encountered, glide through a person's musings. Empty beaches are excellent places for brooding and if occasionally accessing one requires stepping past a "No Trespassing" sign, I fight off whatever qualms would slow me down, ownership being one of the most implausible fictions we write, however useful some of us may find it. I found a fine puddingstone that way one day, in front of an under-construction lake-mansion and, farther down the beach, the skull of a trespassing small animal, washed up by the lake and polished clean. Both of them had backstories, the conglomerate rock's a tale of minerals and glaciers and tides, the skull's a yarn of thirst, perhaps, and flight and undertow. I sat with them in the sand and thought about the narratives that converged in that place. The puddingstone had been making its way to that beach for about 50 million years, give or take. The skull, maybe half a dozen. Me, I was in my forties then. But we'd all been parts of other things before we met up and we all could trace our family tree back to that single Bang.

Beckie, who earned a degree in biology at Cornell before she swapped the Finger Lakes for Michigan's Great Lakes, argues that Homo sapiens has removed itself from the processes of evolution, that our big, reasoning lobes have given natural selection the slip. And in all that subsequent, Wordsworthian getting and spending and laying waste, we have sealed our doom. She may be right. "In the year 2525," I think. Like the misguided men in mustaches you occasionally see, I can't always shake off the seventies.

The stories we tell are rife with numbers. Three Magi. Twenty-two Catches. One Hundred Years of Solitude. And numbers affirm multiplicity.

But, as the truly great story-tellers—our Darwins and Gandhis and

Greta Thunbergs—insist, with their long, clear vision and oversized courage, there really is only one story. The ending depends on whether or not we figure that out.

Brian Doyle, who was an unabashedly *hopeful* writer as well as an avid listener, was enamored of stories. Recalling his conversation with a young girl who was, despite her mere handful of years, a passionate raconteur, committed to the arc of a plot, deeply invested in character and the play of cause and effect, he recounts the story she told him about her grandfather and his fishing boat. "Her grandfather still owned the boat, she said, though he was too old to go fishing. He would go sit in the boat sometimes when it was at the dock, though. It took him a long time to get in and out of the boat but he wouldn't let anyone help him...because he was a Mule-Headed Man." She must have heard her parents grumble, "Mule-Headed Man!" which was how he'd live on in the story she was passing down.

In the world's vast canon of tragedies, Brian Doyle died young and that little girl is presumably grown, but her grandfather haunts me and I thought about him when I was chopping vegetables the other night, feeding my family from farther down the food chain than I had been raised to do, in that way deploying my puny, dubious will to bend our narrative arc.

It's a pretty stock trope: the mule-headed man. In the natural selection of narrative, some trait keeps passing it down. There's a romance to his stubbornness—staying his course to the final hour. But that's not a plot we can afford anymore. And the way we see stories does change, after all.

Perhaps, it's his spirit that points our way. Maybe we'll find our No in his no, take to new channels, steer into new seas. Perhaps if we reframe his refusal, we'll write a new ending from the end of the dock.

ACKNOWLEDGMENTS

Visible	Meat For Tea	March, 2021
Curiosities	Broken Plate	2018
A Better View	Upstreet	Spring, 2015
Through the Dark	Pinyon	Spring, 2021
Grace	River Teeth	Fall, 2019
Through the Trees	Evening Street Review	Summer, 2020
What the Whelk Shells Tell	River Teeth	Spring, 2016
Slow Learner	Still Point Arts Quarterly	Summer, 2017
At Sixty	The Pinch	Fall, 2016
A Crack in Everything	Fourth Genre	Fall, 2020
What's Happening Now	Main Street Rag	Spring, 2019
Caper	Steam Ticket	Spring, 2021
The C-Word	Evening Street Review	Summer, 2021
Pavlova	Still Point Arts Quarterly	Summer, 2021
Doe	Meat for Tea	Vol 15, Issue 3
Nest	River Teeth	Vol 23, No. 1

www.ingramcontent.com/pod-product-compliance
Lightning Source LLC
Chambersburg PA
CBHW041201150726
48006CB00016B/2056